FLAGS OF THE WORLD

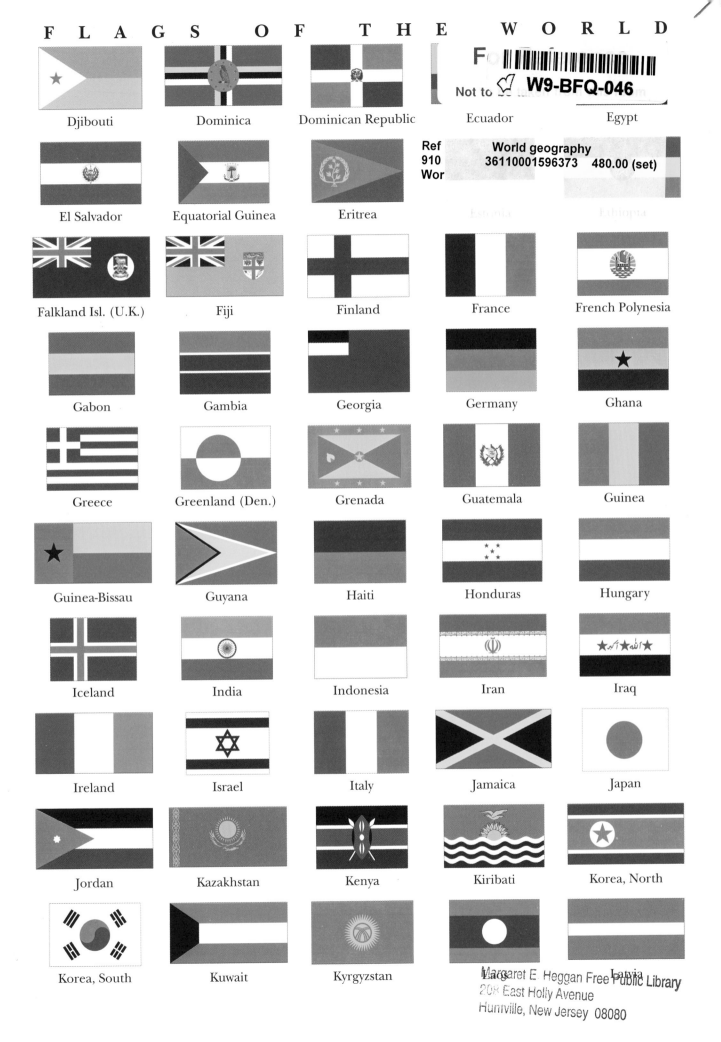

Djibouti	Dominica	Dominican Republic	Ecuador	Egypt
El Salvador	Equatorial Guinea	Eritrea	Estonia	Ethiopia
Falkland Isl. (U.K.)	Fiji	Finland	France	French Polynesia
Gabon	Gambia	Georgia	Germany	Ghana
Greece	Greenland (Den.)	Grenada	Guatemala	Guinea
Guinea-Bissau	Guyana	Haiti	Honduras	Hungary
Iceland	India	Indonesia	Iran	Iraq
Ireland	Israel	Italy	Jamaica	Japan
Jordan	Kazakhstan	Kenya	Kiribati	Korea, North
Korea, South	Kuwait	Kyrgyzstan	Laos	Latvia

WORLD GEOGRAPHY

WORLD GEOGRAPHY

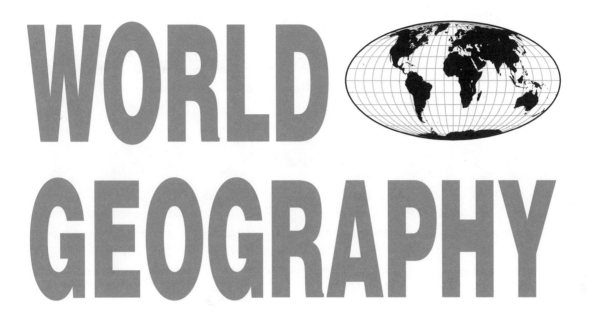

Volume 7

Antarctica, Australia, and the Pacific

Editor
Ray Sumner
Long Beach City College

Managing Editor
R. Kent Rasmussen

SALEM PRESS, INC.
Pasadena, California   Hackensack, New Jersey

Editor in Chief: Dawn P. Dawson

Managing Editor: R. Kent Rasmussen   *Research Supervisor:* Jeffry Jensen
Manuscript Editor: Irene Struthers Rush   *Acquisitions Editor:* Mark Rehn
Production Editor: Cynthia Beres   *Page Design and Layout:* James Hutson
Photograph Editor: Philip Bader   *Additional Layout:* William Zimmerman
Assistant Editors: Andrea Miller, Heather Stratton   *Graphics:* Electronic Illustrators Group
Cover Design: Moritz Design, Los Angeles, Calif.

Frontispiece: Australia from space. *(Corbis)*

∞ The paper used in these volumes conforms to the American National Standard for Permanence of Paper for Printed Library Materials, Z39.48-1992 (R1997).

Library of Congress Cataloging-in-Publication Data

World geography / editor, Ray Sumner ; managing editor, R. Kent Rasmussen.
    p. cm.
    Contents: v. 1. The World. — v. 2. North America and the Caribbean. — v. 3. Central and South America. — v. 4. Africa. — v. 5. Asia. — v. 6. Europe. — v. 7. Antarctica, Australia, and the Pacific. — v. 8. Glossary and Appendices.
    Includes bibliographical references (p.).
    ISBN 0-89356-024-3 (set : alk. paper) — ISBN 0-89356-276-9 (v. 1 : alk. paper) — ISBN 0-89356-277-7 (v. 2 : alk. paper) — ISBN 0-89356-335-8 (v. 3 : alk. paper) — ISBN 0-89356-336-6 (v. 4 : alk. paper) — ISBN 0-89356-399-4 (v. 5 : alk. paper) — ISBN 0-89356-650-0 (v. 6 : alk. paper) — ISBN 0-89356-699-3 (v. 7 : alk. paper) — ISBN 0-89356-723-X (v. 8 : alk. paper)
    1. Geography—Encyclopedias. I. Sumner, Ray.

G133.W88 2001
910′.3—dc21

2001020281

First Printing

PRINTED IN THE UNITED STATES OF AMERICA

CONTENTS

ANTARCTICA, AUSTRALIA, AND THE PACIFIC

REGIONS

PHYSICAL GEOGRAPHY

BIOGEOGRAPHY AND NATURAL RESOURCES

HUMAN GEOGRAPHY

ECONOMIC GEOGRAPHY

GAZETTEER 2063

WORLD GEOGRAPHY

REGIONS

AUSTRALIA

*Map
Page 1839*

The only continent occupied by a single nation, Australia is roughly the size of the forty-eight states of the continental United States. Located entirely in the Southern Hemisphere, it covers about 3 million square miles (7.8 million sq. km.). In the northwest, it is about 250 miles (400 km.) from Timor across the Timor Sea, and 500 miles (800 km.) from the tip of Indonesia across the Indian Ocean. Papua New Guinea is across the Coral Sea, 315 miles (500 hundred km.) north of Queensland's Cape York Peninsula. Due south of the Australian state of Victoria, 380 miles (610 km.) across the Bass Strait, lies Tasmania, the only Australian state not on the mainland. About the size of Scotland, Tasmania, even in its interior, is green, whereas the Outback, as the interior of the mainland is called, is a vast desert.

Australia has eighteen million inhabitants. Except for Antarctica, it is Earth's least populated and most isolated continent. Along the coast of Queensland in the east runs the Great Barrier Reef, the largest such reef in the world. It extends more than 1,200 miles (2,000 km.) from south to north and, in places, is more than 50 miles (80 km.) wide. It has more than 350 species of coral, the world's greatest variety, and teems with sea life, particularly shellfish.

THE GEOLOGICAL PAST.

Australia's geological past is well documented. Long ago, Earth was one huge landmass. Over millions of years, enormous cracks developed, causing parts of it to break off. The largest piece to separate from the whole in this early break-up was Gondwanaland,

which became a supercontinent that, with various nearby islands, constitutes modern Australia, geographically the sixth-largest country in the world. Despite its proximity to Asia, Australia resembles Europe more than Asia in its peoples' outlook and life style.

Australia is the oldest, flattest, and driest continent. Because its interior is parched, the Outback supports only a small population. The country's east and southeast coasts are more heavily populated than those in the north and west. The uplands that separate the coastal areas from the Outback are between 20 and 200 miles (80 to 320 km.) wide.

AUSTRALIA'S SIX STATES.

Modern Australia consists of five contiguous states—New South Wales, Queensland, Victoria, South Australia, and Western Australia—and the island state of Tasmania. The country has two territories, the sprawling Northern Territory on the Timor and Coral Seas, and the relatively small Australian Capital Territory, located within New South Wales. The national capital is Canberra.

Although all five contiguous states except Victoria have considerable land in the Outback, 80 percent of the total population lives near or along the coasts. Even in Tasmania, which has a lush, green interior, the majority of residents are centered in Hobart and other coastal cities. Most Australians live in cities, with the capital city of each state attracting two-thirds of its total population.

NOTABLE GEOGRAPHICAL FEATURES.

The best known geographical feature in

*Victoria
coastline
Page 1850*

*Great
Barrier
Reef
Page 1840*

Whitsunday Passage, which separates Whitsunday Island from the mainland of Queensland, along the Great Barrier Reef. (Corbis)

Uluru
Pages
1849, 1906

the Outback is Uluru, commonly called Ayers Rock. It is located in the Northern Territory, not far from the desert outpost of Alice Springs in Australia's red center. In this area are the MacDonnell Mountain Ranges, as well as King's Canyon, dramatic cliffs and gorges, and the rounded sandstone forms of Kata Tjuta.

Lake Eyre in South Australia, at 52 feet (16 meters) below sea level, is Australia's lowest point and is incredibly dry. It has an area of about 3,600 square miles (5,800 sq.

km.), but fills only three or four times each century. It is so flat and dry that automobile races are held in its bed.

Australia's highest point is New South Wales's Mount Kosciusko in the Australian Alps, which reaches about 7,300 feet (2,228 meters) at its summit. In winter, between May and October, the Australian Alps are generally covered with snow, drawing skiers to them.

Other popular mountains are the Dandenongs of Victoria, less than an hour's drive south of Melbourne. Although the Dandenongs are less dramatic than the Australian Alps, Dandenong Ranges National Park attracts many tourists, particularly during the summer (November to March), when it is much cooler than the surrounding lowlands.

The Nullarbor Plain in the southern part of South Australia and Western Australia is an enormous, arid plain. It is so flat that the Indian-Pacific that runs from Sydney to Perth, a sixty-four-hour train trip, has one stretch of track that is completely straight for more than 200 miles (320 km.).

THE EARLIEST AUSTRALIANS. When British explorer James Cook first landed on the Australian continent, it had been inhabited for more than fifty thousand years by nomadic people. These Aborigines presumably sailed primitive boats to the continent from the nearby Indonesian islands. They were hunters and gatherers, probably numbering about 300,000 in 1788. They constituted an estimated 650 tribes. These earliest inhabitants of Australia spoke more than 250 Aboriginal languages and some 750 dialects. About 50 of the Aboriginal languages survived at the start of the twenty-first century.

The Aborigines inhabited both the main continent and Tasmania. Cave drawings and other Aboriginal artifacts have been reliably dated to before 30,000 B.C.E. The Aborigines moved from place to place in search of food. Their dwellings were usually temporary, although some wooden structures existed in the coastal regions and particularly in Tasmania, which has the heaviest rainfall and the coolest climate of all the states.

Aborigines inhabited much of Australia. Those in the coastal regions, where fishing, hunting, and natural vegetation assured an ample food supply, had relatively comfortable lives. Because the inland areas could not support substantial populations, the coastal tribes were larger than those inhabiting the arid interior. The Aboriginal tribes practiced conservation and had a reverence for the land. They used controlled burning of brush to enrich the soil on which grass would later flourish to provide food for the animals upon which these nomads depended for sustenance.

HYDROLOGY. From the days of the Aborigines, water has been a major problem for those in the interior. Australia has no natural, permanent lakes. Even such large bodies of water as Lake Eyre and Lake Frome are dry much of the time. Artificial reservoirs, such as Lake Argyle in Western Australia's eastern extreme, have eased water shortages in their areas. Long rivers such as the Darling (about 1,700 miles/ 2,740 kilometers long) and the Murray (about 1,600 miles/2,570 kilometers long), were once dry or reduced to a trickle much of the year, but now maintain a more steady flow through a series of dams and locks.

Tasmania Page 1840

Aboriginal hunter Page 1969

Lock on the Murray River in South Australia. (Tom McKnight/Joan Clemons)

Cape York
Page 1839

Queensland
Page 1912

Western Queensland's semiarid plain extends over half the state. Its Great Artesian Basin, at nearly 770,000 square miles (2 million sq. km.), is the largest artesian basin in the world. Rain that falls into it trickles down and collects in subterranean layers through which water is naturally transported to drier regions in the west. Unlike the drier parts of this state, the Cape York Peninsula of northern Queensland is a tropical rain forest.

GROWING AS A NATION. Life in Australia was rugged for the early settlers. A wool industry grew up as herdsmen developed herds of sheep to graze on the grasslands of New South Wales, Victoria, Queensland, and Tasmania. Nevertheless, by 1840, only about 150,000 Europeans lived in Australia. The population grew rapidly in 1851, when gold was discovered in Victoria's Clune and Ballarat. Prospectors flooded into Victoria. Soon eastern Australia had a population of more than 400,000 Europeans and substantial numbers of Asians, including 40,000 Chinese.

An anti-Asian sentiment soon grew among Australia's European inhabitants. This sentiment was responsible for the White Australian Policy, in effect for three-quarters of a century before its termination in 1973. This policy not only discouraged Asians from immigrating to Australia but also placed the Aborigines in a position of second-class citizenship.

Prior to World War II, 95 percent of Australian residents had British roots, and Australia was decidedly British in its outlook. By 1990 about three-quarters of Australians were native-born. Of those born elsewhere, about 14 percent came from Europe, mostly from Italy, Greece, Yugoslavia, Germany, Poland, and the Netherlands. Another 5 percent came from Asia, largely from Vietnam, Laos, the Philippines, and Korea, and 5 percent came from North and South America. Between 1945 and 1975, more than 3.5 million people immigrated to Australia.

AUSTRALIA'S NEW MULTICULTURALISM. Australia's government since the 1970's has sought to create a hospitable atmosphere for immigrants. Its stated aim is to integrate immigrants into society but not to encourage assimilation. Areas within cities reflect the ethnicity of the people living in them. Every major Australian city has sections to which Italians, Greeks, Vietnamese, Koreans, and persons from other national groups gravitate. These enclaves preserve the cultures of their inhabitants' native countries.

Australia has long needed outsiders to staff its industries, so an influx of foreigners creates few of the problems it might in more populous nations. The country's population has doubled since 1945. Approximately 115,000 new immigrants arrive every year, and most find ready employment. The country's annual growth rate is about 2.6 percent.

MAJOR INDUSTRIES. Sheep and cattle stations have long existed throughout Australia. The Spanish merino sheep that thrive in Australia provide high-quality wool. Because much of the grazing land gets less than 15 inches (381 millimeters) of rain annually, it often takes up to 50 acres (20 hectares) to raise each sheep. Cattle stations spawn a prosperous beef industry.

Agriculture is also important, with Australia raising some 20 million tons (18 million metric tons) of wheat annually. New South Wales and Queensland produce considerable rice, and Queensland has the most productive sugarcane fields in Australia. Because of its isolation, Australia has flora and fauna found nowhere else in the world.

Mining is a profitable enterprise in Australia. It began in 1851 with the discovery of gold in Victoria. Western Australia has some of the world's largest deposits of iron ore, and oil has been found off Australia's coasts. Queensland has deposits of silver, copper, zinc, and lead. Both the Northern Territory and South Australia have some of the world's largest deposits of uranium, much of it unmined because of environmental concerns. Valuable opal mines flourish around South Australia's Coober Pedy, a city constructed underground so that its residents can escape the intense desert heat. Deposits of lignite or brown coal are mined in Victoria. Black coal, one of Australia's most profitable exports, exists in enormous quantities in New South Wales and Queensland.

Australia occupies an important role in the world community. By the end of the twentieth century, it was more influenced by the United States than by Britain. It was a signatory to the United Nations Charter in 1945, and is currently a member of the Commonwealth of Nations.

R. Baird Shuman

FOR FURTHER STUDY

Cousteau, Jean-Michel, and Mose Richards. *Cousteau's Australia Journey.* New York: Harry N. Abrams, 1993.

Docherty, James C. *Historical Dictionary of Australia.* Landham, Md.: Scarecrow Press, 1999.

Harrell, Mary Ann. *Surprising Lands Down Under.* Washington, D.C.: National Geographic Society, 1989.

Heathcote, Ronald L., ed. *Australia.* 2d ed. New York: John Wiley & Sons, 1994.

Heinrichs, Ann. *Australia.* New York: Children's Press, 1998.

Hughes, Robert. *The Fatal Shore: The Epic of Australia's Founding.* New York: Alfred A. Knopf, 1987.

Lourandos, Harry. *Continent of Hunter-Gatherers: New Perspectives in Australian Prehistory.* New York: Cambridge University Press, 1997.

Terrill, Ross. *The Australians.* New York: Simon and Schuster, 1987.

INFORMATION ON THE WORLD WIDE WEB

The Web site of the Australian Bureau of Statistics Information, Australia's official statistical organization, features a variety of statistics on Australia. (www.abs.gov.au)

Also of use are the Web sites of the Australian government (www.agd.com.au) and of Canberra, the Australian Capital Territory (www.act.gov.au).

NEW ZEALAND

Map Page 1841

Stewart Island Page 2043

Tongariro Page 2045

Southern Alps Pages 1841, 1854

An isolated part of the world, New Zealand is located in the southwest Pacific Ocean, midway between the equator and the icy Antarctic. Its closest continental neighbor, Australia, lies more than 1,000 miles (1,600 km.) to the northwest. Similar in size to Great Britain or Japan, New Zealand consists of two main islands: North Island—44,010 square miles (113,729 sq. km.)—and South Island—58,084 square miles (150,437 sq. km.), which are separated by the Cook Strait. A third, much smaller island, Stewart Island, roughly the same size as the Hawaiian island of Oahu, sits to the south of South Island.

New Zealand is long and narrow: more than 1,000 miles (1,600 km.) in length and 280 miles (450 km.) at its widest part. If positioned along the West Coast of the United States, New Zealand would stretch from Los Angeles, California, to Seattle, Washington. No place in New Zealand is more than 75 miles (120 km.) from the ocean.

PHYSICAL GEOGRAPHY. Part of the Pacific Ring of Fire, New Zealand sits on a collision zone between the Indo-Australian and Pacific tectonic plates. The grinding motion of these two plates is responsible for New Zealand's mostly rugged terrain. South Island is dominated by a large mountain chain, the Southern Alps, which runs almost the entire length of the island in a north-south direction. The Alps are home to the largest mountain peak in Australasia, Mount Cook, at 12,317 feet (3,754 meters), as well as 360 glaciers.

Tasman Glacier, the largest glacier in New Zealand, flows down the eastern slopes of Mount Cook. Glaciers from previous ice ages carved out the great fjords, called "sounds" in New Zealand, that make up Fiordland National Park, located in the remote southwest corner of the island. Built by erosion, the Canterbury Plains, the country's largest lowland area, stretches along the midsection of the South Island's east coast.

Volcanoes and thermal activity are the main features of North Island. At the heart of the island is Lake Taupo, an ancient volcanic crater. Today the country's largest natural lake, Lake Taupo sits in an active tectonic region called the Volcanic Plateau, which runs in a line from the center of North Island northeast to White Island off the Bay of Plenty. To the south of Lake Taupo lie three major volcanoes: Mount Ruapehu, the highest peak in North Island at 9,177 feet (2,797 meters), Mount Nguruhoe, and Mount Tongariro.

In 1995 Mount Ruapehu erupted, sending ash, steam, and car-sized rocks into the atmosphere. All three volcanoes are part of Tongariro National Park. The site of geysers, boiling mud pools, and hot springs, Rotorua, situated along the Volcanic Plateau between Lake Taupo and White Island, is the country's prime geothermal hot spot. The Waikato, New Zealand's largest river, flows northward across central North Island.

HUMAN GEOGRAPHY. The Maori, from Polynesia, were the first humans to occupy Aotearoa—the Maori word for New Zealand, which means "long white cloud"—beginning around 700 to 1400. In 1642 the Dutch navigator Abel Tasman was the first

European to reach New Zealand. After a brief offshore incident with the Maoris, in which some of his men were killed, Tasman sailed off without setting foot on land. European settlement of the country, mainly by the British, occurred after 1769 with the rediscovery of New Zealand by the British naval explorer Captain James Cook. In 1840 New Zealand became a British colony with the signing of the Treaty of Waitangi in the Bay of Islands on North Island.

Of the 3.8 million people now living in New Zealand, 15 percent are Maori, with Europeans, mainly of British descent, making up 79 percent of the entire population. Given the country's rugged terrain, most of the population lives in centers along or near the coast. Thus, the country is highly urbanized, with 85 percent of the population living in cities. More New Zealanders live on North Island than on South Island. By 1999 more than half the population was living in four urban areas, three of which were located on North Island: Auckland, the largest city in New Zealand, with 1.1 million people; Hamilton (141,800), located to the south of Auckland; and Wellington (346,000), the capital. Christchurch was the third-largest city in New Zealand, with 341,00 people, and the largest city on South Island.

New Zealand has a strong history of promoting equal rights and social benefits for all its citizens. In 1893 New Zealand became the first country in the world to give women the right to vote. On December 8, 1997, Jenny Shipley became the country's first woman prime minister. During the twentieth century, the country established an extensive social welfare system, including public housing, universal health care, and support benefits—such as retirement pensions—which became a model for the rest of the world. The 1990's brought efforts by the government to address grievances by the Maori dating back to early European settlement of the country.

On the world stage, New Zealand has gained international recognition for its antinuclear policy. With widespread support from the public, the fourth Labour government declared New Zealand a nuclear-free zone in 1984. Under New Zealand law, no nuclear-armed vessels or nuclear-powered ships are allowed in its waters. The country also has no nuclear weapons or nuclear-generated power stations. Its antinuclear policy, along with its natural beauty, low population, and rural-based economy, has earned New Zealand a reputation as a "clean and green" county.

Huia Richard Hutton

Wellington Page 2046

TE IKA A MAUI: THE FISH OF MAUI

Maori legend tells of how New Zealand's North Island was a great fish hauled up from the ocean floor by the Polynesian god Maui. The name given to North Island by the Maori was Te Ika a Maui—"the Fish of Maui." The canoe from which the fish was caught was South Island, and Steward Island was the anchor of Maui's canoe. The two eyes of the fish were located at the bottom of North Island, with one of its eyes at Wellington Harbor and the other at Lake Wairarapa. The fins were Mount Taranaki on the North Island's west coast and East Cape on its eastern shore. The fish's long tail was the Northland Peninsula in the far north of North Island. A map of the North Island of New Zealand turned sideways actually looks a bit like a great fish.

FOR FURTHER STUDY

Cumberland, Kenneth B. *Landmarks.* Surry Hills: Reader's Digest, 1981.

Jackson, Keith. *Historical Dictionary of New Zealand.* Landham, Md.: Scarecrow Press, 1996.

McKnight, Tom L. *Oceania: The Geography of Australia, New Zealand and the Pacific Islands.* Englewood Cliffs, N.J.: Prentice Hall, 1995.

Rapaport, Moshe, ed. *The Pacific Islands: Environment and Society.* Honolulu, Hawaii: Bess Press, 1999.

Shadbolt, Brian. *Reader's Digest Guide to New Zealand.* Sydney, Australia: Reader's Digest Service, 1988.

Sinclair, Keith, ed. *The Oxford Illustrated History of New Zealand.* Oxford, Great Britain: Oxford University Press, 1990.

INFORMATION ON THE WORLD WIDE WEB

The Statistics New Zealand site features a wealth of information about New Zealand geography and climate, in the section titled "Yearbook." (www.stats.govt.nz)

A Web site titled "New Zealand Geographical Map" allows viewers to explore various geographical regions around New Zealand by clicking on place names on the map that link to information and pictures about each area. (www.channel8.net/newzealand/nzmap.htm)

PACIFIC ISLANDS

*Maps
Pages 1842-
1843*

To understand the geographical setting of Oceania, one must first appreciate the immensity of the Pacific Ocean itself. The world's largest ocean, the Pacific covers nearly 70 million square miles (181 million sq. km.), about a third of the total surface of the earth. Its area is more extensive than all the world's landmasses combined. Because the continents of Asia and North America are closer to each other than Southeast Asia and South America are, the southern half of the Pacific stands out as a particularly vast body of water. Its widest zone lies along the equatorial belt.

Although the northern zones of the Pacific contain a number of important islands, it is in the southern, and particularly the southwestern, zone of the Pacific that one finds not only the largest but also the most numerous island formations. If one follows the line of the equator or the tropic of Capricorn eastward from the heavy concentration of islands in the southwest and central Pacific, the occurrence of islands drops markedly. There are only two significant sites—the Galápagos Islands on the equator and Easter Island further south—on the eastern fringe of Oceania.

Geographers have identified three major subregions of generally smaller to medium-size islands for concentrated study: Melanesia, Micronesia, and Polynesia. These terms mean "black islands," "small islands," and "many islands," respectively.

MELANESIA. The area of Oceania lying north and northeast of Australia, Melanesia contains most of the island land surface in the southern Pacific Ocean. In part this is because it includes Papua New Guinea,

the largest island of Oceania and the second-largest in the world, after Greenland. The two halves of New Guinea taken together cover approximately 316,000 square miles (820,000 sq. km.). Papua New Guinea is the most densely populated island in Melanesia. Its culturally diversified inhabitants are divided into hundreds of different language groups and must rely on a form of New Guinea pidgin dialect to communicate with one another. Although a diversity of cultural groups live in Melanesia, most inhabitants are dark skinned, with frizzy hair. Such dark skin pigmentation prompted early observers of these islands to coin the term "Melanesia."

The modern nation state of Papua New Guinea is the eastern half of New Guinea island itself. The dominant geographical feature of Papua New Guinea is the long central mountain chain that runs almost the entire length of the country. The populations north of the main mountain ridges are culturally distinct from those living to the south of the mountains, the Papuans. Western New Guinea came under Indonesian control in the 1970's, and was named Irian Jaya.

Several islands adjacent to New Guinea are still known as the Bismarck Archipelago, since their earliest colonizers were German. After World War I, the biggest islands came under British and Australian control, gaining names that were appropriate to their new status: New Britain and New Ireland.

Due west of the Bismarck Archipelago is Bougainville Island, named after the French navigator Louis Antoine de Bougainville who first explored it. Bougainville is the first of the long chain of the Solomon Islands, stretching more than 1,000 miles (1,600 km.) to the southeast. The Solomons are geologically similar to the Bismarck Archipelago. Ten quite large islands and many small islands make up the chain. The largest of the Solomon Islands after Bougainville is Guadalcanal, whose Spanish name is a reminder of the variety of European maritime explorers who discovered the South Pacific islands following Magellan's ill-fated but historic voyage westward across the Pacific early in the sixteenth century.

Fiji
Pages
1845, 1903

The Fiji Islands, located on the westernmost fringe of Melanesia, number more than three hundred. Only about one hundred islands are inhabited. Until they came under British colonial administration in the last quarter of the nineteenth century, they were populated by a number of rival chieftaincies. Great Britain chose Fiji's main city, Suva on the island of Viti Levu, as the seat of their colonial presence in the South Pacific after World War II. Before that date, the British already had begun encouraging Indian immigration to the Fiji Islands as part of plans to expand sugar production under a plantation regime.

Most of Fiji's population has concentrated on its two largest islands, Viti Levu and Vanua Levu. Viti Levu is nearly as big as the well-known Polynesian island of Hawaii. Fiji's main islands are high islands whose eastern slopes receive significant quantities of rainfall, while the western slopes are considerably drier. Viti Levu's main peak, Mount Victoria, is more than 4,265 feet (1,300 meters) high and is not a great distance from beautiful, although limited, zones of untouched mahogany forest.

MICRONESIA. Micronesia lies within the broad zone due north of Melanesia beyond the equator. As its name suggests, Micronesia consists of a multitude of small islands, some so tiny that they were never, or only very recently, named. Micronesia is bounded on the west by the open seas next to the Philippine Islands and stretches northward to 30 degrees, which is about the same latitudinal location as the Hawaiian Islands. No clear border marks the end of Micronesia to the east and the beginning of the vast zone of Polynesia. Convention has drawn a line through open Pacific Ocean waters between the Gilbert Islands (now known as the Republic of Kiribati) and the Ellice Islands (the independent country of Tuvalu).

Micronesia contains twenty-five islands spread over a vast zone of more than 3 million square miles (7.8 million sq. km.). Most of these are small, low-lying atolls. Even taken together with a few larger islands, Micronesia's total land surface is only one-third of 1 percent of the Pacific Islands' land area.

One of the longer-term results of United Nations' recognition of newly independent states in Southeast Asia was an incentive for the United States to group many of these small islands to form constitutional governments. This ended Washington's post-World War II trusteeship over the single "unit" of Micronesia (earlier controlled by Japan and, before that, Germany) and created four distinct constitutional regimes, all with some form of continuing dependency on the United States. These include the Republic of Belau (formerly Palau) immediately north of Indonesia's Irian Jaya (Western New Guinea), the Federated States of Micronesia in the center of the region, and the Republics of the Marshall Islands and Kiribati to the northeast and southeast, respectively.

The island of Guam and the Commonwealth of the Northern Marianas to the northwest (the latter extending almost to the tropic of Cancer due east of Taiwan)

THE HAWAIIAN ISLANDS

The Hawaiian Islands, originally called the Sandwich Islands after the British Earl of Sandwich, include eight major islands and a number of smaller islands, with a total area of nearly 6,500 square miles (17,000 square km.). All the main islands are of volcanic origin and most are surrounded by coral reefs. Hawaii itself, the largest island, is notably younger geologically than the other islands. The capital city of Honolulu is on the island of Oahu. The islands were discovered in 1778 by the English sea captain James Cook. Apparently, growing U.S. concern over British and French colonial interest in the Hawaiian Islands—even after a local independent monarchy was recognized in 1842—led to increasing U.S. involvement. This involvement peaked in 1898 when the United States claimed the Hawaiian Islands as its territory.

remained more formally tied to the United States. Beyond the Northern Marianas are the Ogasawara, or Bonin Islands, the southernmost part of Japanese territory.

The largest and most heavily populated island in Micronesia is Guam. Nearly half the people of Micronesia live on Guam. At the end of the twentieth century, almost a third of Guam's population consisted of military or military support personnel from the United States.

POLYNESIA. The last geographical zone of Oceania, Polynesia, represents only about 1 percent of the total land area of the Pacific island world, but its dozen or more island groups are heavily populated by comparison with the other areas. It is the largest subzone of Oceania, forming a vast triangle with its southwestern tip well below 40 degrees south latitude, midway through New Zealand and south of Australia. The sides of the Polynesian triangle extend some 5,000 miles (8,000 km.) through the central and southeastern Pacific. The northern tip of Polynesia reaches the Hawaiian Islands (since 1959 a state of the United States), and its eastern point includes Easter Island (part of Chile's territory) near the tropic of Capricorn.

Although the Hawaiian Islands may be the most famous of the Polynesian island groups, several other island complexes are important and quite well known. Western Samoa, which is much larger than the half dozen islands constituting the United States territory of American Samoa, was the first independent island nation of Oceania. Its two medium-sized and seven small islands became independent in 1962, after more than six decades of U.S. control.

To the southeast of the Samoas are the seven Cook Islands, named after the British navigator James Cook. They are nominally a self-governing unit with close formal associations with New Zealand. The entire region's economy remains closely tied to New Zealand, and the Cook Islands, already rather sparsely populated, have lost many immigrants to the work market in New Zealand.

Southwest of the Samoas is the complex of more than one hundred islands known as Tonga, divided by their still-existing kingly authority into three sections: Tongatapu (Sacred Tonga) with its capital, Nuku'alofa; the low-lying coral islands of Ha'apai; and Vav'u. Several islands some 600 miles (960 km.) to the north are also part of Tonga.

French Polynesia is, like New Caledonia in Melanesia, one of France's overseas

Samoa Pages 1845, 1904

Tahiti
Page 2044

Bora-Bora
Pages
1843, 1844

Mooréa
Page 2036

territories. Among its more than 130 islands, Tahiti is the largest, most populated, and best known, although Bora-Bora has the reputation of being among the most beautiful islands of the entire Pacific. Bora-Bora combines the spectacular profile of twin volcanic peaks with a surrounding coral reef structure.

There are a number of lesser-known islands in the Polynesian group, including Wallis and Futuna, a far-flung extension of French overseas territory; British-controlled Pitcairn Island, whose several dozen inhabitants are descendants of mutineers from the famous ship HMS *Bounty*; and Niue, a tiny self-governing country that is closely associated with New Zealand.

The most remote of the Polynesian islands is Easter Island, 2,000 miles (3,200 km.) off the coast of Chile. Easter Island became famous after European explorers discovered its mysterious great stone figures, the origin of which is still being debated.

PHYSICAL AND FLORAL DIVERSITY IN OCEANIA. Islands in the different geographical subregions of Oceania show different physical characteristics, depending on how they were formed geologically. One category, referred to as continental islands, applies to only one island of Oceania as defined here, namely Papua New Guinea. Continental islands share not only geological origins with the large landmass next to them (in this case Australia), but also a notable diversity of ecological features. These features may be the result of the broad ranges of altitudes found on such large islands, or differentiations in soil composition produced by extensive erosion.

The case of Papua New Guinea in the Melanesian zone fits this observation quite well. The highlands in the interior of New Guinea contain fertile mountain valleys whose elevations range between 4,000 and 6,000 feet (1,200-1,800 meters), with a diversity of plant and animal life on the even higher slopes surrounding them.

The second category of islands in Oceania is referred to as "high islands." These include fairly large islands, most of which owe their geological origins to volcanic eruptions. Because of their volcanic origins, most high islands have sharply sloping mountainous features. Some high islands are a single volcanic peak, like the visibly spectacular island of Mooréa in French Polynesia.

Other islands, like Bougainville in Melanesia (where most of the high islands of Oceania are found), have a series of volcanic peaks, or, in the case of New Caledonia, an extensive range of mountains forming the backbone of an elongated island formation. Although the elevation of

---

THE MYSTERY OF EASTER ISLAND

There are many theories concerning the origin of Easter Island's numerous carved volcanic, or tufa stone, heads and the inscriptions on them. Some have argued, unsuccessfully, that the petroglyphs found on Easter Island were derived from ancient Egyptian or Hindu writing systems, or hieroglyphs. The stone heads range in height from 10 to 40 feet (3 to 12 meters) and weigh up to fifty tons. Most scholars agree that the stones were carved by people of Polynesian stock that arrived on the island from the central Pacific. When Europeans first arrived in 1722, the sparse population of the island was visibly of Polynesian origin.

Bougainville's peaks is impressive (reaching 10,000 feet/16,000 meters), the highest volcanic peaks in Oceania, some reaching 13,000 feet (20,800 meters), are found in the distant Hawaiian Islands at the northern fringe of Polynesia.

The vast majority of islands throughout Oceania are coral atolls. Coral atolls are composed of the long-term accumulation of skeletons of small marine animals (specifically, polyps) that become cemented together by the partial breakdown of their calcareous content. Atolls usually are found in relatively shallow waters close to an already existing island. The neighbor island may owe its origins to totally different geological causes. Its function is to provide an appropriate marine environment for polyps to breed and multiply. Nearly all Pacific islands have some form of coral reef nearby off their shores. All reefs do not necessarily emerge above the surface to become atolls. It sometimes happens, however, that coral atolls survive as circularly shaped reefs rising above the surface long after the original island at their core has sunk beneath the waters.

Coral formations also can become islands as a result of tectonic uplifting, or upward pressures coming from the earth's tectonic plates under the ocean floor. Uplifted coral islands are less common in Oceania than the typical flat, low-lying atoll formations. Although the mass of coral material may have been essentially a flat subsurface platform, effects of tectonic uplifting can produce varied results. There may be tilting slopes (not actual mountain chains) and fissures or faults, much like the effects of uplifting of sections of the larger landmass on the continents. In such cases, medium-size coral islands have varied topographical features, ranging from low-lying coastal fringes to fairly high mountainous elevations with valleys caused by erosion. Two of the most

prominent examples of uplifted coral islands appear in the Polynesian region of Oceania: Tongatapu in the Tonga group and Makatéa in the Tuamotu group.

Because all three regions of Oceania are subject to high levels of precipitation, and sometimes even major typhoons, one might expect plant life to be dense and varied. Both density and variation depend, however, on a variety of factors that are unique to the Pacific Island world.

First, the heaviest rainfall accumulates mainly on the high islands that are characteristic of the Melanesian area. These include New Guinea, New Britain, Bougainville, and Guadalcanal, where mountain slopes are covered by extensive rain forests. Rain forest conditions are otherwise rather rare, occurring on the windward slopes of Fiji and a few islands in American Samoa. Another form of island forest in areas of high humidity, especially on the larger islands like New Guinea, occurs because of near perpetual mist. Here the trees of the so-called moss, or cloud, forest never grow very high, and most of the misty humidity is absorbed by thick carpets of moss on the forest floor.

Guadalcanal Page 2031

Savanna-like (drier and less dense) tree and scrub vegetation is more characteristic of most islands in Oceania. The nature of such vegetation depends on relative elevation and soil conditions. Larger islands, such as New Guinea, can have fairly extensive grassland zones, especially at middle elevations (4,000-6,000 feet/1,200-1,800 meters) where rainfall is seasonal and moderate by comparison to higher forested areas.

The spread of different plant species also depends on degrees of geographical isolation from other islands. Wide expanses of ocean water separate the different island groupings, and this has served to block transmission of floral species from one region to another. In some

Coconut palms Page 1842

places, the seeds of certain species may have been carried considerable distances across the water by birds. The spread of the coconut palm to almost all parts of Oceania is due in large part to the fact that coconuts have floated, sometimes for years, before washing up on distant shores where soil conditions were conducive to their growth. A similar pattern of dispersion by means of floating seeds has spread another typical Pacific island tree, the pandanus (referred to as the "screw pine") throughout Oceania.

When vast distances or patterns of oceanic currents and winds have prevented the spread of plants across the Pacific, the opposite phenomenon may occur—concentrations of endemic plant species that are found only in certain areas. This is the case of the Hawaiian Islands and New Caledonia in Melanesia, where up to 70 percent of plant species exist in isolation only in those subregions of Oceania. While volcanic soils in particular possess high levels of fertility, other soils typical of Oceania do not contain adequate nutrients to support a diversity of plants. This is particularly true of the smaller coral island formations, due not only to their low elevations above sea level (and resultant low rainfall "catch"), but also to the porous nature of the subsoils underlying thin layers of topsoil. Many such islands are completely barren, or support only a few species of grasses and bushes.

Byron D. Cannon

FOR FURTHER STUDY

McKnight, Tom L. *Oceania.* Englewood Cliffs, N.J.: Prentice-Hall, 1995.

Spate, O. H. K. *The Pacific Since Magellan: Paradise Lost and Found.* Canberra: Australian National University Press, 1988.

Stanley, David. *South Pacific Handbook.* Chico, Calif.: Moon Publications, 1984.

Stevenson, Robert Louis. *In the South Seas.* New York: Scribner's, 1901.

Turner, Ann. *Historical Dictionary of Papua New Guinea.* Landham, Md.: Scarecrow Press, 1994.

Ward, Gerald R., and A. Proctor, eds. *South Pacific Agriculture: Choices and Constraints.* Canberra: Australian National University Press, 1980.

Wuerch, William L., and Dirk Anthony Ballendorf. *Historical Dictionary of Guam and Micronesia.* Landham, Md.: Scarecrow Press, 1994.

INFORMATION ON THE WORLD WIDE WEB

The Web site of the Pacific Islands Development Program of the East-West Center for Pacific Islands Studies at the University of Hawaii at Manoa links to dozens of useful Pacific Island sites. (pidp.ewc.hawaii.edu/PIReport/news_links.htm)

PHYSICAL GEOGRAPHY

PHYSIOGRAPHY AND HYDROLOGY

ANTARCTICA

The fifth largest of the earth's seven continents, Antarctica is an enormous island with a network of other islands along its 18,648-mile (30,010 km.) coastline and farther out in the three oceans that adjoin its shores, the Atlantic, Pacific, and Indian Oceans. Because more than 98 percent of Antarctica is covered with ice and snow that has not melted for more than 170,000 years, most of the adjacent islands look from the air as though they belong to the mainland.

PHYSICAL DIMENSIONS. The continent is roughly circular, with indentations for the Ross Sea on the western side and the Weddell Sea 3,000 miles (4,828 km.) to the north. Antarctica has a landmass of about 5.1 million square miles (13.2 million sq. km.)—the size of the United States and Mexico combined. The Transantarctic Mountains run like a great spine from the Ross Sea to the Weddell Sea, crossing the geographic South Pole at 90 degrees south latitude. They divide Antarctica into East (Greater) Antarctica and West (Lesser) Antarctica.

The Antarctic Peninsula, consisting of Palmer Land and Graham Land, juts from the mainland and extends north from about 85 degrees south latitude to about 60 degrees south latitude and longitude 60 to 80 degrees west. Its mountains are part of the range that includes South America's Andes and the submarine mountains of the South Atlantic Ocean. South Orkney, South Georgia, and Elephant Island are mountain peaks of that submerged range.

Antarctica has huge ice shelves, fed largely by glaciers, off its coasts. The largest of these is the Ross Ice Shelf, four times the size of the state of New York. It is fed by six glaciers, the largest of which is the Beardmore, which starts at the South Pole and, attaining altitudes of 10,000 feet (3,048 meters), flows into the Ross Sea, depositing huge quantities of ice on the Ross Ice Shelf.

The Lambert Glacier, which runs through the Prince Charles Mountains, feeds the Amery Ice Shelf. Every year it discharges many square miles of ice into the Amery Ice Shelf, which is 125 miles (200 km.) wide.

Antarctica rises to a height of 16,859 feet (5,139 meters) at the Vinson Massif of the Ellsworth Mountains in Maria Byrd Land. Antarctica also has the lowest point on the earth: the Bentley Subglacial Trench, which lies 8,325 feet (2,538 meters) below sea level. This is 7,000 feet (2,134 meters) lower than the Dead Sea in

*Map
Page 1846*

*Weddell
Sea
Page 1846*

*Trans-
antarctic
Mts.
Page 1848*

Israel, the lowest point on the six continents other than Antarctica. Much of Antarctica is below sea level, gradually having been sunk by the constant weight of an ice cover, often 2 miles (3.2 km.) thick, which has not melted for more than 170,000 years. Nevertheless, Antarctica's average altitude is 6,000 feet (1,830 meters), excluding its ice cover, whose average thickness of 8,000 feet (2,440 meters) increases the continent's average altitude to 14,000 feet (4,270 meters).

Antarctica has three major dry valleys—Taylor Valley, Wright Valley, and Victoria Valley—sheltered from the harsh climate by the Royal Society Mountains. They were once filled with ice, but over time, the ice dissipated, leaving the earth exposed. The climate is so dry there that snow does not fall. Each of these dramatic oases amidst the great ice fields of the continent is 3 miles (5 km.) wide and about 25 miles (40 km.) long.

Besides the Ross Ice Shelf, major ice shelves off the Antarctic coast include the Amery, at longitude 70 degrees east and 70 degrees south latitude; the Filchner, at longitude 40 degrees west and 80 degrees south latitude; the Larsen, at longitude 65 degrees west and 65 degrees south latitude; and the Ronne, at between longitude 50 and 75 degrees west and 80 degrees south latitude. Other large ice shelves are the Shackleton, Voyeykov, Getz, and West.

GEOLOGY. The geological history of Antarctica reveals that more than 170,000 years ago, the continent had a moderate climate that sustained a broad range of plant and animal life. There is evidence that once trees grew in the area, it had swamps, and many varieties of animals roved about in it. The Ice Age that covered the continent with a coating of ice that grew to an average thickness of about 8,000 feet (2,440 meters) changed the entire face of the continent, turning it into the frozen mass that it is now.

East Antarctica south of the Indian Ocean is a single landmass composed largely of igneous rock. It appears to have been formed more than a billion years ago during the Precambrian period. A deep trough filled with 2 miles (3.2 km.) of ice runs along the Great Antarctic Horst into West Antarctica, which is a collection of islands, many below sea level because of the weight of the ice that has accumulated on them. They are covered by an ice cap that makes them look a solid mass from the air. The northern portion of West Antarctica, which resulted from volcanic action, developed in the third period of Antarctica's geological time.

The Ellsworth Mountains, located in West Antarctica and extending northward to the Antarctic Peninsula, are composed partly of granite and sedimentary rock. The mountains on the Antarctic Peninsula are part of the mountain chain that

ANTARCTICA'S GEOGRAPHICAL DIVISIONS

Unlike the other continents, Antarctica has no large cities, no towns or villages, and no permanent human residents. The Transantarctic Mountains, also known as the Great Antarctic Horst, divide the continent into East (Greater) Antarctica, the continent's larger land area, and West (Lesser) Antarctica, the smaller. The Transarctic Mountains cut through the continent for a distance of more than 3,000 miles (4,800 km.).

forms the Andes in South America.

The Antarctic Peninsula, with oceans on its coastline, has the most moderate climate in Antarctica. In summer, it can have temperatures of 50 degrees Fahrenheit (10 degrees Celsius). Some rudimentary plant life—types of grasses, pennywort, lichens, and mosses—grow here, but Antarctica is without the plant life that characterizes the earth's other six continents. Trees cannot grow anywhere on Antarctica.

VOLCANIC ACTIVITY. Major parts of Antarctica were attached at one time to the South American continent. In prehistory, large segments of the landmass detached from the mainland and drifted slowly south to what is now Antarctica. Other parts of the continent, however, appear to be of volcanic origin, particularly in the north reaches on the Antarctic Peninsula immediately below the Antarctic Circle, which lies at 65° 32′ south latitude. There also has been recent volcanic activity near the Ross Sea: Mount Erebus, at an altitude of 13,200 feet (4,023 meters), still spews smoke and flame into the air to a height that Sir James Clark Ross estimated in 1841 to reach 2,000 feet (600 meters) above its cone.

It is indisputable that Mount Erebus underwent a major eruption around 1500. Lava and volcanic ash from such an eruption have been found by scientists and dated with reasonable accuracy. Eight of the eleven South Sandwich Islands, north of the Weddell Sea, originated from volcanic action that occurred an estimated four million years ago. Volcanic activity also is evidenced by major splits in rock formations found in West Antarctica that date from between twenty-five and thirty million years ago.

> ### THE WORLD'S BIGGEST ICEBERG
>
> The largest iceberg ever seen by humans was calved from the Ross Ice Shelf and first spotted in 1956. It was 208 miles (335 km.) long and 60 miles (97 km.) wide, and its total area was six times the size of the state of Delaware.

The Marie Byrd Land volcanic area shows evidence of volcanoes from the Cenozoic period, dating back over sixty-five million years. The lower beds of volcanic rock are overlaid with other layers of volcanic rocks that suggest continued volcanic activity in the period from sixty-five million to about thirty million years ago.

When what is now Antarctica broke loose from the South American continent, great heat and gas were released violently as blisteringly hot molten rock from the earth's core flowed into the cold waters to the south. Scientists have speculated on the effect a major contemporary eruption of either of Antarctica's two active volcanoes might have upon the surrounding environs. Some have speculated that such eruptions might, over the next millions of years, make the continent habitable, as recent archeological evidence indicates that it once was.

ANTARCTICA'S ICE COVER. Antarctica contains 90 percent of the earth's permanent ice, which amounts to hundreds of billions of tons. This ice sheet, which has built up over at least 170,000 years without any substantial melting, is the largest accumulation of fresh water on the planet, holding 68 percent of the earth's fresh water. It is estimated that this amounts to 7.2 million cubic miles (30 million cubic km.) of fresh water.

At times, it has been suggested that huge icebergs might be hauled to countries where water is in short supply. Icebergs are constantly being calved from the

Icebergs Page 1847

huge ice shelves that abound in Antarctica. These icebergs are often of unimaginable size.

The ice shelves that occur off 30 percent of the coastline of Antarctica contain 7 percent of the continent's total ice cover. Ice shelves exist only in Antarctica; the Arctic regions north of the equator, which have a more temperate climate than Antarctica, do not have them.

In 1986 the ice shelf on the northeastern side of the Filchner Ice Shelf calved, and the resulting iceberg drifted into the Weddell Sea, carrying with it two important research stations. This demonstrates how unstable the ice cover can be. Although the ice cover looks like a solid mass, when water is beneath it, it often is an enormous iceberg rather than an ice cover over a land base. The area that floated away from the Filchner Ice Shelf totaled about 5,000 square miles (13,000 sq. km.), about the size of Belgium.

Icebergs extend far below sea level, so what one can see with the naked eye might, depending on its size and weight, be only 10 percent of the total mass. When ice covers form on land, particularly on islands like those that lie beneath the ice of West Antarctica, their great weight, which increases every year as more snow falls and more ice accumulates, depresses the land mass on which it rests, often forcing it below sea level. As the ice cover overflows the land beneath it, it comes to rest on a less stable base than land provides. In time, fissures occur and large portions of the ice shelf break away.

THE ANTARCTIC OCEAN. A line of demarcation between warm and cold water in the Antarctic Ocean called the Antarctic Convergence occurs. Ocean currents running along the ocean's floor from the Northern Hemisphere to the Antarctic Ocean carry small bits of sediment they encounter on their way south. This sediment, rich in nutrients, ends up in the upper layers of the frigid Antarctic between the fiftieth and sixtieth degrees south latitude. The warm water currents rise, as heat does, pushing the colder Antarctic waters deep into the sea, where they continue as cold, deep-water currents.

HYDROLOGY AND ANIMAL LIFE. Antarctica's hydrology supports what animal life is found on the continent. The Antarctic Ocean has an abundance of plankton and crustaceans. At the Antarctic Convergence, there is a drop of about 5 degrees Fahrenheit (2.8 degrees Celsius) in the surface temperature of the water. Its salt content also drops appreciably.

The Antarctic Ocean's murky, gray-green color is caused by the presence of microorganisms that make its waters nutritionally rich. Fish and mammals, particularly seals and whales, abound in the Antarctic waters, although whale hunting has

---

ANTARCTICA: THE WINDIEST PLACE ON EARTH

Antarctica has the distinction of being the windiest place on Earth, although, in some areas of the Antarctic, the wind is no stronger than in parts of the midwestern United States. Commonwealth Bay on the George V Coast east of the Ross Sea is the windiest place in Antarctica. The wind speeds there sometimes reach 50 to 90 miles (80 to 145 km.) per hour for several consecutive days. Winds as high as 200 miles (320 km.) per hour have been clocked in the region. These winds reach their greatest intensity during storms.

brought some kinds of whales to the point of extinction. The strong surface winds that blow from out of the west, often cyclonic in their speed and intensity, cause the surface water to move rapidly from west to east around Antarctica.

Antarctica has a variety of birds. Some, like the blue-eyed shag and various species of gulls and albatrosses, come during the long summer to mate; a few, such as the snow petrels, stay in Antarctica through the long winter, sometimes sitting on their eggs when they are covered by snow almost up to their beaks. The best-known animal of Antarctica is the penguin, which moves about easily on its slippery surfaces, dives into its frigid waters to catch the fish that constitute the major part of its diet, and generally delights people who watch them. The penguin is one of the few birds that cannot fly, but the lack of predators and the abundance of food from the sea makes Antarctica an environment in which these playful creatures can survive and prosper.

The four kinds of Antarctic penguins are the Adélie, chinstrap, emperor, and gentoo. Adélie and gentoo penguins are considered the most authentic Antarctic penguins because they seldom stray from the continent. The chinstraps are found often on the Antarctic Maritime Islands and on the Antarctic Peninsula. The gentoo usually breeds in the sub-Antarctic islands. Gentoos number about 350,000 and live mostly on South Georgia Island.

A HYDROLOGICAL DISCOVERY. Russian scientists at the Vostok Research Station, 625 miles (1,000 km.) from the geographic South Pole, have done pioneering studies of the microorganisms found in deep ice core samples that have been retrieved by using instruments developed in Russia to bring samples up with no contamination. Some of the ice in these samples is more than 400 million years old and reveals extremely interesting information about the microorganisms that existed then and the chemical composition of their environments.

Even more interesting is the discovery in 1996, while deep core ice samples were being taken, of a huge liquid lake that exists under 2 miles (3.2 km.) of glacial ice. This lake is presumably pristine, and efforts are being made to keep it from contamination of any sort. The ice cover directly above it has not been breached and will not be until there is evidence that the lake can be opened without the risk of contamination. Scientists involved in this project compare this hydrological find to the possibility of finding water or ice on Mars and slush on Jupiter's moon Europa, which could be possible in the near future.

The experiments and discoveries at Vostok may bring humans one step closer to understanding how and when the universe came into being. These investigations pose interesting puzzles to be solved. In the deep ice core samples, along with the elements one would expect to find—oxygen, nitrogen, carbon—are large quantities of antimony, a highly toxic heavy element that is not found in current earthly atmospheres in nearly the concentration found in the deep ice core samples.

Because of the harsh climatic conditions in Antarctica, scientists still know relatively little about its composition and about what lies beneath its surface. With year-around research stations being operated by several countries on Antarctica, this information gap could eventually decrease or even disappear.

R. Baird Shuman

FOR FURTHER STUDY

Billings, Henry. *Antarctica.* Chicago: Children's Press, 1994.

Caras, Roger A. *Antarctica: Land of Frozen Time.* Philadelphia: Chilton Books, 1962.

Fogg, G. E., and David Smith. *The Explorations of Antarctica: The Last Unspoiled Continent.* London: Cassell, 1990.

Hansom, James D., and John E. Gordon. *Antarctic Environments and Resources: A Geographical Perspective.* New York: Addison Wesley Longman, 1998.

Kerry, Knowles R., and Hempel, Gotthilf, eds. *Antarctic Ecosystems: Change and Conservation.* Berlin: Springer Verlag, 1990.

McDonald, Kellie. *Antarctica.* Crystal Lake, Ill.: Heineman, 1997.

May, John. *The Greenpeace Book of Antarctica: A New View of the Seventh Continent.* New York: Doubleday, 1989.

Pringle, Laurence. *Antarctica: The Last Unspoiled Continent.* New York: Simon and Schuster, 1992.

Tingey, Robert J., ed. *The Geology of Antarctica.* Oxford, England: Clarendon Press, 1991.

Winckler, Suzanne, and Mary M. Rodgers. *Antarctica.* Minneapolis: Lerner, 1992.

INFORMATION ON THE WORLD WIDE WEB

One of the best sources for on-line information about Antarctica is Polar Challenges: Adventure and Research, a Web site devoted to polar expeditions, environments, and ecotourism, with specific reference to Antarctica. (www.antarctica.org)

Other useful and informative sites include NASA's South Pole Adventure Web Page (www.southpole.com), which has valuable information about research occurring at the Vostok Research Center; the Web site of New Zealand's International Antarctic Centre (www.iceberg.co.nz), and the Web site of the Antarctica Project (www.asoc.org), which reports on the organization's conservation activities.

AUSTRALIA

*Maps
Pages 1848-1849*

*Cape York
Page 1839*

The only country in the world that occupies a whole continent by itself, Australia is about the same size as the forty-eight contiguous states of the continental United States. Australia's area of 2.97 million square miles (7.7 million sq. km.), which includes the island of Tasmania, makes it the world's sixth largest country.

The tropic of Capricorn runs through the center of Australia, placing the northern half of the country within the Tropics.

The continent's northernmost tip, Cape York, reaches a point only 10 degrees south of the equator. Australia's southernmost point, located on the island of Tasmania, is South East Cape. It reaches 43 degrees south latitude. Australia extends farther south than the African continent, but not as far south as South America or New Zealand. The distance between Cape York and South East Cape is 2,287 miles (3,680 km.).

Australia's most easterly point is Cape Byron in New South Wales, at 153 degrees east latitude. Its most westerly tip is Steep Point in Western Australia (113 degrees east). The east-to-west distance across Australia is 2,486 miles (4,000 km.)—roughly equivalent to the distance between the East and West Coasts of the United States.

LANDFORMS AND PHYSIOGRAPHIC RE-GIONS. The landforms of Australia are millions of years old. They have evolved as a result of unique physical circumstances and have influenced the patterns of flora and fauna on the Australian continent. They continue to affect the human geography of this part of the world. Australia is not only the world's smallest continent, it is also the flattest. It has few mountains, and those it does have are comparatively small. The continent's average elevation is 1,085 feet (330 meters) above sea level. More than a third of the continent lies below 656 feet (200 meters) in elevation. The low-lying regions are mostly narrow coastal plains and interior lowlands. Half of Australia is between 200 and 500 meters (1,640 feet) above sea level. Less than 1 percent of the continent rises more than 1,000 meters (3,281 feet) above sea level.

The history of Australian landscapes has been traced back to the Permian period, over 280 million years ago. At that time a huge ice cap covered most of the continent. After the ice melted, central parts of the continent had subsided so much that they were covered by shallow seas. There sediments were laid down that became sedimentary rocks. By the Cretaceous period, over 100 million years ago, seas rose over the flat land, separating Australia into three separate sections of land.

Many Australian rocks contain fossils of very large animals, both land and marine creatures. In other basins, deposits developed that later formed coal, oil, and natural gas fields. These features show that the climate was warm and quite wet for long periods of geological history.

The extreme aridity now characteristic of interior Australia is thought to be geologically relatively recent, occurring between 10 and 55 million years ago, during the Tertiary period, as the continent moved northward from its earlier position in the Antarctic. The Indo-Australia Plate is still moving northward, but very slowly—at a rate of about two centimeters (one inch) a year.

VOLCANISM. Queensland is an area of relatively recent volcanic activity, as is the Western District of Victoria. Although there are no active volcanoes in Australia, there are lava flows and other signs of volcanic activity, dating from the Tertiary period to as recently as 5,000 years ago at Mount Gambier. Australia's island neighbors—New Zealand, New Guinea, and Indonesia—all have active volcanoes, as they are located at the boundaries of tectonic plates, but Australia is located centrally on the Indo-Australian Plate.

WESTERN PLATEAU. Australia can be divided into three fairly distinct physiographical regions: The Western Plateau, the Central Lowlands, and the Eastern Highlands. More than half of the continent is part of the great Western Plateau. This plateau covers all of Western Australia and most of South Australia and the Northern Territory and has an average elevation of 300 meters (984 feet).

The plateau contains great expanses of desert. Some of the world's oldest rocks—over three billion years old—are found in western Australia in the area known as the Australian Shield. The size and shape of the continent has changed greatly throughout the earth's history. Over 200 million years ago, it was part of the supercontinent Pangaea. Around 100 million years ago, it started to separate from Antarctica and to move northward.

Great Sandy Desert Page 1851

The Great Sandy Desert, the Gibson Desert, and the Great Victoria Desert occupy much of the Western Plateau. Huge fields of longitudinal sand dunes, aligned in the direction of the prevailing winds, cover parts of these deserts. A great part of these deserts is stony desert or reg, known in Australia as "gibber plains."

Around the continent's ocean edges the Western Plateau is rimmed by escarpments. The most interesting of these is the Nullarbor Plain. It is a limestone area with no surface streams but many underground caves. Its rocks were a seafloor about 25 million years ago. Since then the area has been uplifted to form the present landscape.

At the southeastern edge of the western Plateau are the Flinders and Mount Lofty Ranges, a series of fault-block mountains.

They have an unusually distinctive appearance and are sometimes called the Shatter Belt. Most of these mountains are about 1,000 meters (3,281 feet) high and contain some very old rocks. Two places in the Western Plateau are rich in minerals—the goldfield area around Kalgoorlie in Western Australia and the Mount Isa area in western Queensland, where copper and lead are mined.

A few mountains and smaller plateaus rise above the generally flat landscape of the Western Plateau. In the west is the Hamersley Range, from which a number of rivers flow west to the Indian Ocean: the De Grey, Fortescue, Ashburton, Gascoyne and Murchison.

In the northwest is the Kimberley Plateau, from which the Fitzroy River flows west, and the Drysdale and Ord flow north

Western Queensland's Channel Country. (Corbis)

Section of the Murray River in Victoria. (Tom McKnight/Joan Clemons)

to the Timor Sea. In the Northern Territory, the Victoria, Daly and Roper are important rivers. The rugged areas of Arnhem Land and the Macdonnel Ranges are prominent higher areas, as are the Musgrave Ranges in South Australia.

In the center of Australia is one of the world's famous landforms, Uluru, once known as Ayers Rock. This sandstone monolith rises 345 meters (1,132 feet) above the very flat surrounding plains, and covers 1.3 square miles (3.3 sq. km.). To the east, the Western Plateau slopes down into the Central Lowlands, a series of three basins running from the Gulf of Carpentaria to the South Australia-Victoria border.

CENTRAL LOWLANDS. The northernmost basin of the Central Lowlands drains to the Gulf of Carpentaria. Long rivers

here include the Leichhardt, Cloncurry, Flinders, Norman, Gilbert and Mitchell. In the center of the Lowlands is the Lake Eyre basin, where the streams of the western Queensland Channel Country drain to the lowest point on the Australian continent, Lake Eyre. That lake's surface is 50 feet (15 meters) below sea level and covers almost 3,861 square miles (10,000 sq. km.). This salt lake is normally dry, but it has been filled three times in the twentieth century. Other large salt pans, or salinas, in South Australia are Lake Torrens and Lake Gairdner.

Many Australian rivers are intermittent, containing water only for a short period each year. In the dry period, they shrink to a series of waterholes, or billabongs, and sometimes a river is only a sandy bed for very long periods.

Uluru
Pages
1849, 1906

Rivers
Page 1909

The third basin of the Central Lowlands is occupied by Australia's largest and most important river system, the Murray-Darling. The Murray River is over 1,560 miles (2,500 km.) long and forms part of the New South Wales-Victoria border. The Darling and its tributaries, known as the Upper Darling, are another 120 miles (2,000 km.) in length. One tributary of the Darling, the MacIntyre River, forms part of the New South Wales-Queensland border.

Although the Murray-Darling drainage basin covers 386,000 square miles (1 million sq. km.), or about one-seventh of the continent, its discharge of water is small. Because of climatic variability, it is also extremely variable. Nevertheless, during the nineteenth century the Murray River was used as a waterway on which a steamboat trade flourished. In the twentieth century, large dams, weirs and barrages were constructed to make water available for agriculture throughout the Murray-Murrumbidgee agricultural area.

ARTESIAN WATER. Although the interior of Australia is extremely arid, it contains a valuable resource in the form of groundwater. This is the Great Artesian Basin, the world's largest aquifer, or reservoir of underground water. The Great Artesian Basin stretches under the Central Lowlands, from the Gulf of Carpentaria to northern New South Wales and South Australia, covering an area of 656,000 square miles (1.7 million sq. km.) and containing over 7 million acre feet (8,700 million megaliters) of water. The intake beds for the basin are located along the western slopes of the Eastern Highlands. Because artesian water is under pressure, it rises to the surface without needing to be pumped. The average depth of the bores is about 1,640 feet (500 meters). Artesian water is warm and contains minerals, but it is suitable for animals to drink.

The discovery of the Central Lowland's artesian water in the 1870's prompted a great expansion of cattle and sheep farming, especially in Queensland. These developments created two new problems. Native plant species began declining because of the overgrazing of cattle and sheep. This in turn led to declines in numbers of native animal species. The sinking of thousands of bores—many of which flow without restriction—to tap underground water severely decreased the water's flow. Hundreds of bores have dried up. Recharge is smaller than demand, so attempts are now being made to conserve the water of the Great Artesian Basin, and to prevent environmental damage.

EASTERN HIGHLANDS. Running the length of the east coast, from Cape York in the north to Melbourne in the southeast, are the Eastern Highlands. These uplands also continue on to the island of Tasmania. This area was uplifted during the Tertiary period, between 2 and 65 million years ago. This region is often called the Great Dividing Range. However, this is a misleading term, as much of the high land consists only of tablelands and plateaus. Moreover, there are many different ranges, ridges, and mountains.

The Eastern Highlands do, however, form a true divide, separating the short rivers flowing across the coastal plains to the Pacific Ocean from the rivers that flow inland. Rainfall is plentiful, so these streams are permanent, and they have provided the initial sites for the founding of Australia's cities. Near their headwaters waterfalls and gorges are common. Some of the longer coastal rivers are the Burdekin and Fitzroy in Queensland and the Hunter River at Newcastle, which is the heart of a wine-growing district.

The steep cliffs and slopes on the eastern side of this region form a long escarpment, running from Queensland to Victoria, with a gentle slope on the western side, down over the interior plains. The coastal plains lying between the Pacific Ocean and the Eastern Highlands are as narrow as 31 miles (50 km.) in some places and as wide as 497 miles (800 km.) in others. In Queensland, the highest peak is Mount Bartle Frere, which rises only to 5,322 feet (1,622 meters). The New England Tableland of northern New South Wales is one of Australia's coldest environments. The Atherton Tableland in north Queensland has a cool climate, enabling dairying, even though it is within a tropical region.

EXPLORATION. The Blue Mountains, on the inland side of Sydney, are not a high escarpment, but are highly dissected and quite rugged. For this reason, they presented a formidable barrier to the early European settlers in the British colony of New South Wales. The explorers Gregory Blaxland, William Lawson, and William Charles Wentworth crossed the mountains in 1813 and discovered the wonderful grasslands of the interior which became sheep pastures. As later explorers ventured into the strange new environment they were often deceived by misinformation and preconceived ideas.

A myth that a great river flowed to a large inland sea persisted into the 1840's, when Thomas Mitchell, the surveyor-general of New South Wales, traveled into central Queensland along what is now called the Barcoo River. In 1861 Robert Burke and William John Wills died at Cooper's Creek, after crossing Australia from Melbourne to the Gulf of Carpentaria without finding any major rivers or lakes. Ludwig Leichhardt discovered the Burdekin River in 1845 during an epic journey from the Darling Downs to Port Essington, near

Gorge in the New England Tableland, near Armidale in New South Wales. (Tom McKnight/Joan Clemons)

modern Darwin in the Northern Territory. On another expedition, three years later, his party vanished in the central Queensland desert.

MOUNTAINS. Australia's ten tallest mountains all stand in an area of the Eastern Highlands known as the Australian Alps, near the border between New South Wales and Victoria. The tallest of these is Mount Kosciusko, which is only 7,313 feet (2,229 meters) high. In comparison, the world's highest mountain, Mount Everest, is four times higher than Kosciusko. Covered with snow during the winter months, the alps are the source of important rivers.

New South Wales Page 1852

EASTERN HIGHLANDS AND TASMANIA. On Australia's mainland, the Eastern Highlands end in the Grampians of western Victoria. The rugged mountains of Tasmania form the southernmost portion of the Eastern Highlands. Much of the island is a plateau, while the island's tallest peak is Mount Ossa which rises to 5,305 feet (91,617 meters). During the Quaternary period, over a million years ago, the earth experienced its most recent ice age. Huge areas of North America, Asia and Europe were covered by ice, which advanced and retreated numerous times.

Tasmanian mountains Page 1840

Like the northern continents, Australia also experienced glaciation, which left glacial lakes and other typical features in Tasmania. A small part of the Australian Alps also was affected by this glaciation. At this time too, sea level was some 330 feet (100 meters) lower than at present; what is now the continental shelf was part of the mainland. The Great Barrier Reef now marks this outer edge. Three parts of the Eastern Highlands have been designated World Heritage Areas—the Wet Tropics of Queensland, the Central Eastern Rain Forest Reserves, and the Tasmanian Wilderness. The Great Barrier Reef is another marine World Heritage Area.

WATER RESOURCES. The flat topography of Australia affects the rainfall, because there are no high mountain barriers to block winds and produce what is called orographic rainfall. Australia's drainage patterns are clearly the result of topography. The main divide of the Eastern Highlands separates the moist coastal plains from the dry basin and plains of the interior. Most permanent streams in densely populated areas have their flows regulated by dams, creating surface storage in artificial lakes and reservoirs. A drawback to this is that large amounts of water are lost to surface evaporation.

Permanent streams in the unpopulated north are too remote for development to be economically practical. The availability of water resources has been a major influence on human settlement patterns throughout Australia's history, and has resulted in the concentration of population around the moist east, southeast and far southwest coastal areas. The percentage of the population living in rural areas declined from 43 percent in 1911 to 14 percent in the late 1990's. Only 5 percent of Australian workers are employed in agriculture, forestry and fishing.

Ray Sumner

FOR FURTHER STUDY

Arden, Harvey. "The Land of Northwest Australia: Journey into Dreamtime." *National Geographic* (January, 1991): 8-41.

"Australia: A Bicentennial Down Under." *National Geographic* (February, 1988): 157-294.

Haynes, Rosslynn D. *Seeking the Center: The Australian Desert in Literature, Art, and Films.* New York: Cambridge University Press, 1999.

Heathcote, Ronald L. *Australia.* 2d ed. New York: John Wiley & Sons, 1994.

McKnight, Tom L. *Oceania: The Geography of Australia, New Zealand and the Pacific*

Islands. Englewood Cliffs, N.J.: Prentice Hall, 1995.

Manuel, Mark. *A Geography of South Australia.* New York: Cambridge University Press, 1995.

Newman, Cathy. "Cape York Peninsula." *National Geographic* (June, 1996): 2-33.

Serventy, J. *Landforms of Australia.* New York: American Elsevier, 1968.

Pacific Islands

Map Page 1853

Most islands of the Pacific Ocean are located between the tropics of Cancer and Capricorn. While there are some large islands, most are quite small in size and population and poor in natural resources, but with beautiful tropical landscapes, conducive to travel and tourism. New Zealand is larger than all but Papua New Guinea, and is located south of the main island region, yet its indigenous culture, the Maori, is similar to some island peoples in cultural and physical characteristics; thus, it is included in the Pacific Island region.

The west-to-east extent of the Pacific Island region is from Palau (Belau) in the west, at 7° 30′ north latitude and longitude 134° 30′ east, to Easter Island in the east, at 28° 10′ south latitude and longitude 109° 30′ west. The north-to-south extent is from Midway Islands in the north at 28° 13′ north latitude and longitude 177° 22′ west, to New Zealand in the south, with the southernmost tip of the southern island at 47° south latitude and longitude 168° east. This is more than 1,000 miles (1,600 km.) southeast of Australia.

PHYSIOGRAPHIC REGIONS. Three physiographic regions define the Pacific Islands and New Zealand. The first is Melanesia (black islands in Greek), which includes the culturally rich and generally darker-skinned peoples of Papua New Guinea, Solomon Islands, Vanuatu, New Caledonia, and Fiji. These islands are diverse both physically and culturally. They are primarily mountainous, but differ greatly in size. Papua New Guinea is by far the largest at 174,849 square miles (452,860 sq. km.). All Melanesian territories are large by Pacific standards, which gives them relatively more regional and international political influence.

The second region, Micronesia (the little islands in Greek), consists of more than two thousand coral atolls and volcanic islands scattered across the western Pacific, primarily north of the equator. The main island groups are the Federated States of Micronesia, including Palau (Belau); Kiribati (the Gilbert Islands); the Mariana Islands, including Guam; the Republic of Marshall Islands; and the island of Nauru. Although covering an ocean area larger than the continental United States, the islands of Micronesia have a combined land area of only 1,120 square miles (2,900 sq. km.)—roughly the size of the state of Rhode Island. Fewer than one hundred of these resource-poor islands are inhabited.

Polynesia (Greek for many islands), the third region, is vast in terms of sea area, covering the largest expanse of ocean. A

RECENT VOLCANIC ERUPTIONS IN THE PACIFIC

Volcanic eruptions and related earthquakes and tsunamis, or seismically induced sea waves, are common events across the Pacific Island region, and they impose major environmental hazards upon its inhabitants. A summary of recent volcanic activity in the Pacific Islands region follows.

1832-1984:   Hawaii's Mauna Loa erupts thirty-nine times.

1983-:   Hawaii's Mount Kilauea begins erupting continuously.

1994:   Eruptions and earthquakes on Papua New Guinea's island of New Britain force more than 100,000 people from their homes, destroying Rabaul and nearby villages.

1995:   New Zealand's Mount Ruapehu erupts.

1995:   Mariana Islands' Mount Ruby, a prominent, active submarine volcano, erupts.

1995:   Mount Alba on Vanuatu's Ambae Island erupts.

1995:   Tonga's Metis Shoal erupts.

1996:   Mount Loihi, the youngest volcano in the Hawaiian chain, erupts.

1996:   Gemini Seamount on the New Hebrides Island Arc erupts.

*Kilauea
Pages
1903, 2034*

triangular shape defines the area, with the Hawaiian Islands in the north, New Zealand in the south, and Rapanui to the east. Polynesia also includes the French-controlled Society Islands (French Polynesia), and the smaller political states of Tonga, Tuvalu, Cook Islands, and Samoa. Excluding New Zealand and the Hawaiian Islands, the total land area of these small island groups, or archipelagos, is only about 3,189 square miles (8,260 sq. km.). The largest island is Tahiti at 402 square miles (1,042 sq. km.).

*Tahiti
Page 2044*

LANDFORMS. The landforms of the Pacific Islands and New Zealand are divided into high islands and low islands or atolls. They are primarily volcanic in nature and geologically fairly young. The high islands are mountainous and spectacularly scenic, with steep slopes and peaks of 3,300 to 13,000 feet (1,000 to 4,000 meters), but with great local variations in elevation,

slope, soil, rainfall, and plant life. Papua New Guinea, for example, is dominated by extensive, east-west trending volcanic mountain ranges separated by rugged, elevated plateaus and bordered by coastal lowlands.

The Hawaiian Islands, on the other hand, contain several more classic-looking shield volcanoes, relatively gently sloping mountains produced from numerous fluid lava flows, and rimmed at the top by volcanic cones that reveal the inner core of the volcano. All larger islands of Melanesia and several Polynesian islands are volcanic high islands.

The low islands are generally quite small and lacking in vital resources such as fertile soils and drinking water; therefore, they are sparsely populated. Coral reefs, sandy beaches, and coconut palms, typical of a picturesque island paradise, characterize the low islands. These islands, called atolls, are made of broken pieces of coral and usually form an irregular ring around a lagoon, with the coral pieces separated by channels leading into the lagoon.

The world's largest atoll, Kwajelein, in Micronesia's Marshall Islands, is 75 miles (120 km.) long and 15 miles (24 km.) wide. Polynesia, Micronesia, and parts of Melanesia are dotted with extensive atoll systems. Some major archipelagos, such as the Marshall Islands in Micronesia and Tuamotus in Polynesia, are composed entirely of atolls.

New Zealand consists of two large islands, North Island and South Island, plus several small islands. Cook Strait separates North and South Island. The two main islands are rugged in terrain. North Island primarily comprises high volcanoes, many exceeding 5,000 feet (1,500 meters), and a central highland plateau; South Island is formed of a range of high mountains, called the Southern Alps, and an eastern lowland plain.

The highest and most rugged mountains are found on the western side of the South Island. Aoraki (Mount Cook) is New Zealand's highest peak, cresting at more than 12,000 feet (3,660 meters). The Southern Alps, known to the Maori as Te Tapu Nui (the Peaks of Intense Sacredness), are one of the world's most visually spectacular mountain ranges, complete with high mountain glaciers and steep, narrow, fjord-like valleys that cut into much of South Island's isolated western coast.

GEOLOGIC HISTORY. Island geology varies across the Pacific Island region. The high islands were formed by undersea volcanic or tectonic mountain-building activity. The large islands of Melanesia, along with New Zealand, are composed of continental rock and are geologically quite complex. When the Indian continental plate collided with the Pacific continental plate, a series of mountain ranges formed in Papua New Guinea, extending across the Solomon Islands to Vanuatu and New Caledonia, and down to New Zealand to form a mountainous island chain or arc.

Most of the islands of Polynesia and Micronesia originated from volcanic activity on the ocean floor without any geological connection to continental landmasses. These volcanic islands are formed by oceanic crust sliding over a hot spot in the earth's mantle where molten magma (hot liquid rock), relatively close to the crust, rises and cools to form new volcanic islands. The Hawaiian Islands, the largest and youngest of the Pacific's high islands, are an excellent example with several young, active and recently active volcanoes rising to more than 3980 meters (13,000 feet). Many French Polynesian islands are smaller examples of high volcanic islands. In tropical latitudes, most high islands are ringed by coral reefs that quickly establish themselves in the shallow waters near the shore.

High islands are limited in geological lifespan. Volcanic activity gradually decreases, and the volcanoes eventually become extinct. These high islands slowly subside or sink, and erode away to begin formation of low island atolls. After a few hundred years, only a few low peaks, called seamounts, or underwater volcanoes, may rise out of a shallow, reef-rimmed lagoon. Eventually, even remnant peaks erode away, leaving only the reef surrounding the lagoon. Reefs tend to persist because they are composed of living organisms that constantly create new coral, even as the island base subsides. Atoll formation continues as large waves periodically break off and crush large pieces of coral, then deposit them on adjacent sections of the reef to form narrow sandy islands. An atoll, therefore, comprises the combination of circular or oval-shaped barrier coral reefs, narrow sandy islands, and shal-

Southern Alps Pages 1841, 1854

Lava from the island of Hawaii's Mauna Ulu volcano enters the sea west of the island's Apua Point. (U.S. Geological Survey)

geologic development through undersea mountain building from "hot spots" beneath the ocean crust. The North Island of New Zealand, for example, contains several volcanic peaks and geothermal features as a result of volcanic formation.

The Hawaiian Islands were produced by the Hawaiian hot spot, presently located under the Big Island of Hawaii. Each has at least one primary volcano, although many islands are composites of more than one. The Big Island, for instance, is constructed of five major volcanoes: Kilauea, Mauna Loa, Mauna Kea, Hualalai, and Kohala.

HYDROLOGY. Many Pacific Islands are located in a tropical wet/dry climate region where abundant rains and tropical cyclones can bring heavy seasonal precipitation. High islands are particularly noted for their heavy rainfall, with frequent snows on the higher peaks (13,000 feet/3,980 meters). Drainage patterns are established in mountainous terrain according to rock type and slope steepness. Steep, volcanic slopes erode easily during heavy rains, developing deep drainage channels that transport rainwater to lands below. Major populations are located in the coastal lowland regions and urban areas of the high islands where fresh water is abundant. Inhabitants of the highlands have ample fresh water as well.

Low-lying atolls have significantly less precipitation than high islands, and limited water storage capacity as well; thus, they often experience water shortages. When it does rain, small "lenses" of fresh water often float above the salt water. In dry periods, the salt water in the center of each sandy island quickly depletes the stores of fresh water. Limited availability of

low central lagoons. The nineteenth century scientist Charles Darwin developed this explanation for the geological formation of atolls.

VOLCANISM. Most of the Pacific Islands have a volcanic core that developed from eruptions of lava deep beneath the ocean floor during tectonic movement of the Pacific Plate. Much of Melanesia and Polynesia, including New Zealand and the Hawaiian Islands, are part of the seismically active Pacific Rim of Fire, so named for its

*Hawaii
Pages
1853, 1903*

fresh water limits human settlement on the low islands and atolls. Most fresh water must be imported to support inhabitants of atolls.

New Zealand's highlands lie in the Southern Hemisphere belt of westerly winds and receive abundant precipitation, with local variations within the rain shadows of east-facing slopes. Moderate marine weather keeps year-round temperatures fairly warm, causing glaciers to flow on both islands. The glaciers, lakes, and mountain streams of the highland regions provide plenty of fresh water for New Zealand's population. Rugged terrain and heavy precipitation in the Southern Alps and mountainous core of the North Island limit highland settlement. The well-populated areas are restricted to the fringing lowlands of the North Island and along the drier east and south coasts of the South Island where fresh water flows naturally from the highlands.

Island hydrology also provides transportation routes for human settlement. In some high islands, rugged terrain and lack of roads make canoe travel by navigable river a necessity. The large and powerful Fly and Sepik Rivers of Papua New Guinea, for example, are widely used as travel and trade routes between villages in these southern and northern coastal regions, respectively.

Laurie A. Garo

FOR FURTHER STUDY

Bradshaw, Michael. "South Pacific." In *A World Regional Geography: The New Global Order.* Madison, Wis.: Brown and Benchmark, 1997.

Brookfield, H. C., and Doreen Hart. *Melanesia: A Geographical Interpretation of an Island World.* London: Methuen, 1971.

Browne, Christopher, and Douglas A. Scott. *Economic Development in Seven Pacific Island Countries.* Washington, D.C.: International Monetary Fund, 1989.

Rowntree, Les, et al. "Australia and Oceania." In *Diversity Amid Globalization: World Regions, Environment and Development.* Englewood Cliffs, N.J.: Prentice Hall, 2000.

Salter, Christopher L., et al. "A Geographical Profile of the Pacific World." In *Essentials of World Regional Geography.* 2d ed. Fort Worth, Tex.: Saunders, 1998.

INFORMATION ON THE WORLD WIDE WEB

The World Factbook 2000 Web site, maintained by the U.S. Central Intelligence Agency (CIA), features profiles of Pacific Island nations and New Zealand. (www.odci.gov/cia/publications/factbook/es.html#geo)

CLIMATOLOGY

AUSTRALIA

Map
Page 1905

Australia
from space
Page 1905

The dominant feature of Australia's climate is its general aridity. Indeed, the continent is the world's driest. More than a third of its area has a hot desert climate. Another third has a semiarid climate. Average annual precipitation throughout the continent is only 17.7 inches (450 millimeters). Thanks to the low rainfall, clear skies are characteristic of most Australian weather.

PRECIPITATION ZONES. Australia's precipitation zones can be seen as rings encircling the north, east, and south portions of the continent. In the west the dry desert extends all the way to the coast. The outermost ring is the wettest, getting more than 31 inches (800 millimeters) of rain a year. That ring encompasses the Kimberly region, Arnhem Land, and the entire east coast—from Cape York to the South Australia border. It also includes most of the island of Tasmania and a small section of the southwest corner of Western Australia.

As one moves inland, away from the imaginary outer rings, rainfall decreases sharply. A large area in the interior gets less than 5.8 inches (200 millimeters) of precipitation annually. Eighty percent of Australia receives less than 23.6 inches (600 millimeters) of rainfall annually.

SUNSHINE AND HEAT. The second important feature of Australian climates is their high temperatures. Indeed, heat is such a pervasive part of Australian life that all Australians are familiar with Dorothea McKellar's poem "My Country," which begins: "I love a sunburnt country."

Almost all of Australia has at least 3,000 hours of sunshine every year. The central and western desert areas receive even more. Heat waves, or successive days of temperatures over 104 degrees Fahrenheit (40 degrees Celsius), are frequent during summer months (December through March) over much of inland Australia.

As a general rule, mean temperatures decrease as one moves from the northwest to the southeast. Between Broome and Darwin on the west, average annual temperatures are around 82 degrees Fahrenheit (28 degrees Celsius). Throughout the rest of tropical Australia (the northern half), annual average temperatures range between 70 and 79 degrees Fahrenheit (21 and 26 degrees Celsius). Between Perth and Sydney, annual averages range between 59 and 68 degrees Fahrenheit (15 and 20 degrees Celsius). Victoria and Tasmania experience annual average temperatures below 59 degrees Fahrenheit (15 degrees Celsius).

Australia's coldest regions are in its southeastern corner: the Australian Alps—the only region where snow falls regularly—and in Tasmania. Frost is common in winter in elevated areas of Australia, such as the Darling Downs and New

England Tableland and throughout inland Victoria and Tasmania. At the opposite corner of the continent, in northwestern Australia, temperatures above 104 degrees Fahrenheit (40 degrees Celsius) are common throughout the summer. The highest recorded temperature in Australia, 127.4 degrees Fahrenheit (53 degrees Celsius), was recorded at Cloncurry in western Queensland. However, the hottest inhabited place in Australia is the small settlement of Marble Bar in western Australia. There temperatures have risen above 100 degrees Fahrenheit (37.5 degrees Celsius) as many as 160 days a year.

WINDS. Because it lies across the line of the tropic of Capricorn, Australia is in the belt of subtropical highs, where dry descending air dominates the climate. During winter, large anticyclones, or highs, move across the continent, from west to east. They move at a rate of about 375 miles (600 km.) per day. Sometimes they remain stationary over the interior for several days.

Australia is in the Southern Hemisphere, where the direction of rotation of winds around subtropical cyclones is counterclockwise. This means that southeast winds, the trade winds, influence northern Australia, while the continent's southern parts are affected by strong westerly winds. These winds are called the "Roaring Forties" because they develop around 40 degrees south latitude. These cool, moist winds and accompanying cold fronts and midlatitude cyclones deliver rainfall to the southern part of Australia during the midyear winter.

The southwest corner of Western Australia receives abundant winter rain of more than 23.6 inches (600 millimeters), followed by intense summer drought when the high pressure cells are further south, producing dry easterly winds. This region has a typical Mediterranean climate, similar to southern California. Moving further east, there is a similar but drier region around Adelaide in South Australia, which also has a Mediterranean climate.

In summer, when the highs move further southward, the southern parts of Australia experience dry conditions, and heat waves are common. Southeast trade winds dominate the climate of southeast and east Australia. This is the humid subtropical climate region, where temperatures are moderate and rain falls in every month. This type of climate is also found in the eastern United States and in Western Europe, where most Australian immigrants came from in the nineteenth century. It is still the most densely populated part of Australia, containing the two largest cities, Sydney and Melbourne. The rainfall here is reliable, although there are occasional droughts, as well as occasional flooding in the tropical parts, brought by hurricanes.

Temperatures vary greatly throughout this long region, from tropical conditions in the north to cool conditions in the south, where frosts are common, and winter precipitation falls as snow in the Alps and in Tasmania, and even on the Blue Mountains and the New England Plateau. Some patches of snow may remain through summer, but there are no permanent snowfields in Australia. Seasonality of precipitation also varies, with northern regions receiving more rain in summer, and the southernmost regions receiving a winter maximum.

RAIN PATTERNS. Where the warm moist southeast trades meet mountains close to the coast, orographic rainfall occurs, making the small region of North Queensland from Ingham to Cooktown the wettest in Australia. This is a tropical wet or tropical rain forest climate. Annual rainfall totals exceed 157.2 inches (4,000 millimeters) in smaller towns like Tully and Innisfail, while the tiny settlement of Deeral claims

Queensland Page 1912

Thunderstorm cloud forming over Western Australia. (Tom McKnight/Joan Clemons)

Snowy Mts.
Page 1906

the record of over 275.1 inches (7,000 millimeters) of rainfall per year. Only the mountainous western coast of Tasmania has a similar rainfall, with around 137.6 inches (3,500 millimeters) annually.

The Snowy Mountains also receive over 117.9 inches (3,000 millimeters) of precipitation a year. The record for the highest rainfall in Australia in a single year was recorded at Mount Bartle Frere in 1979: 442 inches (11,251 millimeters). This station also holds the record for the highest rainfall in a twenty-four-hour period: 37.7 inches (960 millimeters). Temperature and humidity are high in this region throughout the year. Tropical cyclones are also common along the whole of the tropical Queensland coast, bringing heavy rains in the summer months.

The northernmost part of Australia has a tropical savanna climate, and is part of the monsoon system which dominates life in India and Southeast Asia. Starting in October and continuing till April, moist northwesterly winds bring heavy rainfalls accompanied by dramatic thunderstorms to the northern coastal regions of Australia's Northern Territory, Queensland and Western Australia.

Darwin has more than seventy thunder days per year. Since temperatures are high year-round in the Tropics, people of the Northern Territory describe their climate as having two seasons, the wet and the dry. Tall tropical grasses thrive in the wet summer, but dry out quickly during the rest of the year, when the wind comes from the opposite direction, bringing dry south-westerly winds from the arid heart of the continent. Evaporation is very high, and bushfires are common. These conditions are similar to those of Southern California's Santa Ana winds.

TROPICAL STORMS. Hurricanes are frequent in northern and eastern tropical Australia during the summer wet. They develop over the warm oceans south of 5 degrees south latitude, and on average three hurricanes affect the Queensland coast and three affect the northern coast during a season. These storms are called tropical cyclones in Australia, and have wind speeds of over 46 miles (74 km.) per hour. The highest wind speed recorded in Australia was 166 miles (267 km.) per hour, during tropical cyclone Olivia in April, 1996.

Because northern Australia has a very small population, there is generally little loss of life during these storms, but severe flood damage is common. An exception to this was tropical cyclone Tracy, which struck the city of Darwin around midnight on December 24, 1974, killing 65 people and injuring 500. Because of health problems in the devastated city, most of the inhabitants were evacuated within a week. Many never returned, even though Darwin was rebuilt, using strict building codes to lessen wind damage should another tropical cyclone occur.

DESERT INTERIOR. The interior of Australia is a true desert, where temperatures are high, evaporation rates are high, and rainfall is very low. About half the continent has a desert climate, a belt extending from the west Australian coast to western Queensland, and extending from the Great Australian Bight into the Northern Territory. The driest part of Australia, around Lake Eyre, receives only 4.9 inches (125 millimeters) of rainfall annually.

Surrounding the desert interior is a semiarid belt; the northern parts receive

most of their scanty rainfall in the summer, while the southern parts receive their rainfall in the winter. Many towns in the south of Australia experience an interesting weather pattern in the summer: a low pressure trough causes hot dry winds from the center to bring very high temperatures which persist for several days. These winds are sometimes called brick-fielders. The situation can even affect coastal areas.

Lightning strike Page 1906

Sydney and Melbourne have recorded January temperatures above 113 degrees Fahrenheit (45 degrees Celsius). City-dwellers suffer the scorching heat and dusty conditions until a cold front brings welcome relief with a very rapid drop in temperature and usually thunderstorms. This abrupt and dramatic change is common in summer in Melbourne, where it is called a "cool change."

UNPREDICTABLE WEATHER. With rainfall and temperature data that have been collected over a long period of time, climatologists have come to understand that rainfall seasonality and variability are themselves important climatic factors in Australia. Australia is a country of climatic extremes: Droughts have long alternated with great floods, and both have seemed unpredictable. Using new technology such as the Topex-Poseidon

---

AUSTRALIAN SEASONS

Because Australia lies in the Southern Hemisphere, summer runs from December to February; autumn from March to May; winter from June to August; and spring from September to November. For most of the country the hottest month is January, and the coldest months are July and August. Because this pattern of seasons is opposite to that of the Northern Hemisphere, people who live in the Northern Hemisphere might find it difficult to imagine a winter with sweltering heat.

satellite, scientists have begun to understand and even predict years of flood or drought.

The extreme variability of precipitation over much of the continent is linked to what is called the El Niño-Southern Oscillation (ENSO) phenomenon, which affects large parts of the earth. The term "El Niño" relates to the unusually warm waters in the southwestern Pacific Ocean, off the coast of Peru. "Southern Oscillation" relates to changes in atmospheric pressure in the western Pacific region, from Tahiti to Indonesia—a large region that includes Australia.

During the 1980's scientists realized, for the first time, that El Niño and Southern Oscillation are linked. Moreover, they affect large parts of the world—not just regions around the Pacific Ocean. For example, when California experiences exceptionally heavy El Niño rains, lands on the opposite side of the Pacific experience severe droughts, with added danger from fires. During the El Niño event of 1997-1998, mudslides and floods in the western United States occurred while great fires burned Indonesian rain forests and droughts afflicted Australia, New Guinea, and even Southern Africa.

Long-term climate forecasting, using modern technology and computational modeling, is an area of research with great interest and significance for Australians. Much of the Australian environment is vulnerable to great climatic variation, and a better understanding of climatic processes can help protect people and resources in extreme events.

Ray Sumner

House built on stilts as a precaution against flooding in the Northern Territory's chief city, Darwin. (Tom McKnight/Joan Clemons)

Continued on page 1855

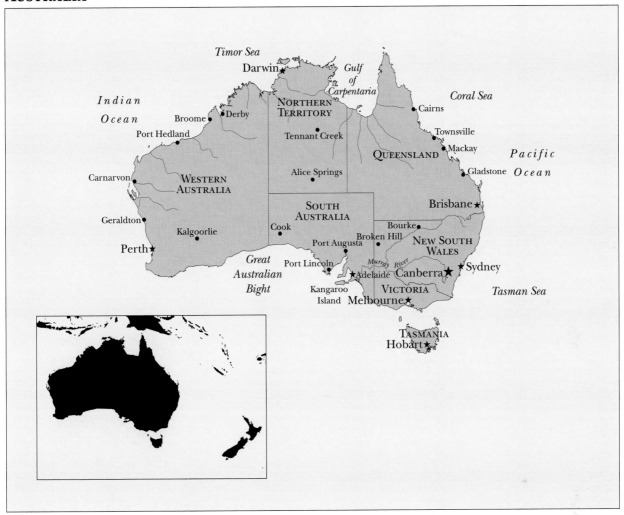

The northern tip of Cape York—the northernmost point of Australia—is only ten degrees south of the equator. (Tom McKnight/Joan Clemons)

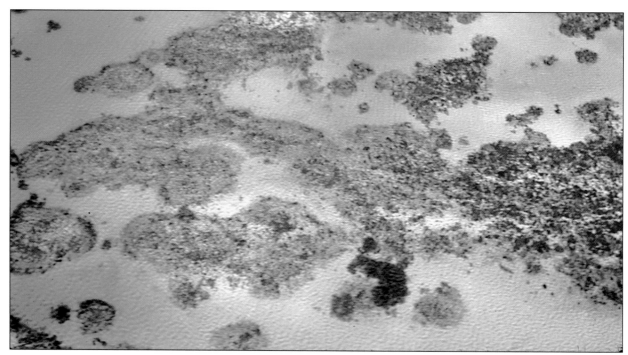

One of Australia's most famous natural sites is the Great Barrier Reef, off the east coast of Queensland. (Tom McKnight/Joan Clemons)

Mountain terrain in Tasmania, which has the greenest landscapes and coolest climate of any Australian state. (Tom McKnight/Joan Clemons)

1840

NEW ZEALAND

New Zealand's South Island is dominated by a large range called the Southern Alps, which runs almost the entire length of the island in a north-south direction. (Corbis)

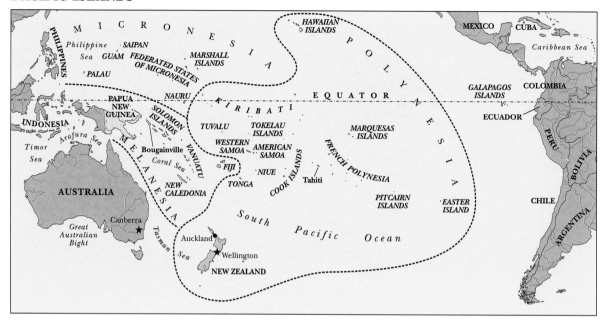

Coconut palms. (Digital Stock)

A volcanic island in French Polynesia, Bora-Bora is part of the Society Islands group. (PhotoDisc)

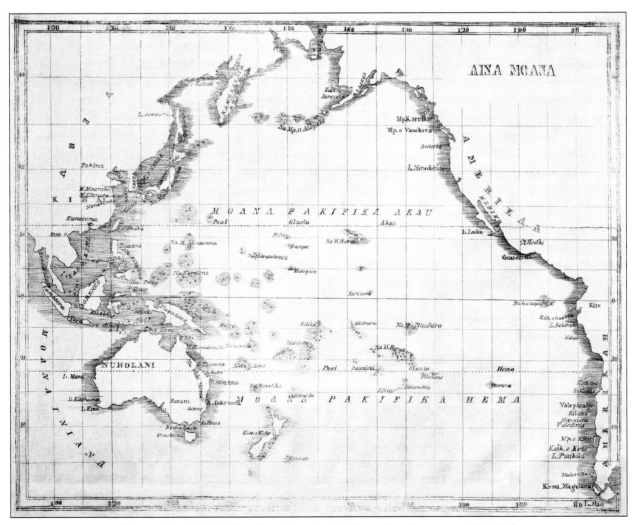

Map of the Pacific Islands written in the Hawaiian language. (Corbis)

Bora-Bora has the reputation of being among the most beautiful islands of the entire Pacific. It combines the spectacular profile of twin volcanic peaks with a surrounding coral reef structure. (American Stock Photography)

Samoan beach. (Clyde L. Rasmussen)

A South Pacific sunset in Fiji. (Tom McKnight/Joan Clemons)

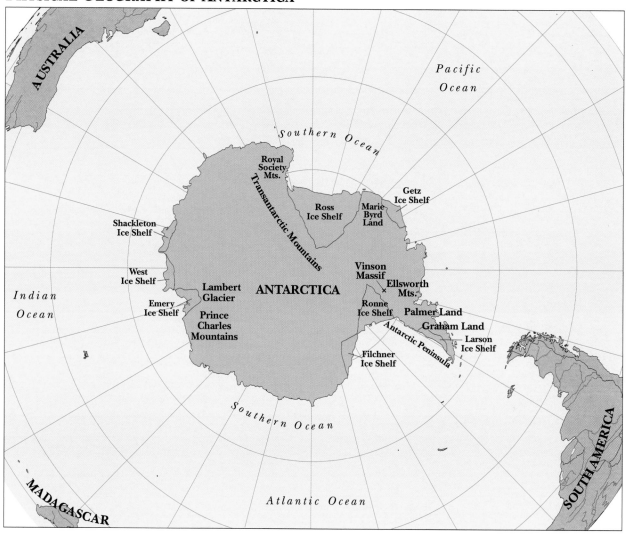

A crack in the Weddell Sea in early 1997. Satellite images revealed that a huge chunk of the Larsen B ice shelf had separated from the Antarctic Peninsula, an event that many scientists saw as evidence of global warming. (AP/Wide World Photos)

This award-winning photograph by Cherry Alexander shows a group of Antarctic penguins on a rare "blue iceberg"—the name given to ancient, highly compressed ice masses that reflect blue light. (AP/Wide World Photos)

The Transantarctic Mountains cross Antarctica from the Ross Sea to the Weddell Sea, passing through the South Pole. (AP/Wide World Photos)

MAJOR WATERSHEDS OF AUSTRALIA

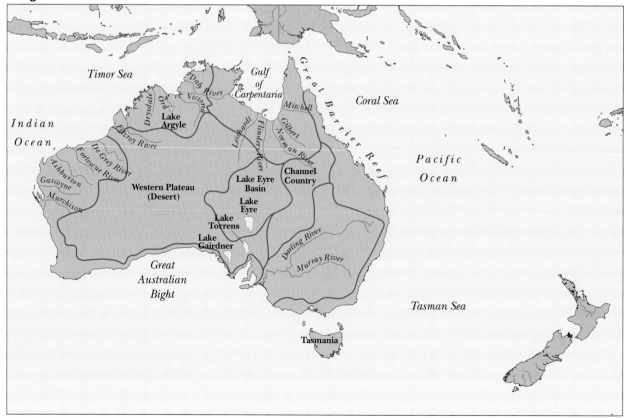

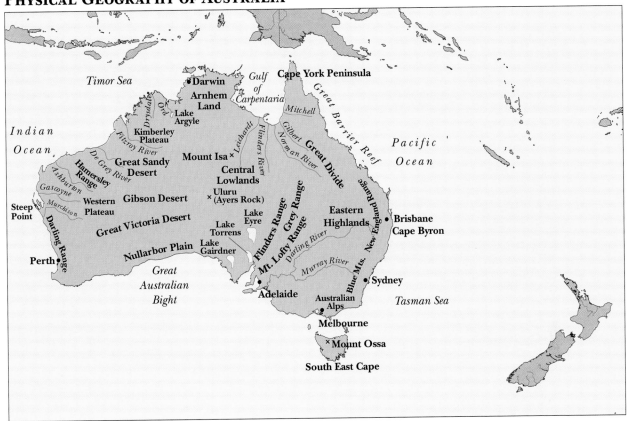

Australia's most famous landform, Uluru—also known as Ayers Rock—is a sandstone monolith that rises 1,132 feet (345 meters) above the surrounding plains, covering 1.3 square miles (3.3 sq. km.). (Digital Stock)

Rugged coastline of Victoria. (Corbis)

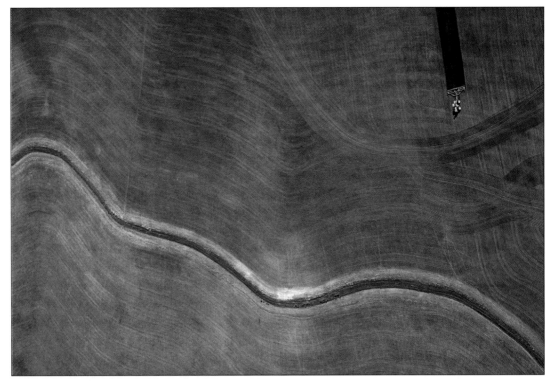

The Great Sandy Desert of Western Australia is a vast, flat expanse of sand hills and salt marshes with no significant human settlements. Daytime temperatures in the summer are some of the hottest in Australia. (Corbis)

Pounding waves produce spectacular cliffs and stacks and horizontal beds of sedimentary rock along Australia's Victoria coast. Called the Twelve Apostles, these erosional remnants are in Port Campbell National Park, 150 miles west of Melbourne. (Tom McKnight/Joan Clemons)

Wollomombi Falls, near Armidale in New South Wales. (Tom McKnight/Joan Clemons)

PHYSICAL GEOGRAPHY OF THE PACIFIC ISLANDS

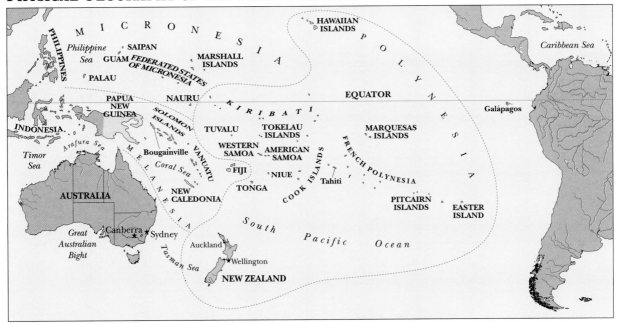

This satellite photograph of the island of Hawaii reveals some of the island's topography. (Hilo is hidden by clouds on the island's upper-right corner.) (PhotoDisc)

New Zealand's alpine South Island. (Corbis)

FOR FURTHER STUDY

Australian Bureau of Statistics. "Australia Now: A Statistical Profile." (http://www.statistics.gov.au)

Berra, Tim. *A Natural History of Australia.* Sydney: New South Wales Press, 1998.

Jeans, Dennis N., ed. *Australia: A Geography.* Volume 1: *The Natural Environment.* Sydney: Sydney University Press, 1986.

McKnight, T. M. *Oceania: The Geography of Australia, New Zealand and the Pacific Islands.* Englewood Cliffs, N.J.: Prentice Hall, 1995.

Ollier, Cliff. "Landforms and Their History." In *Year Book Australia 1988.* Canberra: Commonwealth Government Printer, 1988.

Read, Ian. *Continent of Extremes: Recording Australia's Natural Phenomena.* Sydney: New South Wales Press, 1998.

Sturman, A. P. and Tapper, Nigel J. *The Weather and Climate of Australia and New Zealand.* Melbourne, Australia: Oxford University Press, 1996.

Taylor, Griffith. *Australia: A Study of Warm Environments and Their Effect on British Settlement.* 7th ed. London: Methuen, 1966.

Webb, Eric K., ed. *Windows on Meteorology: Australian Perspective.* Melbourne: CSIRO Publishing, 1997.

Whitaker, D. P., et al. *Area Handbook for Australia.* Washington, D.C.: U.S. Government Printing Office, 1973.

ANTARCTICA

Antarctica is the coldest, windiest, driest continent on Earth. The cold is so extreme that it is known as a "heat sink," because warm air masses flowing over Antarctica quickly chill and lose altitude, affecting the entire world's weather. Most of Antarctica (98 percent) is ice cap with a few bare, rocky coastal areas, dry valleys, and mountain peaks blown free of snow by persistent winds. Annual precipitation on the ice cap is scant—between 1.25 and 3 inches (3-7 centimeters). The high-altitude central plateau is a frozen desert, with annual mean temperatures between –58 to –76 degrees Fahrenheit (–50 and –60 degrees Celsius)—identical to the average surface temperature on the planet Mars. Even on a summer's day at the South Pole, temperatures hover around –22 degrees Fahrenheit (–30 degrees Celsius). In comparison, the temperature of the average home freezer is a mere +5 degrees Fahrenheit (–15 degrees Celsius).

The Antarctic Peninsula is known as the Banana Belt of Antarctica. The summer temperature can hit a balmy 59 degrees Fahrenheit (15 degrees Celsius) on its northwest coast, with as much as 30 inches (76 centimeters) of annual precipitation. The temperatures of the islands ringing Antarctica, warmed by the sea, range from a few degrees below freezing up to around 37 degrees Fahrenheit (3 degrees Celsius). These warmer regions are much windier than the interior, however.

Antarctica holds the record for the coldest temperature ever recorded on Earth: –128 degrees Fahrenheit (–89 de-

THE OZONE HOLE

Ozone is a molecule composed of three atoms of oxygen instead of two. At the earth's surface, it is one of the ingredients in smog. In the upper atmosphere, however, ozone forms a protective chemical shield against deadly cosmic radiation. In 1981 atmospheric scientists became alarmed when September and October (Antarctic springtime) ozone readings over an area of Antarctica the size of the continental United States registered 20 percent below normal. This drop in ozone coincided with the increased presence in the upper atmosphere of artificial chemicals called chlorofluorocarbons (CFCs), which contain chlorine, an element that destroys ozone. The chlorine is released when ultraviolet light strikes CFC molecules in the upper atmosphere. Each chlorine atom remains in the atmosphere an average of forty years, destroying tens of thousands of ozone molecules.

The ozone hole began to develop over Antarctica because of the continent's extremely cold atmosphere. Polar stratospheric clouds, composed of ice particles containing water and nitrogen compounds, only occur when the air temperature drops below –112 degrees Fahrenheit (–80 degrees Celsius). These clouds occur during the Antarctic winter when the cold air circulates in a swirling pattern called the polar vortex at altitudes between 6 and 15 miles (10 to 24 km.). The clouds persist throughout the long winter without any influx of air from warmer areas. The surfaces of their ice crystals store chlorine compounds such as CFCs.

In the spring, the sun melts the ice crystals, freeing enormous amounts of chlorine to rapidly deplete the ozone layer, thus creating the ozone hole. In the summer, warm air breaks up the polar vortex and replenishes the ozone from other areas in the Southern Hemisphere. Bubbles of the ozone hole can break away, however, and drift north over populated areas. After 1987, CFC production decreased, but the ozone hole remained.

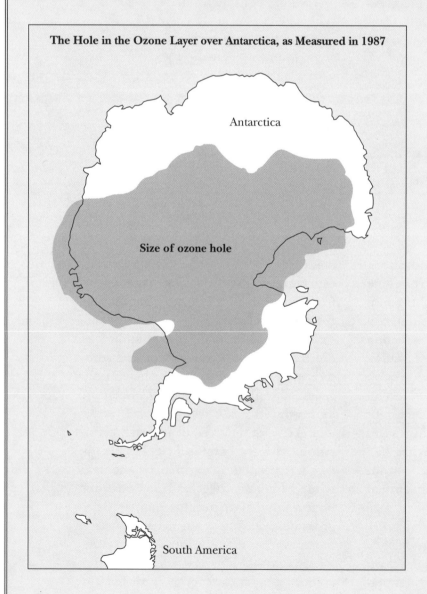

The Hole in the Ozone Layer over Antarctica, as Measured in 1987

Antarctica

Size of ozone hole

South America

grees Celsius), measured at the Russian research station of Vostok in July, 1983. Even colder temperatures could be measured at higher elevations on mountain summits if recording devices were present, but Vostok is definitely the coldest inhabited place on Antarctica, partly because of its location at what is called the Pole of Inaccessibility, the point on the ice cap furthest inland from the ocean's moderating influence. In addition, both its latitude (78 degrees south) and its altitude (11,320 feet/ 3,450 meters) are quite high.

Latitude and altitude both contribute to the continent's extreme coldness. At such low temperatures, water sprayed into the air freezes before striking the ground. Frozen water in the form of ice crystals suspended in the frigid atmosphere scatters light rays to create spectacular optical effects unique to Antarctica. Among them are vertical sun pillars, ice and fog bows, haloes, arcs, multiple suns and moons, and mirages.

HIGH LATITUDE. The primary reason both polar regions are cold is their high latitude. The earth is tilted on its axis, so the poles receive less of the sun's direct radiation than the lower latitudes. Even in midsummer, the Sun never rises very high above the horizon, so the air stays cool— like early morning or late afternoon in the temperate zones. The poles never experience the heat of high noon. In addition, winters are long and dark. At the Arctic Circle (66° 32′ north latitude) and the Antarctic Circle (66° 32′ south latitude), the Sun does not rise above the horizon on midwinter's day.

As latitude increases from the Arctic and Antarctic Circles to the poles, the winter night lengthens until, at the poles, the Sun sets just once a year. Once the last light fades, around March 21 at the South Pole, the poles are left in darkness for half the year with no direct solar warming at all. Although the Sun stays above the horizon for six months when it finally returns in late September, the warmth Antarctica receives in summer cannot make up for the heat it loses in winter. In fact, only at the height of summer (November and December in the Southern Hemisphere) does the South Pole actually gain heat by absorbing more solar radiation than it reflects away.

SOLAR REFLECTION. Antarctica actually receives about 7 percent more solar radiation annually than the Arctic because of the earth's elliptical orbit, bringing it closest to the Sun in January, the height of the Southern Hemisphere's summer. However, the climate of Antarctica is much harsher and far colder than the climate of the Arctic. The Arctic is an ocean surrounded by land. The ice covering the Arctic Ocean melts every summer, partly because the continents that surround the Arctic Ocean heat up considerably then and radiate warm air north. In addition, the dark waters absorb heat from the sun, keeping them warmer than the surrounding snow-covered continents in winter. Warm currents flowing from the south also raise temperatures there.

In contrast, the Antarctic is land surrounded by ocean. Land does not retain heat as well as water. The sea reflects back only about 5 percent of incoming solar short-wave radiation into the atmosphere. Exposed land reflects between 15 and 35 percent back. In the Antarctic, reflection from the land is intensified by the permanent mass of ice that covers all but 2 percent of the surface. The ice cap reflects back up to 90 percent of the sunlight it receives in the summer, so little heat can be absorbed. Because Antarctica reflects away more total radiation than it absorbs, it would get colder and colder if not for the structure of its atmosphere, which is separated into three layers. The

ICE CORES: FROZEN TIME CAPSULES

Scientists use special drills to remove samples of ice from deep within the Antarctic ice cap. These ice cores hold clues to the earth's climate and environment, dating from the present to hundreds of thousands of years ago. As each snowflake forms and falls, it acquires a tiny sample of the atmosphere's chemistry and is compressed into ice by the weight of successive snowfalls. The ice preserves a record of the conditions that existed when it was formed, such as traces of past volcanic eruptions, lightweight pollen grains blown by winds, and air bubbles. When the sources of the pollen can be identified, knowledge about the plants' present requirements for growth gives hints about past climates. When air bubbles are analyzed, chemists can determine changes in the percentages of different gases such as carbon dioxide and methane, both linked to possible global warming.

bottom and top layers transport cold air away from the continent. The middle layer is warm, moist air flowing in from temperate regions. As the water vapor in this layer condenses and freezes, it gives up its heat, providing a stabilizing influx of warm air.

Like the Arctic Ocean, the ocean that surrounds Antarctica is warmer than the land, but it cannot help to raise the land's temperature much because it, too, is blanketed most of the year by sea ice up to 6 feet (1.8 meters) thick, extending hundreds of miles out from shore. About 6.2 million square miles (16 million sq. km.) freeze and thaw every year, the biggest seasonal change to occur anywhere. When the southern ocean freezes in winter, about 8 percent of the Southern Hemisphere is covered by ice. The pack ice almost doubles the size of the continent in winter and also reflects solar energy back into the atmosphere.

OCEAN CURRENTS. Pack ice around Antarctica deepens its frigid temperatures, not just by reflecting the sun's energy back into space but also by insulating the mainland as bags of ice do in a cooler. The sea ice also dampens wave motion and creates downward-flowing ocean currents of cold, dense water that affect ocean circulation. Powerful currents in the southern ocean flow around the entire globe unhindered by land, generating huge waves, intense winds, and powerful low-pressure weather systems. Antarctica is surrounded by the planet's stormiest seas, so treacherous and wild that sailors call these latitudes the Roaring Forties, the Furious Fifties, and the Screaming Sixties.

To add to the commotion, a current called the Antarctic Convergence, a belt of water about 25 miles (40 km.) wide, encircles Antarctica where the cold currents streaming away from the ice cap meet the warmer currents flowing south from the Tropics, creating cold, wet, windy weather offshore. People sailing across the Antarctic Convergence can immediately feel the difference when the air and sea temperatures suddenly drop and mist appears. Its location shifts north every winter and south every summer, but it is always there somewhere between 50 and 60 degrees south latitude. These ocean currents together form an effective barrier isolating Antarctica from the moderating influences of currents and air masses from warmer latitudes.

WIND AND ALTITUDE. Another reason Antarctica is so cold is its high altitude. Higher altitudes are generally colder than lower altitudes, and Antarctica has the highest average altitude of any continent—8,039 feet (2,450 meters) because of its thick ice cap. By contrast, most of the Arctic is at or near sea level.

Closer to shore, frigid winds are constantly blowing down from the high altitudes of the ice cap because the relatively warmer, lighter air flowing at high altitudes over the interior quickly chills and sinks as it becomes colder and denser. These katabatic or gravity winds gain power as they accelerate down the slopes of the ice cap toward the coast. Faster and stronger than any other winds on Earth, they commonly travel at more than 50 miles (80 km.) an hour and have been recorded reaching 186 miles (300 km.) per hour, twice the velocity of the average hurricane.

ARIDITY. Prevailing ocean currents and winds prevent moist air masses from reaching Antarctica while the cold temperatures allow little evaporation to occur, so most of Antarctica experiences little precipitation even though it holds more then two-thirds of the planet's fresh water locked in its frigid embrace. The explanation for this apparent contradiction is simply that the snow, too cold to melt, has been accumulating for millions of years. What appear to be raging blizzards are actually like the sandstorms of the Sahara Desert. Most Antarctic snowfalls consist not of flakes but of pellets of loose, already fallen snow compacted into icy fragments that are then blown about by the fierce winds.

Sue Tarjan

FOR FURTHER STUDY

Campbell, David G. *The Crystal Desert: Summers in Antarctica.* Boston: Houghton Mifflin, 1992.

Chester, Jonathan. *Antarctica. Beauty in the Extreme.* London: Grange Books, 1991.

Fothergill, Alastair. *A Natural History of Antarctica: Life in the Freezer.* New York: Sterling Publishing, 1995.

Heacox, Kim. *Antarctica: The Last Continent.* Washington, D.C.: National Geographic Society, 1998.

Johnson, Rebecca. *Science on the Ice: An Antarctic Journal.* Minneapolis: Lerner, 1995.

Linacre, Edward, and Bart Geerts. *Climates and Weather Explained.* London: Routledge, 1997.

May, John. *The Greenpeace Book of Antarctica: A New View of the Seventh Continent.* 2d ed. New York: Doubleday, 1989.

INFORMATION ON THE WORLD WIDE WEB

The Web site of the Antarctica Meteorology Research Center at the University of Wisconsin Space Science and Engineering Center features weather data and many links to images and information from research sites in Antarctica. (uwamrc.ssec.wisc.edu/amrc/realtime.html#syn)

Virtual Antarctica, a Web site maintained by a commercial expedition company, features a gallery of images and dispatches from trekkers, allowing viewers a virtual experience of the Antarctic climate. (www.terraquest.com/antarctica/)

PACIFIC ISLANDS

The Pacific Islands stretch from Palau in the west to Pitcairn in the east and from the Hawaiian Islands in the north to New Zealand in the south. The islands generally fall into two types, high and low. The high islands consist of hills and mountains, some of which are active volcanoes. They are the larger islands, such as New Zealand and New Guinea, and the main islands in groups such as the Hawaiian Islands, Solomons, and Marianas. The low islands are formed of coral reefs and are generally small, some rising only a few feet above sea level. When a number of low islands surround a lagoon, they are called atolls. Low islands include the Marshall and Gilbert Islands. Their relatively small size and their dispersion across the ocean means that none of them has a truly continental climate; rather, their climates are governed by the ocean waters that surround them and the trade winds that blow over them.

TEMPERATURES AND RAINFALL. Most of the Pacific Islands are within the Tropics and thus are warm, humid, and temperate the entire year. The temperature in the islands ranges from about 70 to 80 degrees Fahrenheit (21.1 to 26.7 degrees Celsius). However, the climate in parts of New Zealand, which lies on the fortieth parallel of south latitude, can be termed temperate oceanic. In New Zealand, average temperatures range from 56 to 66 degrees Fahrenheit (13.3 to 18.9 degrees Celsius) in January and from 42 to 50 degrees Fahrenheit (5.6 to 10.0 degrees Celsius) in July. The mountain areas in New Guinea, New Zealand, and some other high islands are somewhat cooler; the tallest mountains on the largest islands retain their snow caps all year.

In general, the Pacific Islands near the equator experience high humidity and abundant rainfall distributed evenly through the year; islands more distant from the equator and more affected by winds have greater seasonal fluctuations in rainfall. In the Marshall Islands, where the climate is equatorial, rain falls year-round, surpassing 117 to 156 inches (3,000 to 4,000 millimeters) per year. Rains in the interior of Pohnpei Island in Micronesia can reach 390 inches (10,000 millimeters) per year. The amount of rain received in a particular area also depends on whether it is exposed to the trade winds or is on the leeward side. For example, the southeastern slopes of the main Fiji islands, on which the trade winds blow, receive more than 117 inches (3,000 millimeters) of rain per year.

Many islands have wet and dry seasons. In Melanesia (the larger, mountainous islands from New Guinea to Fiji) and Polynesia (the islands within the triangle formed by Hawaii, New Zealand, and Easter Island), the wet season is from December to March and the dry season is from April to November. In Micronesia (the small islands and atolls reaching from Palau and the Marianas toward Kiribati), the wet season is from May to December and the dry season is from January to April.

EFFECT OF THE WINDS. Most of the Pacific Islands lie in the intertropical zone, between the trade winds, air currents that flow from the subtropical high-pressure zones found between the thirtieth and fortieth parallels both north and south of the equator. North of the equator, the trade winds, diverted by the earth's rotation from their southward path, turn to the southeast; south of the equator, the north-bound winds turn to the northeast. In the eastern Pacific, the southeast trade winds lie between the twenty-fifth parallel south and slightly north of the equator, moving slightly farther north in summer. The northeast trade winds lie between the fifth and twenty-fifth parallels north.

Overall, the climatic conditions in the Pacific Islands are uniform, lacking a great deal of seasonal variation, because of the steadiness of the trade winds. The trade winds are relatively cool air, moving at an average wind speed of 13 knots. They become increasingly humid and warm as they near the equator and produce light to moderate showers, although the weather is generally fine in these areas. The windward sides of the higher islands tend to be cloudy and wet, with the leeward side relatively dry.

In the intertropical zone, the winds become generally easterly, particularly in the east Pacific, where the zone diminishes to a width of only 200 to 300 miles (322 to 483 km.). In the part of the equatorial region known as the doldrums, where the trade winds converge, the wind is generally calm or light and variable. The doldrums are over the equator, which receives the most heat from the Sun of any place on Earth. This heat causes the air to expand and creates a belt of low pressure. In the doldrums, the sky is often cloudy and humidity is particularly high. Thunderstorms or showers are common, and rainfall is abundant in the western Pacific although much scarcer in the east.

In the far western Pacific Islands, the effect of the trade winds is mitigated by that of the monsoon winds. The seasonal heating and cooling of the Asian continent produces a reversal of winds that blow across the islands. From November to March, northwest monsoonal winds bring rain to Papua New Guinea, the Solomon Islands, and the western Carolinas; in the

AVERAGE TEMPERATURES IN SELECTED PACIFIC ISLANDS

City/Country	January Degrees Fahrenheit	January Degrees Celsius	July Degrees Fahrenheit	July Degrees Celsius
Suva, Fiji	80	26.7	73	22.8
Tarawa, Kiribati	83	28.3	82	27.8
Majura, Marshall Islands	81	27.2	81	27.2
Yap, Micronesia	81	27.2	81	27.2
Auckland, New Zealand	66	18.9	50	10.0
Wellington, New Zealand	60	15.6	47	8.3
Madang, Papua New Guinea	82	27.8	81	27.2
Honiara, Solomon Islands	81	27.2	79	26.1
Vava'u, Tonga	80	26.7	73	22.8
Fongafale, Tuvalu	84	28.9	81	27.2
Vila, Vanuatu	80	26.7	72	22.2

Source: Parker, Sybil P., ed. *World Geographical Encyclopedia.* Vol. 5. New York: McGraw-Hill, 1995.

HURRICANES, TYPHOONS, AND TROPICAL CYCLONES

Tropical cyclones are called either hurricanes or typhoons, depending on where they occur. Tropical cyclones are low-pressure systems over tropical or subtropical waters, with organized convection, such as thunderstorm activity and surface winds that rotate counterclockwise in the Northern Hemisphere and clockwise in the Southern Hemisphere. These storms are termed tropical depressions until the maximum sustained (for one minute) surface winds reach 39 miles (62.9 km.) per hour, at which point they are called tropical storms. Once the winds reach 74 miles (119.3 km.) per hour, the storm becomes either a hurricane, typhoon, or tropical cyclone, depending on where it occurs. Tropical storms in the North Atlantic Ocean, in the Northeast Pacific Ocean east of the International Dateline, or in the South Pacific Ocean east of longitude 160 degrees east are called hurricanes; those in the Northwest Pacific Ocean west of the dateline are called typhoons. Those that occur in the southwest Pacific Ocean west of longitude 160 degrees east or in the Southeast Indian Ocean east of longitude 90 degrees east are called severe tropical cyclones. Those in the North Indian Ocean are severe cyclonic storms, and those in the Southwest Indian Ocean are tropical cyclones.

summer, the monsoonal winds reverse, becoming southeast winds.

From July to November, typhoons frequently occur in western Micronesia. Typhoons produce gale force winds, torrential rains, and sometimes tidal waves, which can damage the low islands. Tropical cyclones also occur in the southern Pacific Islands.

Just below the trade winds, from the latitudes of about 30 degrees south to 40 degrees south, high-pressure zones known as anticyclones occur. They rotate and move, either toward the subpolar latitudes or in the same direction as the trade winds. In these high-pressure areas, known as the horse latitudes, the weather is generally fair.

Below the fortieth parallel south, where part of New Zealand lies, the winds are generally westerly. These warmer westerly winds converge with cold easterly winds from the polar regions, producing tropical depressions noted for their gale force winds. This phenomenon is most pronounced in winter, when the contrast in air humidity and temperature is greatest.

THE OCEAN'S EFFECT. The climate of the Pacific Islands is also influenced by the movement of the waters of the ocean, particularly the tides, currents, wind-produced waves, and the rising and sinking waters produced by differences in water temperature. The temperature of the water affects that of the air above it, producing changes in atmospheric pressure. Cold surface water tends to produce high-pressure zones, and warmer water produces low-pressure zones.

The trade winds and westerlies create drifts of warm ocean water. In the northern Pacific, the northeast trade winds create a drift that splits at Hawaii to form two clockwise circulating drifts, the western of which is the larger. In the south Pacific, trade winds produce a similar, counterclockwise-moving drift that flows around many of the Pacific Islands. The trade winds also produce an equatorial current that flows in a westerly direction on both sides of the doldrums. These two currents meet around Palau and the Carolines, where part goes north and feeds the north Pacific drift and part turns eastward through the doldrums to create the Equatorial Countercurrent.

CLIMATE AND CULTURE. The trade winds and currents of the Pacific Islands are believed to have carried people to the islands from southeastern Asia. However, experts do not know how groups as diverse as the Asiatic Micronesians and Polynesians developed. The early islanders survived by fishing, agriculture, and hunting, but their ways of life differed greatly, reflecting the climatic differences among the islands, which produced flora and fauna that were often unique to a particular island. The Pacific Islands were far from Europe, small, and spread out across the ocean; they also had varying climatic conditions, such as heat and humidity, that required adaptations in Western living styles and few easily tapped resources. Therefore, European exploration and colonization came fairly late. Although the islands were discovered by Europeans in the sixteenth century, colonization did not take place on a large scale until the late nineteenth century. Fishing and agriculture still play a large part in the lives of the inhabitants of the Pacific Islands.

GLOBAL WARMING. In the late twentieth century, concerns arose about the effects of global warming on the low islands of the Pacific. Large parts of these islands are not far above sea level, and rising ocean levels caused by the melting of glacial ice may severely reduce the land mass above water, disrupting residential patterns and interfering with how people make their living. At a United Nations climate change conference in late 1999, a number of Pacific Islanders reported det-

rimental effects believed to stem from global warming. Tonga, a group of 175 small islands, reported that the rise in sea levels had contaminated drinking water on its central and northern islands. Strong winds accompanied by salt-water spray had reduced farm production, warmer waters had reduced the supply of fish, and beaches had experienced erosion, making them less attractive to tourists. Vanuatu reported that rising seas had ruined low-lying coconut plantations, and Palau said global warming had damaged its coral reefs. At a separate conference, representatives from Tuvalu reported higher salt content in its aquifers, more dry spells, and more ferocious cyclones.

Rowena Wildin

FOR FURTHER STUDY

Campbell, I. C. *A History of the Pacific Islands.* Berkeley: University of California Press, 1990.

Houghton, J. T. *Global Warming: The Complete Briefing.* New York: Cambridge University Press, 1997.

Howe, K. R. *Nature, Culture, and History: The "Knowing" of Oceania.* Honolulu: University of Hawaii Press, 2000.

Lal, Brij V., and Kate Fortune, eds. *Encyclopedia of the Pacific Islands.* Honolulu: University of Hawaii Press, 2000.

Nunn, Patrick D. *Oceanic Islands.* The Natural Environment series. Cambridge, Mass.: Blackwell, 1994.

Nunn, Patrick D., William Aalbersberg, and Asesela D. Ravuvu, eds. *Climate and Agriculture in the Pacific Islands: Future Perspectives.* Suva, Fiji: Institute of Pacific Studies, 1993.

Rapaport, Moshe, ed. *The Pacific Islands: Environment and Society.* Honolulu: Bess Press, 1999.

BIOGEOGRAPHY
AND
NATURAL
RESOURCES

NATURAL RESOURCES

ANTARCTICA

The most isolated of the seven continents, Antarctica generally has been written off by scientists and mineralogists as a place where productive mining and drilling cannot be done. Its natural resources fall into three categories: animal, mineral, and hydrological. The first has been over-exploited. The other two have not yet been developed significantly.

What is known about the continent's mineral resources is largely speculative. The conclusions reached are based upon comparisons with mineral deposits in other parts of the world, but one cannot easily or relevantly compare Antarctica with any other place on the earth. It is the only continent that has no cities and towns, no conventional infrastructure, and no permanent human inhabitants. Its severe climate and isolation make it unique. Strides have been made, however, in assessing the hydrological resources underlying Antarctica. It has long been known that the continent holds approximately 68 percent of the world's fresh water in its glaciers and ice shelves.

ANIMAL RESOURCES. The animal resources of Antarctica begin with plankton and krill in the waters around the continent's 18,648-mile (30,010 km.) coastline. These creatures at the lower end of the food chain nourish, directly or indirectly, the fish, birds, penguins, seals, and whales

that constitute part of Antarctica's treasure of animal resources.

The exploitation of Antarctica's animal resources began not with whaling, which was a major, worldwide industry in the eighteenth century, but with sealing. The English navigator James Cook, who sailed into southern waters, wrote about the profusion of seals there. This launched a period of sealing activity by the British, beginning in 1778 and continuing with the arrival of American sealers into the area shortly afterward. The hunters sought seals mostly for their fur, for which ready European, Chinese, and American markets existed. They hunted the elephant seal for its oil as well. By the 1850's, seals were almost extinct in the southern polar regions.

Whaling was not a major activity in the Antarctic until the whale population in more climatically hospitable areas had been depleted almost to the point of extinction by nineteenth century whalers. In 1892 Christen Christensen, a Norwegian, sent a whaling expedition into Antarctic waters. By 1904 a whaling station had been established on South Georgia Island. This lucrative industry prospered and grew during World War I, when whale oil was in great demand.

The blue whale, the largest known creature on the earth, was plentiful in Antarc-

Map Page 1907

Seals Page 1910

tic waters until the 1950's. The International Whaling Commission, established in 1946, introduced zero-catch quotas for all commercial whaling so that the whale population could replenish itself. Some nations, however, failed to honor their quota agreements and hunted the blue whale almost to extinction.

In 1912-1913, an official catch of 10,670 whales in the Antarctic waters was documented. In 1930-1931, a record forty thousand whales were taken from the Ross Sea and the South Atlantic Ocean bordering Antarctica. With the depletion of the whale population, the South Georgia Whaling Station closed in 1965, giving way to ship-based processing plants. By 1990 seal hunting and whaling were no longer commercially profitable in Antarctica and its adjacent waters.

MINERAL RESOURCES. Most of what is known about the mineral resources of Antarctica is based on informed speculation by mineralogists and other scientists who must base their conclusions on comparative data from other areas where mining and drilling take place. Such conclusions must be assessed in the light of Antarctica's uniqueness as a continent and, therefore, must be viewed with some skepticism.

To evaluate the mineral wealth of any large landmass, it is necessary to analyze what is in the rocks that constitute that landmass. Ninety-eight percent of Antarctica is under an ice sheet whose thickness averages 8,000 feet (2,440 meters). The conjectures that have been made are based upon what has been found in a sampling of rocks from the 2 percent of the continent that is exposed and accessible.

From this small sample, it has been established that the continent probably has coal and iron ore in significant quantities. Among the minerals found in much smaller quantities are gold, silver, lead,

nickel, molybdenum, antimony, zinc, copper, cobalt, and chromium. Nodules on the sea floor off Antarctica contain iron, manganese, copper, nickel, and cobalt, but in quantities too small to consider them viable mineral resources.

During the Ernest Shackleton expedition to the Ross Sea in 1909, one of Shackleton's party found in the sedimentary rock of the Beardmore Glacier that terminates in the Ross Sea the first coal deposits ever discovered in Antarctica. Some scientists cite geological evidence suggesting that Antarctica has no significant petroleum resources, although the waters off the continent apparently have considerable reserves of oil beneath them. Getting to such reserves is hindered by three major factors: Antarctica's lack of cities, towns, and conventional infrastructure; its lack of permanent inhabitants; and the rough seas with their frigid cyclonic winds that surround the continent. As long as petroleum reserves exist in parts of the world that are more accessible, reserves that lie beneath Antarctica's surface or beneath its adjacent waters will likely remain untapped.

Technology does not currently exist for making mining and drilling in Antarctica and off its shores a profitable enterprise. From a long-term perspective, it is likely that many of the problems currently related to climate and lack of a permanent population will be overcome. As shortages of various minerals develop, means of unlocking Antarctica's mineral resources will be developed. When the necessity arises, it is probable that means will be found for controlling the climate to the point that workers can spend extended periods of time in Antarctica and possibly even live there.

One restraint on exploiting Antarctica's mineral resources in the immediate future is the Antarctic Treaty's Protocol on

*Icebergs
Page 1847*

Environmental Protection, enacted in 1991. This legally binding international act, which can be modified by the Consultative Parties, imposes an indefinite ban on all activities involving mining or drilling for minerals in Antarctica's fragile ecosystem. The act will be reviewed in 2041. It is unlikely that any substantial mining or drilling activities will occur in Antarctica before that review.

HYDROLOGICAL RESOURCES. With 68 percent of the world's total supply of fresh water, Antarctica could supply other parts of the world with water for agriculture, drinking, bathing, and industry. Recent developments at Russia's Vostok Research Station have suggested that even more fresh, liquid water may lie beneath Antarctica's surface than was originally suspected.

In 1996, while drilling through an ice cover 2 miles (3.2 km.) deep, scientists from Vostok uncovered evidence of a huge underground lake, perhaps one of many, resting beneath the earth and the deep ice cover above it. To date, this newly discovered lake has not been breached because the scientific community does not wish to risk contaminating it in any way. Research is now under way to determine how this resource can best be studied without compromising its pristine qualities.

It has been suggested that huge icebergs that are calved from Antarctica's many ice shelves might, in time, be hauled to parts of the world that have water shortages. Some speculate that it would be possible not only to do this but also to create electrical power in the process by converting the ocean's thermal energy to electrical power. At present, the technology to accomplish this does not exist, but once the idea was articulated, creative minds began to work on its possible implementation.

Among the problems to be solved before such an undertaking could occur is that of keeping the icebergs from melting as they move into warmer waters and from breaking apart as they are subjected to the relentless pounding of waves in rough seas before they reach the processing plants. The hydrological resources of Antarctica are greater than those of any other continent. It is inconceivable that they would not one day be put to use, regardless of the difficulties involved in accomplishing this objective.

R. Baird Shuman

FOR FURTHER STUDY

Australian Government. *Impact of Climate Change: Antarctica.* Canberra: Australian Government Printing Office, 1992.

Hansom, James D., and John E. Gordon. *Antarctic Environments and Resources: A Geographical Perspective.* New York: Addison Wesley Longman, 1998.

Herr, R. A., H. R. Hall, and Marcus G. Haward, eds. *Antarctica's Future: Continuity or Change?.* Hobart, Tasmania: Australian Institute of International Affairs, 1990.

Stewart, John. *Antarctica: An Encyclopedia.* Jefferson, N.C.: McFarland, 1990.

Thomson, Michael R. A., J. Alistair Crame, and Janet W. Thomson, eds. *Geological Evolution of Antarctica.* Cambridge, England: Cambridge University Press, 1991.

Tingey, Robert J., ed. *The Geology of Antarctica.* Oxford, England: Clarendon Press, 1991.

INFORMATION ON THE WORLD WIDE WEB

NASA's South Pole Adventure Web Page has valuable information about research occurring at the Vostok Research Center. (www.southpole.com)

AUSTRALIA

*Map
Page 1908*

*Rutile
mining
Page 1908*

Although the smallest continent, Australia is rich in mineral and hydrocarbon (petroleum and natural gas) resources. Since the gold rushes in the middle of the nineteenth century, Australia has maintained its proud tradition as one of the world's major mining nations. It is in the top six producing countries for bauxite, gold, iron ore, lead, zinc, mineral sands, uranium, copper, diamond, lithium, manganese, nickel, silver, tantalum, tin, and vanadium. New discoveries of mineral resources and hydrocarbon resources happen frequently, but the new finds sometimes are located in remote areas and thus are difficult to exploit.

Australia is not so blessed when it comes to water resources. The continent is dry except for the tropical north. True rivers are few. Australia's water supply consists mostly of fossil water that has lain underground for millions of years and is seldom or never replaced. Problems with salinity—the salt content of the water and soil—are becoming common. More than 6 million acres (2 million hectares) of soil have been damaged by salinity.

Increasing population, urbanization, agricultural production, and mining have placed pressure on limited resources, causing land and water degradation and loss of biodiversity. Australia's twenty largest cities have 65 percent of the population of eighteen million. Half of Australia's vegetation has been cleared or disturbed, and farmers use 70 percent of Australia's water. In 1993 approximately 8,140 square miles (21,070 sq. km.) of land were irrigated.

HYDROCARBON RESOURCES. In 1995-1996, mineral fuels and lubricants accounted for 16.6 percent of the value of

*Snowy Mts.
Pages
1906, 1981*

Australia's exports. As of 1998, commercial oil reserves were 1,910 million barrels and gas reserves were 26.9 million cubic feet (760,000 cubic meters). At that time, new unanalyzed discoveries had been made in the Bonaparte and Carnarvon Basins of offshore northwestern Australia. There have been fifteen new petroleum discoveries in five onshore basins in New South Wales (Clarence-Morton, Sydney, and Gunnedah Basins), Queensland (Clarence-Moreton and Georgina Basins), and the Northern Territory (Georgina and McArthur Basins). Australia's first commercial oil discovery was Surat Basin's Moonie Number 1 well, in 1961. Australia's oil production in 1997 was 250 million barrels, expected to peak at 280 million barrels in 2002 and decline to 60 million barrels per year in 2040.

The offshore conversion of natural gas to liquid fuel is believed to be the key to Australia's energy future. Pipeline sales will be made to urban and industrial centers. As an additional benefit, Australia will be energy independent for at least another one hundred years. The move away from coal and oil and toward the use of natural gas as a primary energy source also will help to curb greenhouse emissions.

RENEWABLE ENERGY RESOURCES. Great variation in river volumes and relatively flat land limit the opportunities for the production of hydroelectric power. Tasmania is exceptional in its reliance on a type of hydro-economy that has exploited the natural advantages of the island state. On the mainland, there is the world-renowned Snowy Mountains Project, a hydroelectric and irrigation complex serving New South Wales and Victoria, and

Queensland's Burdekin Falls dam. Approximately 75 percent of Australia's total generated electric power comes from thermal stations that draw on the country's abundant coal reserves.

MINERAL RESERVES. The mineral industry generates a high proportion of Australia's export income. In 1996-1997, mineral exports earned more than 36.5 billion dollars (Australian). In 1995-1996, mineral ores and scrap metal accounted for 11.4 percent of the value of Australia's exports. Australia's greatest mineral reserves are located in Western Australia (iron ore, nickel, bauxite, diamonds, gold, and mineral sands), Queensland (bauxite, bituminous or black coal, lead, mineral sands, zinc, and silver), New South Wales (bituminous coal, lead, zinc, silver, and mineral sands), and Victoria (brown coal or lignite and offshore oil and natural gas).

The largest known uranium reserves are in northern and northwestern Queensland, the Northern Territory, Western Australia, and South Australia. Iron ore is produced in Australia for domestic iron and steel production, but most production is for export, mainly to Japan, Taiwan, and South Korea. Remoteness has blunted the effect of the staggering scale of modern discoveries. Western Australia's Hamersley iron province contains billions of tons of iron ore, but the ore is located in an isolated area. Tungsten has been mined since colonial times and is a major export. It has been produced in Queensland from wolframite and scheelite located on King Island in the Bass Strait. The rich Kambalda nickel deposits, 35 miles (56 km.) southeast of Kalgoorlie, were discovered in 1964. Other nickel deposits are at Greenvale (Queensland) and in the Mus-grave region on the borders of Western Australia, South Australia, and the Northern Territory.

Enormous deposits of bauxite have been located at Weipa on the Cape York Peninsula, at Gove in the Northern Territory, and in the Darling Range in Western Australia. Their exploitation made Australia the world's leading producer of bauxite and alumina in the late 1980's. Australia ranks as the Western world's third-largest gold producer. Silver occurs in good quantities in rich lead-zinc ores. Small amounts of platinum and palladium have been located.

Iron ore mine in Western Australia's Hammersley Range. (Corbis)

AUSTRALIA'S SHARE OF WORLD MINERAL RESOURCES

Mineral	Percentage of World Resources
Bauxite	12
Black coal	7
Brown coal	13
Copper	7
Diamonds (industrial grade)	21
Gold	11
Ilmenite (oxide of iron and titanium)	22
Iron ore	12
Lead	27
Lithium	8
Manganese	8
Nickel	8
Rutile	35
Silver	14
Tantalum	31
Uranium	30
Vanadium	12
Zinc	23
Zirconium	44

The Windimurra Vanadium Project of Precious Metals Australia Limited is located near Mount Magnet in Western Australia. The Windimurra Project is the world's largest primary producer of vanadium pentoxide. Vanadium is a rare silver-white metal that is alloyed with steel, to which it adds tensile strength, and used in nuclear applications. With a production capacity of 17.2 million pounds (7.82 million kilograms) per year, Windimurra can supply 12 percent of the world vanadium market.

Australia has abundant deposits of industrial minerals such as clays, mica, salt, dolomite (limestone), refractories, abrasives, talc, and asbestos. Gem minerals occur in many localities. Unique black opals are found in Lighting Ridge in New South

Wales and Mintable in South Australia. Sapphires and topaz come from Queensland and the New England district of New South Wales. In 1979 a vast deposit of diamonds, mostly of industrial quality, was discovered in the Kimberley region of Western Australia.

Tasmania has some important mineral deposits, including iron at Savage River; high-grade lead-zinc-silver at Hellyer, Que River, and Rosebery; low-grade copper at Queenstown; low-grade tin at Renison Bell; and tin and tungsten in the northeast.

WATER. The average annual rainfall is approximately 18 inches (45 centimeters), and more than one-third of the mainland, principally the interior, receives less than 10 inches (25 centimeters) per year. Aridity or semiaridity prevails over most of Australia, and evaporation rates are extremely high. Due to the high evaporation rates, less than 2 inches (5 centimeters) of the average annual rainfall contributes surface runoff for natural and artificial systems.

Permanently flowing rivers are found only in eastern Australia, southwestern Australia, and Tasmania. The major exception is the Murray River, a stream that rises in the Mount Kosciusko region in the Eastern Uplands and is fed by melting snows. It acquires a volume sufficient to survive the passage across the arid and semiarid plains that bear its name and to reach the Southern Ocean southeast of Adelaide. However, the combined discharge from all Australian rivers, including the principal river system, the Murray-Darling, is only about one-fourth that of the Mississippi River.

There are wide regional disparities in the availability of water. In the sparsely populated northern sector, runoff draining into the Timor Sea and the Gulf of Carpentaria accounts for half the national total. The tropical north as a whole contributes about two-thirds of the national total water runoff. Much of Australia's population, however, is concentrated in New South Wales and Victoria in the southeastern sector of the country.

Many areas such as the Nullarbor Plain, which is underlain by limestone, and the sand ridge deserts are without surface drainage. There are, however, underground streams. A map of Australia can be misleading. Many of the "lakes" depicted in the interior areas are now salt lakes that often contain no water for years at a time.

The Great Artesian Basin, a huge underground aquifer, is the largest of its type in the world and gives security to one-fifth of mainland Australia's population. Groundwater systems extend over 40 percent of Australia's land and in many cases, more water is being extracted than is replenished naturally. In some areas of Australia, people are using three to four times more water than is being recharged, so the water is running out.

Scientists have warned that the quality of Australia's inland water is increasingly at risk. The two main causes are toxins produced by blue-green algae and agricultural chemical residues. Some of the algae in Australia produce unique toxins, which can be long-lived and potentially toxic to humans and animals. The algal toxins, known as paralytic shellfish poisons, could accumulate in the food chain, affecting human health, the rural industries, and Australian plants and animals.

Dryland salinity is becoming a serious problem in Australia. In 1998 the country had 6.2 million acres (2.5 million hectares) of salt-affected land. Western Australia, one of the worst affected states, has 4.5 million acres (1.8 million hectares) of salt-affected land, and this is increasing at a rate equal to one football field an hour. Much of the dryland salinity is due to low rainfall and high evaporation rates. Salts

in groundwater originate either from minute quantities dissolved in rainwater, from the chemical breakdown of rocks, or from direct contact with seawater.

In South Australia, at least 20 percent of surface water resources were sufficiently saline to be above desirable limits for human consumption. In the Northern Territory, which is relatively well watered, the groundwater in the southern half of the state is too saline for most uses. In the northern half of the Northern Territory, groundwaters are mainly fresh because the high rainfall tends to flush away salt before it is concentrated by evaporation. It has been estimated that soil salinity in Australia could expand to 95 percent of total irrigated lands and to one-third of dryland arable area by the middle of the twenty-first century.

Tasmania is well watered and thus the opposite of mainland Australia. It has two major river systems, the Derwent in the southeast and the South Esk in the northeast. There are many small systems flowing to the west coast and innumerable lakes. The Central Plateau is studded with more than four thousand lakes in a landscape similar to northern Canada and Finland.

FORESTS. Approximately 21 percent of Australia's land is forested. The chief commercial forests are in high-rainfall areas on the coast or in the coastal highlands of Tasmania and the southeastern and eastern mainland, and along the southwestern coast of Western Australia. Queensland's forest industries contribute more than 1.7 billion dollars (Australian) annually to Queensland's economy and employ approximately seventeen thousand people. Approximately 80 percent of the industry's plantation and native log timber supplies are derived from the Department of Primary Industries Forestry's sustainable production activities in Crown forests throughout the State.

In Tasmania, there are softwood plantations in the Fingal and Scottsdale areas and inland from the northwest coast. The main types of trees are the eucalyptus, an evergreen genus providing timbers of great strength and durability, and a great variety of rain forest trees such as coachwood, crab apple, and yellow carabeen. Since World War II, several regions both on the mainland and in Tasmania have been intensively exploited for wood pulp, partly for export to Japan.

Dana P. McDermott

FOR FURTHER STUDY

Birrell, Robert. *Quarry Australia: Managing Australia's Resources.* New York: Oxford University Press, 1982.

Blainey, Geoffrey. *Rush That Never Ended: A History of Australian Mining.* Melbourne, Australia: Melbourne University Press, 1993.

Conacher, Jeannette, and Arthur Conacher, eds. *Rural Land Degradation in Australia.* New York: Oxford University Press, 1995.

Darcavel, John. *Fashioning Australia's Forests.* New York: Oxford University Press, 1996.

Dixon, R. A., and M. C. Dillon, eds. *Aborigines and Diamond Mining: The Politics of Resource Development in the East Kimberley, Western Australia.* Portland, Oreg.: International Specialized Book Services, 1990.

Heathcote, Ronald L., ed. *Australia.* 2d ed. New York: John Wiley & Sons, 1994.

Smith, David. *Water in Australia: Resources & Management.* New York: Oxford University Press, 1999.

INFORMATION ON THE WORLD WIDE WEB

The Australian Geological Survey Organization maintains a Web site with information on Australia's hydrocarbon and mineral resources. (www.agso.gov.au)

Another valuable site is Pine Australia, with links to primary industries in Queensland and the Northern Territory leading to specific information on mineral, timber, and water resources. (www.pineaust.asn.au/links.htm)

PACIFIC ISLANDS

Resources are the part of the natural environment that is given value by human knowledge and perception. The Pacific Islands and New Zealand vary greatly in the availability of renewable and nonrenewable natural resources. These, in turn, influence settlement patterns and local economies, including exports, industry, and tourism. The Pacific region is rich in a number of natural resources that often form a basis for the countries' economies. These resources include minerals, water,

New Caledonia nickel smelter during the 1960's. (Tom McKnight/Joan Clemons)

forests, cash crops and plantation agriculture, and ocean fishing. The tourism industry has developed in several islands where the natural resources provide activities and attractions of interest to visitors. Some of the smaller islands, however, have virtually no natural resources apart from those in the ocean surrounding them.

MINERALS. The Melanesian countries located along the Pacific and Indian tectonic plate collision zone are well endowed with mineral resources; the extraction of minerals that are desired by industrial nations has provided significantly for the national wealth of these countries. In Papua New Guinea, one of the most resource-rich countries in the region, mineral resources account for two-thirds of the country's total exports. Two

of the world's largest copper and gold mines are found in Papua New Guinea. The copper deposits on Bougainville Island, an offshore island that is part of the country, contain one of the world's largest reserves and were intensively mined until terrorist activities closed the mine in the early 1990's. Gold and petroleum are found in Papua New Guinea as well, especially along the Fly River. Gold is also mined in Fiji, Palau, and the Solomon Islands.

New Caledonia is the world's third-largest producer of nickel ore, and also contains chrome, iron, cobalt, manganese, copper, silver and lead. The Solomon Islands also have bauxite, lead, zinc, and nickel. Manganese was mined in Vanuatu, but is now depleted. Phosphate, useful in producing manure, was or is con-

Iron roofing
Page 1909

*Nauru
Pages
1910, 1976*

GUANO IN NAURU

The tiny island of Nauru is an extreme example of how the Pacific nations tend to rely for major export earnings on a few primary natural resource products that support their economies. Nauru based its industry and wealth on the mining and processing of phosphate, the product of thousands of years of accumulation of seabird excrement, called guano. Raw phosphate is mined and processed into fertilizer on the island, and then exported.

Because of the phosphate industry, Nauru has one of the highest per capita incomes in the developing world. Nauru's economy depends on annual exports of two million tons of phosphate and on revenues earned from overseas investments of phosphate profits. This resource, however, is said to be near depletion, and because phosphate mining has stripped the island of soil and vegetation, the people of Nauru have sought a new island home.

tained on five great phosphate rock islands in the Pacific region: Kiribati on the island of Banaba (the country's only island that is not an atoll; deposits are now depleted), Makatea in French Polynesia, the Solomon Islands, the Marshall Islands, and Nauru. Phosphate deposits in Nauru are nearing depletion.

WATER. Fresh water is a necessary resource for any area with human settlement. The Pacific Islands are split in terms of water resources. Because of their location in a tropical wet/dry climatic region, heavy seasonal precipitation is common. The high islands are especially well endowed with water, as the mountainous terrain provides conditions conducive to heavy, frequent rainfall, and snow on the higher peaks. Water in these countries can be tapped for energy as well. The steep terrain and heavy rains in the highlands of Papua New Guinea, for example, enable the development of reservoirs and hydroelectric power plants that supply city dwellers and much of the rural population with water and electricity. Low-lying atolls are deficient in precipitation and limited in water-storage capacity; thus, they must import most of their water to support their populations.

New Zealand's highland glaciers, lakes, and mountain streams supply its people with abundant fresh water as well as with hydroelectric power. Increasing urban population, however, continues to place greater demands on domestic water use. To deal with this problem, storage lakes and treatment plants have been built to increase the country's water storage capacity, and water conservation measures are in effect in Wellington and Auckland, New Zealand's two largest cities.

TROPICAL RAIN FORESTS. Tropical rain forests are botanically complex. At lower elevations, they consist of several layers of canopy (different heights of plants) and a wide variety of plant and tree species. At higher elevations, the lower canopy is absent but several tree species can be found. Sizable expanses of tropical rain forest still exist on most of the larger islands of Melanesia, but some of the drier, flatter islands in the Pacific have only sparse vegetation. Although rain forests still cover 70 percent of Papua New Guinea (one of the few remaining extensive natural tropical rain forests in the world), more than 37 million acres (15 million hectares) have been identified as suitable for logging.

Some of the world's most biologically diverse environments are being threatened in these operations, but landowners see the quick cash sales to loggers as attractive in the short term, even though the long-term practice will damage their traditional lifestyles. The global expansion of commercial lumbering also threatens nearby portions of the Solomon Islands and many unique environmental settings in Polynesia. Much of the subalpine mountainous region of New Zealand is covered with rain forest. This country, too, has a significant forest products industry that involves the logging and processing of its rain forest.

Tropical rain forests contribute greatly to the world's oxygen supply, thus, the cutting of the rain forests depletes the supply of this vital element of air that helps humans breathe. Many plants from rain forests are used for medicinal purposes as well. The cutting of forest, therefore, reduces the availability of medicinal plants.

CASH CROPS AND PLANTATION AGRICULTURE. The tropical and subtropical latitudes of the Pacific islands provide year-round warm temperatures, fertile soils, and adequate rainfall, making these islands ideal for tropical agriculture for subsistence use and for export. As with minerals, specific crops have become the primary export products in certain Pacific Island countries. Coconut, sugar, pineapple, and bananas are grown on small local farms and on large, foreign-owned plantations for mass production and export to industrial nations. Other tropical crops and livestock provide additional export income.

Loggers cutting trees in Samoa. (Tom McKnight/Joan Clemons)

FOLK MEDICINE IN THE SAMOAN RAIN FOREST

The Samoan tropical rain forest is useful for more than timber: The indigenous people of Samoa use many rain forest plants to treat disease. Samoan medicine women use dozens of plant species to treat human ailments and pass down their knowledge of this folk medicine from mother to daughter.

There are some seventy remedies or cures using rain forest plants, including the polo leaf, used for fighting infections; the ulu ma'afala root, for diarrhea; and the bark of a local tree, used to combat hepatitis. Another plant species is being tested for its effectiveness against AIDS. Although these plants are termed "folk medicines," they are not merely local cures. At least 25 percent of the prescription drugs made in the United States are extracted from flowering plants, many of which grow in tropical rain forests.

However, the Samoan rain forest is in danger of extinction; by 1999 commercial logging operations had cut down more than 80 percent of the coastal rain forest, and logging continued. Ethnobotanist Paul Alan Cox, noted for his research on the use of tropical plants for health remedies, won the Goldman Environmental Prize in 1997 for his efforts to save the Samoan rain forest. In honor of his work, the Samoan Islanders gave him the name Nafanuna, after one of their traditional protective gods.

Coconut palms Page 1842

Coconut plantation Page 1976

Pineapple field Page 1974

Coconuts are the most widespread plantation crop in the region. Coconuts require year-round warm temperature, well-drained soil, and plenty of moisture and sunlight; they grow best in low altitudes near the coast. The coastal lowland areas of the tropical Pacific Islands are ideal for large and small-scale coconut plantations. Products from the coconut include copra, the dried meat extracted from the nut; desiccated (finely grated) coconut for cooking and baking; milk and cream to drink or use in cooking; oil used in cooking and for producing margarine, fine soap, and cosmetics; and fiber from the husk of the nut, used to manufacture rugs and cord. In addition, the timber from the tree is used as a building material and to make furniture and utensils.

Coconuts are grown in Tonga, Western and American Samoa, Papua New Guinea, Guam, the Cook Islands, French Polynesia, New Caledonia, Fiji, Vanuatu, Tuvalu, the Solomon Islands, and the Marshall Islands. Copra, extracted from the meat of coconuts, is processed in Western Samoa, Papua New Guinea, the Solomon Islands (where it is the major source of income for smallholder farmers), Vanuatu, Fiji (where coconuts are the second largest crop), Kiribati, Tuvalu, the Marshall Islands, and Tonga. Coconut cream and oil are processed in Western and American Samoa and the Marshall Islands; coconut oil is processed in Tonga.

Sugar is the main plantation crop processed in and exported from the Hawaiian Islands, Fiji, Rapanui (Easter Island), and the Marianas. While sugarcane grows naturally in these countries, the processing industry is far more complex and expensive than that for coconut; therefore, these operations are limited to large-scale, often foreign-owned, plantations. Small farmers cannot compete as they do with coconuts.

Pineapples are grown, processed, and exported from the Hawaiian Islands as well. Bananas grow in the Hawaiian Islands, Western Samoa, Tonga, and other islands of Micronesia. Other cash crops exported from the region include rubber, tea, and coffee in Papua New Guinea; coffee in Vanuatu; cocoa in Western Samoa, Papua New Guinea, Solomon Islands, and Vanuatu; palm oil in the Solomon Islands and Papua New Guinea; rice in Fiji and the Solomon Islands; and vanilla in Tonga. Western Samoa also produces taro and passion fruit.

New Zealand is too far south for tropical agriculture but has climate and terrain that is ideal for raising livestock. Sheep are the main animal raised in the country. Export products from sheep farming include wool, lamb, mutton, cheese, and other dairy products. Cattle are raised in New Zealand, Vanuatu, and Western Samoa,

for export of beef. Poultry and pork are produced in Western Samoa and Papua New Guinea.

OCEAN FISHING. Ocean fish are another important resource for much of the Pacific Islands. This should be no surprise, given the huge expanse of ocean within the Pacific region. Fishing of tuna and other ocean fish occurs from Papua New Guinea, Fiji, the Solomon Islands, Vanuatu, Kiribati (sent for canning to American Samoa), Tonga, Western Samoa (though largely untapped), New Zealand, Vanuatu, Federated States of Micronesia, Tuvalu, the Marshall Islands, Palau, Pitcairn, French Polynesia, Niue, and the Midway Islands.

As with plantation agriculture, fishing influences industrial development in

Passion fruit blossoms Page 1916

Sheep farm Page 1973

New Zealand sheep. (Corbis)

some Pacific Island countries. There are fish canneries, for example, in Papua New Guinea, Fiji, Solomon Islands, Vanuatu, and American Samoa.

TOURISM. Tourism can be considered a resource in that the tourist industry uses a country's natural resources to attract visitors. This builds the economy as tourist-related infrastructure (the communication structures that make it possible for the activity to take place, such as roads and public transportation), facilities (hotels, restaurants, sporting centers, museums), and activities (swimming, camping, and other recreation) are set up to make tourism possible. The Hawaiian Islands and New Zealand have the most well-developed tourist industry, including urban and environmental attractions. Papua New Guinea, Fiji, Tahiti, the Cook Islands, New Caledonia, Tonga, Kiribati, Vanuatu, and the Samoas have invested in airport and hotel facilities and tourist activities to attract visitors to their islands.

RESOURCE-POOR AREAS. The low islands and atolls are all poor in natural resources. Tuvalu, Wake Atoll, and the Marshall Islands, for example, have no streams or rivers, and groundwater is not potable. All water needs must be met by catchment systems with storage facilities. Nauru has limited natural fresh water resources, with roof storage tanks to collect rainwater. Intensive phosphate mining during most of the twentieth century has left the central 90 percent of Nauru a wasteland and threatens the limited remaining land resources. Few other resources exist in Nauru and most necessities, including fresh water, must be imported from Australia. Kiribati is another resource-poor area. With the exception of the island of Banaba, which is of limestone origin, these islands are coral atolls with shallow topsoil and low water-absorption capacity that prevents cultivation of most crops.

Laurie A. Garo

Tahiti
Page 2044

FOR FURTHER STUDY

Brookfield, H. C., and Doreen Hart. *Melanesia: A Geographical Interpretation of an Island World.* London: Methuen, 1971.

Browne, Christopher, and Douglas A. Scott. *Economic Development in Seven Pacific Island Countries.* Washington, D.C.: International Monetary Fund, 1989.

Le Heron, Richard, and Eric Pawson, eds. *Changing Places, New Zealand in the Nineties.* Auckland, New Zealand: Longman Paul, 1996.

Oliver, Douglas L. *The Pacific Islands.* Honolulu: University Press of Hawaii, 1962.

INFORMATION ON THE WORLD WIDE WEB

The World Factbook 2000 Web site, maintained by the U.S. Central Intelligence Agency (CIA), features information on the resources of Pacific Island nations and New Zealand. (www.odci.gov/cia/publications/factbook/es.html#geo)

FLORA AND FAUNA

FLORA AND FAUNA OF ANTARCTICA

The harsh climate of Antarctica makes it one of the most inhospitable places on the earth, allowing only a relatively small number of organisms to live there. Most animals associated with Antarctica, such as penguins, seals, and whales, are actually seasonal visitors or live on the ice and in the ocean surrounding the continent. Permanent terrestrial (land) animals and plants are few and small. There are no trees, shrubs, or vertebrate land animals. Native organisms are hardy, yet the ecosystem is fragile and easily disturbed by human activity, pollution, global warming, and ozone layer depletion.

The Antarctic continent has never had a native or permanent population of humans. In 1998 the United States, Russia, Belgium, Australia, and several other countries signed another in an ongoing series of treaties to preserve Antarctica and keep it for peaceful international uses such as scientific research and ecotourism.

TERRESTRIAL FLORA. There are only two types of flowering plants in Antarctica, a grass and a small pearlwort. These are restricted to the more temperate Antarctic Peninsula. Antarctic hairgrass forms dense mats and grows fairly rapidly in the austral summer (December, January, and February). At the end of summer, the hairgrass's nutrients move underground and the leaves die. Pearlwort forms cushion-shaped clusters and grows

only 0.08 to 0.25 inch (2 to 6 millimeters) per year.

Numerous species of primitive plants, such as lichens, mosses, fungi, algae, and diatoms, live in Antarctica. Lichens are made up of an alga and a fungus in a symbiotic (interdependent) relationship. They can use water in the form of vapor, liquid, snow, or ice. Lichens grow as little as 0.04 inch (1 millimeter) every hundred years, and some patches may be more than 5,000 years old. Mosses are not as hardy as lichens but also grow slowly; a bootprint in a moss carpet may be visible for years. Fungi are found in the more temperate peninsula and most are microscopic.

Algae grow in Antarctic lakes, runoff near bird colonies, moist soil, and snow fields. During the summer, algae form spectacular red, yellow, or green patches on the snow.

Bacteria are not plants, but they are also found in lakes, meltwater, and soils. As elsewhere on the earth, bacteria play a role in decomposition. Because of the extreme conditions, they are not always as efficient in Antarctica, and carcasses may lay preserved for hundreds of years.

TERRESTRIAL FAUNA. Terrestrial animals in Antarctica are limited to invertebrates. There are more than one hundred species, including insects, mites, nematode worms, copepods (tiny crustaceans), and microscopic protozoans. The largest

Research station at Lake Hoare, where an American team is studying photosynthetic bacteria in Antarctic lakes. (AP/Wide World Photos)

is an insect, a long wingless midge only 0.47 inch (1.2 centimeters) long. The invertebrates have adopted various methods of dealing with the cold: Some dry out; others avoid freezing by making antifreeze chemicals in their blood; others do freeze but ice crystals form between cells, not inside them. Many avoid the cold by attaching themselves as parasites to a warm-blooded host.

MARINE LIFE. Unique in the world's oceans, the marine ecosystem of Antarctica is based on shrimplike crustaceans called krill, tiny animals that live in open water and under sea ice and grow up to 2 inches (5 centimeters) long. Nearly all Antarctic vertebrates, such as whales, seals, birds, and fish, depend directly or indirectly on krill. Masses of krill covering 300 square miles (1,000 sq. km.) and 328 feet (100 meters) thick have been seen. Other protozoans, small crustaceans, and larval fish float with the krill to form plankton.

WHALES. Among the creatures that feed on plankton are the largest animals in the world, the baleen whales, which have sievelike plates instead of teeth. Seven species feed in the southern ocean in the austral summer. A whale can eat thousands of pounds of krill per day. All the larger baleen whales were hunted by whalers, and most species are still recovering after decades of protection.

The blue whale is the largest animal ever to live on the earth, growing up to 100 feet (30 meters) long and weighing 150 tons (136,000 kilograms). The most common large whale, the fin whale, grows up to 38 feet (25 meters) long. The fastest whale, the sei whale, grows up to 65 feet (20 meters) long. The southern right whale was named by whalers because it was the "right" whale to catch: They are fat, very slow, and float when killed. They grow up to 56 feet (17 meters) long. Their numbers were severely reduced by whaling.

Humpback whales, up to 62 feet (19 meters) long, have recovered most successfully from whaling. They are known for their haunting songs and unique feeding habits. The minke is the smallest baleen whale, at 26 feet (8 meters) long, and was not hunted extensively. Ironically, it is the only baleen whale that still can be taken legally in Antarctic waters.

There also are toothed whales in the Southern Ocean. Sperm whales are occasionally found south of 70 degrees latitude. Killer whales are found up to the edge of the Antarctic ice. They travel in groups called pods and prey on other whales, seals, and penguins.

SEALS. Five species of true seals live and breed on or near Antarctica. Weddell seals and crabeater seals are the most abundant. Weddell seals are found on fast ice (sea ice that is attached to land) and eat squid and fish. They spend much of the winter under the ice and must chew open breathing holes. Their teeth can become so severely worn that they are unable to catch food or keep their breathing holes open, and some die from being trapped under the ice. Despite their name, crabeater seals feed almost exclusively on krill and live on the pack ice (sea ice not attached to shore).

Named for their spotted coats, leopard seals usually appear on the continent only in summer. About half their diet is krill, but they are impressive predators and will eat penguins, fish, squid, and the young of other seals. The Ross seal is one of the least known of the Antarctic seals. It lives on the pack ice and eats mainly squid. The elephant seal is one of the most recognizable seals, and is found on the continent in summer. They are named for the large proboscis (enlarged snout) of the male seals. Pups suckle for about three weeks, during which time the mother does not feed and may lose over 660 pounds (300 kilograms) in weight.

BIRDS. The most familiar creatures associated with Antarctica are penguins, flightless birds well adapted to the cold. As many as 35 to 40 million penguins live on Antarctica and the sub-Antarctic islands. They are excellent swimmers and, depending on the species, eat fish, squid, and krill.

*Penguins
Page 1847*

Emperor penguins and Adélie penguins are the only species that breed on the continent. Emperors are the largest penguin, at 4 feet (1.2 meters) tall. Adélie penguins are very sensitive to physical and environmental disturbance, and may serve as biological indicators of the health of the Antarctic ecosystem. Other penguin species, the king, gentoo, rockhopper, royal, and macaroni, breed on sub-Antarctic islands and occasionally the peninsula.

*Seals
Page 1910*

ANTARCTICA'S DRY VALLEYS

Found nowhere else on earth, Antarctica's dry valleys are cold, ice-free areas in which nearly all the snow sublimates, or vaporizes, without melting. They are some of the driest areas in the world, but some organisms—such as pockets of bacteria living underground and lichens and algae living inside rocks—manage to survive. Tiny nematode worms can tolerate being frozen solid and even survive the complete loss of body water: They can be freeze-dried and reconstituted. The nematodes lie dormant for long periods of time, then breed wildly when water and warmth become available. Some researchers believe that life in dry valleys may resemble what life could be like on other, very cold astral bodies such as Europa, a moon of Jupiter.

THE HUMAN IMPACT ON ANTARCTIC LIFE

Human activities have major impacts on Antarctica. Some are as obvious as whaling, some are less so. Adélie penguins nest on low earth mounds, often less than 1 foot (30 centimeters) high. If the mounds are bulldozed flat, the penguin colony may not recover, even after the humans have gone. Even so-called green activities such as ecotourism can introduce foreign bacteria and cause wear and tear. Strict regulations require tourists' clothing to be cleaned before they set foot on the continent, and there are high fines for littering. Research stations must burn or carry away all trash. Some impacts are invisible: Global warming may raise the temperature of Antarctica. Warming such a frozen land might seem like a good thing, but native organisms are adapted to the cold environment, and warming could impact them in negative ways.

The majority of the flighted sea birds are albatrosses and petrels. The wandering albatross has the largest wingspan in the world (11.5 feet/3.5 meters), and actually raises its chick during the Antarctic winter. Other albatrosses, storm petrels, diving petrels, terns, skuas, a cormorant, and a gull also live on or visit Antarctica. Virtually all sea birds feed on fish, squid, or krill.

A few land birds are found on the Antarctic Peninsula and sub-Antarctic Islands, including sheathbills, pintails and pipits.

Kelly Howard

FOR FURTHER STUDY

Bowser, Samuel S. "In Cold Mud (Diving in Antarctica)." *Natural History* (November, 1996): 56-59.

Court, S. "The Seal's Own Skin Game. (Predatory Behavior of Leopard Seals)." *Natural History* (August, 1996): 36-42.

Fothergill, Alastair. *A Natural History of the Antarctic: Life in the Freezer.* New York: Sterling Publishing, 1995.

Hodgson, Bryan. "Antarctica: A Land of Isolation No More." *National Geographic* (April, 1990): 2-52.

Reilly, Pauline. *Penguins of the World.* Oxford, England: Oxford University Press, 1994.

Rubin, Jeff. "Survival of the Coldest (Antarctic Penguins)." *Audubon* (November-December, 1996): 62-70.

Stevens, Jane E. "Life on a Melting Continent." *Discover* (August, 1995): 70-76.

INFORMATION ON THE WORLD WIDE WEB

Some of the best starting places on the Web for finding information about life, research, and conservation on the frozen continent are:

"Live from Antarctica 2," a Passport to Knowledge project sponsored by the National Science Foundation (NSF) and NASA, is "an electronic field trip via interactive television and on-line networks." (quest.arc.nasa.gov/antarctica2/index.html)

Encyclopedia Antarctica's Web site features sections on plant and animal life and physical environment. (www.antarctic.com.au/encyclopaedia/EA.html)

The Web site of the Antarctica Project, a conservation organization, reports on the organization's activities. (www.asoc.org/)

FLORA OF AUSTRALIA

Many species of plants in Australia are found nowhere else on earth, except where they have been introduced by humans. Such species are known as endemic species. This distinctiveness is the result of the long isolation of the Australian continent from other landmasses. Australia broke off from the supercontinent Pangaea more than 50 million years ago, and the species of plants and animals living at that time continued to change and adapt to conditions on the isolated island. This led to distinctive plants and animals, differing from those of the interconnected Eurasian-African-American landmass, where new immigrant species changed the ecology. Australian fauna (animals) are mostly marsupials, and Australian flora (vegetation) is dominated by two types of plants—the eucalyptus and the acacia. Nevertheless, a great deal of botanical diversity exists throughout this large continent, with 569 known species of eucalypts and 772 species of acacias.

Climate is a major influence on Australian flora, and the most striking feature of the Australian environment as a whole is its aridity. Nutrient-poor soils also affect the nature of Australia's vegetation, especially in arid areas. Half of the continent receives less than 11.8 inches (300 millimeters) of rainfall per year; small parts of Australia receive annual rainfall of 75 inches (800 millimeters). Therefore, forests cover only a small percentage of Australia. A close correlation exists between rainfall and vegetation type throughout Australia. Small regions of tropical rain forest grow in mountainous areas of the northeast, in Queensland. In the cooler mountains of New South Wales, Victoria, and Tasmania, extensive temperate rain forests thrive.

More extensive than rain forest, however, is a more open forest known as sclerophyllous forest, which grows in the southern part of the Eastern Highlands in New South Wales and Victoria, in most of Tasmania, and in southwest Western Australia. A huge crescent-shaped region of woodland vegetation, an open forest of trees of varying height, with an open canopy, extends throughout northern Australia, the eastern half of Queensland and the inland plains of New South Wales, and to the north of the Western Australian sclerophyllous forest. Beyond this region, the climate is arid, and nontree vegetation is dominant. The tropical north of inland Queensland, Northern Territory, and a smaller part of Western Australia has an extensive area of grassland. Much of Western Australia and South Australia, as well as interior parts of New South Wales and Queensland, are shrubland, where grasses and small trees grow sparsely. In the center of the continent is the desert, which has little vegetation, except along watercourses.

Paperbark trees Page 1911

THE EUCALYPTS. Many people familiar with the song "Kookaburra Sits in an Old Gum Tree," may not realize that "gum tree" is the common Australian term for a eucalyptus tree. When the bark of a eucalyptus tree is cut, sticky drops of a transparent, reddish substance called "kino" ooze out. The explorer William Dampier noticed kino coming from trees in Western Australia in 1688, and called it "gum dragon," as he thought it was the same as commercial resin. Kino is technically not gum, as it is not water-soluble.

The scientific name *Eucalyptus* was cho-

Eucalyptus trees Page 1911

sen by the first botanist to study the dried leaves and flowers of a tree collected in Tasmania during Captain James Cook's third voyage in 1777. The French botanist chose the Greek name because he thought that the bud with its cap (operculum) made the flower "well" (eu) "covered" (kalyptos). The hard cases are commonly called gum nuts. Early in the twentieth century, a series of children's books were written about Gumnut Babies, tiny imaginary beings who lived among the eucalyptus leaves and wore the operculum as a cap.

The more than five hundred species of eucalyptus in Australia range from tropical species in the north to alpine species in the southern mountains. Rainfall, temperature, and soil type determine which particular eucalypt will be found in any area. Eucalyptus trees dominate the Australian forests of the east and south, while smaller species of eucalypts grow in the drier woodland or shrubland areas. It is easier to mention parts of Australia where eucalypts do not grow: the icy peaks of the Australian Alps, the interior deserts, the Nullarbor Plain, and the rain forests of the Eastern Highlands, both tropical and temperate.

The scientific classification of the eucalypts proved difficult to European botanists. Various experts used flowers, leaves, or other criteria in their attempts to arrange the different species into a meaningful and useful taxonomy, or classification scheme. George Bentham eventually chose the shape of the anthers—the tiny stems that hold pollen—together with fruit, flowers, and nuts.

A simpler classification of the eucalypts, commonly used by foresters, gardeners, and naturalists, arranges them into six

AUSTRALIA'S OFFICIAL FLOWERS

In 1988 Australia proclaimed the golden wattle to be its official national floral emblem. Appropriately, the colors worn by Australian sporting teams—green and gold—are reminiscent of the wattle's green leaves and gold flowers. Australia has many beautiful wildflowers, and seven of the states and territories chose a flower as their state floral emblem; Tasmania chose a flowering tree, the Tasmanian blue gum. The waratah, a gorgeous red flower chosen by New South Wales, was once favored to be Australia's national flower, before the wattle was selected.

Queensland's floral emblem, the striking purple Cooktown orchid, is a reminder of that state's tropical rain forests. South Australia's flower, Sturt's desert pea, is a bright red and black plant found throughout a wide area of central Australia. Victoria's emblem is the common heath, a tiny pink flower. The distinctive kangaroo paw of Western Australia grows along the southwestern coasts of that state. The Tasmanian blue gum is a tall tree, 230 feet (70 meters) in height, making it difficult to see up close the tree's beautiful cream-colored flowers. The tree grows naturally in eastern Tasmania and a small area of Victoria and is also abundant in California.

Sturt's desert rose, the flower of the Northern Territory, is found in central Australia. The small shrub produces flowers with mauve petals, a stylized representation of which is on the territory's flag. The Australian Capital Territory was the last administrative division to choose a floral emblem—the royal bluebell, a small perennial herb with violet flowers. Its natural habitat is restricted to the region of the ACT.

Eucalyptus trees lining a street in Perth, Western Australia. (Corbis)

groups based on their bark: Gums have smooth bark, which is sometimes shed; bloodwoods have rough, flaky bark; iron-barks have very hard bark with deep furrows between large pieces; stringybarks have fibrous bark that can be peeled off in long strips; peppermints have mixed but loose bark; boxes have furrowed bark, firmly attached. This system was devised in 1859 by Ferdinand von Mueller, the first Government Botanist of the Colony of Victoria, and the father of Australian botany. After emigrating from Germany in 1847 for his health, he was appointed to the Victorian position in 1853 and served until his death in 1896. He was an eccentric and controversial figure, but devoted to botanical exploration and research.

Many of the native plants of Australia

show typical adaptations to the arid climate, such as deep taproots that can reach down to the water table. Another common feature is small, shiny leaves, to reduce transpiration. Eucalyptus leaves are tough or leathery, described as sclerophyllous. Sclerophyllus forests of eucalypts cover the wetter parts of Australia, the Eastern Highlands, or Great Dividing Range, and the southwest of Western Australia. The hardwood from these forests is generally not of a quality suitable for building, so areas are cleared and the trees made into woodchips that are exported for manufacture of newsprint paper. This has been a controversial use of Australian forests, especially where the native forest has been cleared and replaced with pine plantations.

The southwest corner of Western Australia has magnificent forests featuring two exceptional species with Aboriginal names, Karri and Jarrah. Karri is one of the world's tallest trees, growing to 295 feet (90 meters) tall. This excellent hardwood tree is widely used for construction. The long straight trunks are covered in smooth bark that is shed each year, making a colorful display of pink and gray. These forests are now protected. Jarrah grows to 120 feet (40 meters) in height and is a heavy, durable timber. It was used for road construction in the nineteenth century, but now the deep red timber is prized for furniture, flooring, and paneling.

During the nineteenth century, Australia could also claim to be home to the world's tallest trees, the mountain ash. The tallest tree, which observers claimed was 433 feet (132 meters) high and with the top broken away, was felled in 1872. The tallest accurately measured tree was only 374 feet (114 meters) high. The tallest known tree now standing is in North America—a redwood growing in northern California.

The most widely distributed of all Australian eucalypts is the beautiful river red gum. These trees grow along riverbanks and watercourses throughout Australia, especially in inland areas; their spreading branches provide wide shade and habitat for many animals. Koalas eat leaves from this tree. In the song "Waltzing Matilda," Australia's unofficial national anthem, a man camps "under the shade of a coolabah tree." This word might apply to any eucalypt, but is most likely a river red gum.

In drier interior areas, and in some mountain areas, there are more than one hundred smaller species of eucalypts that are known by the Aboriginal name Mallee. These many-trunked shrubs have an underground lignotuber or root that stores water. Much of this marginal country was cleared for farming, creating a situation

*Queensland
Page 1912*

similar to the Dust Bowl in the United States. In the dry Australian summers bushfires are a great danger, in the mallee and in any eucalyptus forest. The volatile oils of the eucalyptus trees can lead to rapid spread in the tree crowns, jumping across human-made firebreaks. On the other hand, several Australian trees not only can survive fires but actually require fire to germinate.

Eucalypts have been introduced to many countries, including Italy, Egypt, Ethiopia, India, China, and Brazil, and they are common in California, where they have been growing as introduced trees for 150 years.

THE ACACIAS. These plants are usually called "wattles" in Australia, because the early European convicts and settlers used the flexible twigs of the plant for wattling, in which twigs are woven together, making a firm foundation for a thatched roof or for walls, which then are covered inside and out with mud. This style of building, known as wattle-and-daub, was common throughout Australia in pioneering days.

Wattles frequently have masses of colorful flowers, usually bright yellow. One species is the national flower of Australia. Other interesting acacias include the Mulga, which has an attractive wood.

THE RAIN FORESTS. Although rain forest vegetation covers only a small area of Australia, it is exceptionally varied and of great scientific interest. Neither of the two general types of rain forest found in Australia has eucalypts. Rain forests are located along the Eastern Highlands, or Great Dividing Range, where rainfall is heavy. In small areas of tropical Queensland, where rainfall is also heavy, true tropical rain forest is found. The flora are similar to that in Indonesian and Malaysian rain forests. The tropical rain forest contains thousands of species of trees, as well as lianas, lawyer vine, and the fierce "stinging tree," whose touch could kill an unwary explorer. Toward the north of New South Wales, a kind of subtropical to temperate rain forest grows. Cool, wet Victoria and Tasmania have extensive areas of temperate rain forest, where only a few species dominate the forests. Arctic beech are found, as well as sassafras and tall tree ferns.

SCLEROPHYLLUS FOREST. This is the typical Australian bush, which grows close to the coast of New South Wales, Victoria, and Tasmania. The bright Australian sun streams down through the sparse crowns and narrow leaves of the eucalypts. As the climate becomes drier, farther inland from the coast, the open forest slowly changes to a shrubbier woodland vegetation.

GRASSLANDS. Moving further inland, to still drier regions, woodlands give way to grasslands, where cattle are raised for beef in the Tropics, and sheep are raised for wool in the temperate areas. Before Europeans came to Australia, there were native grasslands in the interior—tropical grasslands in the monsoonal north, and temperate grasslands in the south and southwest. Kangaroo grass and wallaby grass grew in the temperate interior of New South Wales, but much of this has been cleared for agriculture, especially for wheat farming. Mitchell grass is another tussock grass, which grows in western Queensland and into the Northern Territory; cattle and sheep graze extensively on this excellent native pasture.

The commonest grassland type in Australia is Spinifex, a spiky grass clump that grows in the arid interior and west. Even cattle cannot feed on spinifex grass, so this environment is less threatened than most other grassland. The northern grasslands are dotted with tall red termite mounds; those that are aligned north-south for protection from the hot sun are built by so-called "magnetic" termites.

OTHER TREES AND PLANTS. Many people think that macadamia nuts are native to Hawaii, which produces 90 percent of the world's crop, but in fact, the tree is native to Australia. It was discovered by Ferdinand von Mueller in 1857 on an expedition in northern Australia. Mueller named the tree after his Scottish friend, John Macadam. The trees were introduced to Hawaii in 1882.

Cycads are plants from an ancient species, but they still thrive in Australia. The *Macrozamia* of North Queensland is a giant fernlike plant. Similarly old are the *Xanthorrhea* grass-trees, which used to be called "blackboys." A single spearlike stem rises from a delicate green skirt on this fire-resistant species.

In northwest Australia, the baobab or bottle tree can be found. This fat-trunked tree collects water in its tissue. One is said to have served as a temporary prison. The only other baobabs are found in Africa, a reminder that these continents were once joined. Bottlebrush is an Australian shrub with colorful flowers that has become popular with gardeners in many parts of the world.

EXTINCT AND ENDANGERED PLANT SPECIES. Human activities on Australia have led to the extinction of more than eighty species of plants, and the list of endangered plants contains more than two hundred species. Many nonnative species have been introduced to Australia by Europeans; some have become pests, such as the blackberry in Victoria, the lantana in north Queensland, and water hyacinth throughout the continent. There are 462 national parks in Australia, as well as other conservation areas, where native flora are protected.

ABORIGINAL PLANT USE. The Australian Aborigines used plants as sources of food and for medicinal purposes. Food plants included nuts, seeds, berries, roots, and tubers. Nectar from flowering plants, the pithy center of tree ferns, and stems and roots of reeds were eaten. Fibrous plants were made into string for weaving nets or making baskets. Weapons such as spears, clubs, and shields, as well as boomerangs, were made from hardwoods such as eucalyptus. The bunya pine or forests of southeast Queensland were a place of great feasting when the rich bunya nuts fell.

Ray Sumner

FOR FURTHER STUDY

Berra, Tim M. *A Natural History of Australia.* San Diego, Calif.: Academic Press, 1998.

Dallman, Peter R. *Plant Life in the World's Mediterranean Climates: California, Chile, South Africa, Australia, and the Mediterranean Basin.* Berkeley: University of California Press, 1998.

Evans, Howard Ensign, and Mary Alice Evans. *Australia: A Natural History.* Washington, D.C.: Smithsonian Institution Press, 1983.

Kirkpatrick, J. B. *A Continent Transformed: Human Impact on the Natural Vegetation of Australia.* New York: Oxford University Press, 1994.

Pyne, Stephen J. *Burning Bush: A Fire History of Australia.* Seattle: University of Washington Press, 1998.

Watkins, T. H. "Greening of the Empire. Sir Joseph Banks." *National Geographic* (November, 1996): 28-53.

Wolinsky, Cary. "Wildflowers of Western Australia." *National Geographic* (January, 1995): 68-89.

Young, Ann R. M., and Ann Yound. *Environmental Change in Australia Since 1788.* New York: Oxford University Press, 1996.

INFORMATION ON THE WORLD WIDE WEB

Information on Australia's floral emblems can be found at (www.anbg.gov.au/emblems/).

FAUNA OF AUSTRALIA

Map Page 1912

Many scientists theorize that until about 300 million years ago, Earth had one supercontinent or landmass, called Pangaea, that covered about 40 percent of the planet's surface. During that time, animal and plant species multiplied and intermixed freely across the great land. Then, nearly 200 million years ago, many factors caused Pangaea to split into two smaller continents, Laurasia and Gondwanaland.

Laurasia evolved from what had been the northern part of Pangaea and included North America, Europe, and Asia. Gondwanaland, formed from the southern part of Pangaea, comprised Antarctica, South America, Africa, India, and Australia. Over millions of years, Laurasia and Gondwanaland continued to fragment and drift apart. Once-related flora and fauna began to evolve separately.

Female kangaroo with her young in her pouch. (PhotoDisc)

When Gondwanaland broke apart sixty million years ago, Australia became Earth's only island continent—completely surrounded by oceans and seas. Isolated from the other major landmasses, Australian plants and animals evolved on their own. Faunal adaptations took place as special habitats demanded change for survival, especially habitats such as the tropical rain forests of North Queensland; the mangrove swamps along the coast; the mountainous Alps of southeast Australia; and the gorges, caves, and deserts of central Australia. Frogs, for example, learned to burrow for water.

Some mammals adapted to the lack of drinking water by metabolizing food differently. All successful species made adjustments in order to survive. As a result, the Australian continent is now home to a rich, varied, and often unique flora and fauna. Nearly 95 percent of its mammals, 70 percent of its birds, 88 percent of its reptiles, and 94 percent of its frogs are found no where else in the world in the wild.

Kangaroo Page 1913

AUSTRALIAN MAMMALS. Australia's distinctive wildlife includes more than 280 species of native mammals. All three groups of modern mammals—marsupials, monotremes, and placentals—are represented. Monotremes (egg-laying mammals) are perhaps the most unusual; two of the three known species (the platypus and the echidna) exist on the island continent. Australia also has several sea mammals, including the humpback and other whale species, the dugong (or sea cow), and a variety of Australian fur seal species.

Marsupials are the most common mammals native to Australia. They give birth to live immature (fetal) young that are then carried in the mother's pouch until fully developed. Marsupials date back thousands of years and have adapted to many habitats related to their preferred foods. These include plants, eaten by the kangaroo and the koala; nectar, eaten by the pygmy possum; and insects and meat, eaten by the quoll and Tasmanian devil. Some marsupials, such as bandicoots, are omnivorous, eating both plants and small animals.

The second group of mammals, the monotremes, are the most puzzling of nature's animal species. Sometimes referred to as "living fossils," these mammals lay eggs, then nurse their hatched young. Scientists believe that monotremes may represent the stage of evolution between reptilian and placental mammals. Australia has two types of monotremes: the platypus and the echidna. Best-known is the platypus, with its duck bill, beaver-like tail, webbed feet, and furry body. Once hunted for its rich pelt, the platypus is now protected from poaching by law. The echidna, also known as the spiny anteater, resembles the porcupine. This rabbit-sized mammal has no teeth and uses its long sticky tongue to penetrate ant and termite nests that it has torn open with its sharp claws. When in danger, it burrows straight into the ground. Echidna are common in Australia and are not a protected species.

*Lorikeet
Page 1914*

The third group of mammals, the placentals, are those species that give birth to fully developed live young. Many Australian species fall into this group, including varieties of native mice.

Most Australian land mammals are nocturnal (active only at night). Australia abounds with wildlife parks and zoos that allow visitors to observe these animals in their own habitats. Examples include the Lone Pine Koala Sanctuary in Brisbane, Queensland; Lamington National Park, Southeast Queensland; and Sydney's Australian Wildlife Park.

BIRDS. Australia has more than eight hundred bird species of many types. Some major categories include birds of prey (owls, eagles, hawks/kestrels), songbirds, and especially parrots and cockatoos. Australia is also home to the smallest penguin species, the little blue or fairy penguin found on Phillip Island in Victoria.

Australia's emu and cassowary are the largest birds in the world; both are flightless. The emu stands nearly 6 feet (2 meters) tall and weighs more than 100 pounds (500 kilograms). Covered with feathers and having a ferocious beak, its wings are only prehistoric remnants. Its long legs can cover the ground at nearly 30 miles (50 kilometers) per hour. The emu is also a good swimmer. Its image (along with that of the kangaroo) is found on the Australian coat-of-arms. The cassowary is also distinctive in appearance. Smaller than the emu (around 5 feet/1.75 meters), it has coarse, hairlike feathers, red fleshy wattles, a bony helmet, and three-toed feet designed for running. Both the cassowary and emu have distinctive, throaty calls.

Parrot species abound in Australia. The budgerigar (often called budgies) is a common pet. The galah (rose-breasted cockatoo), crimson rosella, turquosine, and rainbow lorikeet are among the most colorful and commonly seen species. There are ten native species of kingfishers and kookaburras, famous for their plunging dives for prey. The laughing kookaburra has a distinct call and is the largest of

Australia's kingfisher families. Particularly unusual is the lyrebird, the largest Australian song bird. Sooty brown and the size of a hen, the lyrebird's tail feathers are nearly 2 feet (0.6 meter) long. When raised, the tail feathers take the shape of the lyre, a string instrument used in antiquity.

REPTILES AND AMPHIBIANS. More than 750 reptile species can be found in Australia; almost 90 percent do not exist anywhere else in the world. Of the 2,400 species of snakes recognized in the world, 170 of them are found on the island continent. Australian snakes are grouped into five families: pythons and boas; blind snakes; colubrid snakes; file snakes; and elapids and sea snakes. Many of the land snakes are venomous, such as the taipan, brown snake, and red-belly black snake.

Australian reptiles include nearly five hundred species of lizards. The main families are geckos; legless or snake lizards; dragon lizards (such as the frilled neck lizard found on Australia's old two-cent coin); iguana-like monitor lizards or goannas; and skinks. Australia's most endangered reptile is the western swamp tortoise, with fewer than three hundred in existence in the late 1990's. Since 1988, the Perth Zoo has had a captive breeding program to increase their numbers.

Australia is also home to the freshwater crocodile and the saltwater (estuarine) crocodile. The latter is the biggest reptile in the world. Found along the country's northern coastline, from Rockhampton in Queensland to Broome in Western Australia, "saltys" live mainly where tidal rivers

Sign in Queensland warning visitors to be wary of crocodiles. (Tom McKnight/Joan Clemons)

SELECT ENDANGERED AND THREATENED MAMMALS OF AUSTRALIA

Common Name	Scientific Name	Range	Status
Bandicoot, desert	*Perameles eremiana*	Australia	endangered
Kangaroo, Tasmanian forester	*Macropus giganteus tasmaniensis*	Tasmania	endangered
Koala	*Phascolarctos cinerus*	Australia	threatened
Marsupial, eastern jerboa	*Antechinomys laniger*	Australia	endangered
Mouse, Australian native	*Notomys aquilo*	Australia	endangered
Numbat	*Myrmecobius fasciatus*	Australia	endangered
Possum, mountain pygmy	*Burramys parvus*	Australia	endangered
Rat-kangaroo, desert	*Caloprymnus campestris*	Australia	endangered
Tiger, Tasmanian	*Thylacinus cynocephalus*	Australia	endangered
Wallaby, western hare	*Lagorchestes hirsutus*	Australia	endangered
Wombat, Queensland hairy-nosed	*Lasiorhinus krefftii*	Australia	endangered

Source: U.S. Fish and Wildlife Service, U.S. Department of the Interior.

meet the sea. They are a protected species and are often caught and relocated for their own survival.

Australia's large population of amphibians includes more than two hundred frog species. One of the most striking features of Australian frog fauna is their lack of dependance on permanent bodies of water for reproduction. Species have adapted to breeding in temporary pools of water by shortening their periods of larval development.

SEA MAMMALS AND MARINE LIFE. Australia is famous for its twelve-hundred-mile-long (1,900 km.) Great Barrier Reef and the countless species of fish and other sea creatures that coexist in that habitat. These include anemones, sponges, worms, gastropods, lobsters, crayfish, shrimp and prawns, crabs, and starfish. One starfish species in particular, the crown-of-thorns, has caused much destruction to the reef by eating most of the living coral. Sharks, such as the fiercesome Great White, also live along the Australian coast. These waters are home

to many sea mammal species, including whales (humpback, sei, and fin, among others); dolphins; Australian fur seals, and dugongs. Australia has the largest dugong population in the world, most living in the Torres Strait and in the northern Great Barrier Reef. A slow-moving mammal with little protection against sharks, saltwater crocodiles, or human predators, it is now a protected species in Australia.

INVERTEBRATES. Australia's invertebrate fauna is estimated at nearly 225,000 species. These include families of insects (beetles, wasps and bees, stick insects, praying mantis, grasshoppers, termites) and nearly four thousand species of ants. Snails, earthworms (including some of the world's largest worms), moths and butterflies, dragonflies, and spiders are included in the count. Many invertebrate species have Pangaen origins or can be traced to Gondwanan times.

INTRODUCTION OF DESTRUCTIVE NON-NATIVE FAUNA. With the passage of time and the mobility of human populations,

Sharks Page 1915

foreign plants and animals were introduced into Australia, and many of them thrived. The Aborigines, the first humans to inhabit the Australian continent, arrived there nearly forty thousand years ago. With them they brought the dingo, a wild dog originally from Asia, possibly Thailand. When Europeans began settling in Australia in the late eighteenth century, hoofed species such as horses, cattle, goats, sheep, and deer were introduced into the faunal mix. Domestic cats were imported as well.

Many of these foreign animals had a disastrous impact on the Australian ecology, causing much damage and loss of native species. Without native predators or diseases to control their growing populations, imported species have often caused great destruction by preying on native animals and devouring native plants. Examples of harmful species include the rabbit, camel, cat, dingo, water buffalo, and cane toad. The dingo, a carnivore, competed for the same food sources as the native Tasmanian tiger, leading to the extinction of that species. Feral domestic cats have killed off native rodent species.

Camels are another example. Originally brought to Australia from Afghanistan, they were well-suited to carrying cargo across central Australia's vast arid deserts. With the advent of railroads and automobiles, however, their use ended. Now, descendants of the original camels roam the Outback.

Cane toads were first introduced by farmers in 1935, despite warnings from scientists, to protect Queensland's sugarcane fields from the cane beetle. The experiment failed; today they are a major nuisance. The highly poisonous amphibians multiply rapidly, often live up to twenty years, and have no natural enemies in Australia. They are especially deadly to native animal populations who attempt to feed on them. Rabbits are also considered pests. In 1859 Thomas Austin imported twenty-four rabbits from England and released them on his property in Victoria for sport hunting. Today the total wild rabbit population exceeds two hundred million and is highly destructive to crops and native plants.

Koalas
Page 1913

Koala. (Corbis)

The loss of numbers of Australia's native animal species cannot be blamed only on competitive interaction with imported species. Humans also have caused losses through poaching practices, use of poisonous herbicides, destruction of habitats through increased building and urbanization, and the commercial use of native animal species.

Issues concerning the preservation of native plants, animals, and habitats remain of the utmost importance to Australians. They have great pride in the country's unique faunal heritage. To this end, Australia continues to establish safeguards and pass legislation aimed at protecting the natural environment, the destruction of which would be tragic and have wide-reaching economic and other consequences.

Cynthia Beres

FOR FURTHER STUDY

Breeden, Stanley. *Visions of a Rainforest: A Year in Australia's Tropical Rainforest.* Berkeley, Calif.; Ten Speed Press, 1993.

Bryson, Bill. *In a Sun-Burned Country.* New York: Broadway Books, 2000.

Environment Australia. "Australia's Biodiversity: An Overview of Selected Components." (http://www.environment.gov.au)

Kennedy, Michael, ed. *Australia's Endangered Species.* New York: Prentice Hall, 1990.

National Geographic Society. *Amazing Animals of Australia.* Books for World Explorers series. Washington, D.C.: Author, 1984.

Vandenbeld, John. *Nature of Australia: A Portrait of the Island Continent.* New York: Facts On File, 1988.

FLORA AND FAUNA OF THE PACIFIC ISLANDS

The vast region of the Pacific, collectively called Oceania, comprises thousands of islands. Oceania spreads across the Pacific Ocean from 20 degrees north latitude to 50 degrees south latitude and from longitude 125 degrees east to 130 degrees west. The major groupings are Melanesia, Micronesia, Polynesia, and New Zealand. Melanesia ("black islands") is a group of large islands immediately north and east of Australia, from New Guinea to New Caledonia. Micronesia ("little islands") is made up of hundreds of tiny atolls in the western Pacific. Polynesia ("many islands") covers a huge region in the central Pacific. New Zealand lies east and south of Australia. For biological purposes, these islands can be categorized by climate and formation type. Climates range from tropical to sub-Antarctic, dry to very rainy. Types include volcanic (Fiji, Guam, and Hawaii), tectonic (New Zealand and New Guinea), and low coral atolls (nearly all of Micronesia's islands).

ENDEMIC AND EXOTIC PLANTS AND ANIMALS. Organisms have a hard time reaching the islands across the broad expanses of the Pacific Ocean. This isolation leads

Easter Island

Easter Island (Rapa Nui) lies in the South Pacific 2,400 miles (3,862 km.) from Chile, South America. It is best known for its huge, mysterious stone statues. Archeological evidence proves that Easter Island once was densely forested and supported many animal and bird species. The inhabitants burned or cut down the forests before Europeans discovered the island in the 1700's. The only plants now living on the island are sparse grasses, a few shrubs, and two species of trees. There are almost no land animals larger than insects. The few thousand people who still live on the island must import nearly all their food. The devastation of Easter Island is an extreme example of what can happen to island ecologies when human development exceeds natural capacity.

to trends in the number of species found on any given island: Bigger islands have more species; those farthest from continents have fewer species. To reach the islands, plants must be carried by animals or rely on wind or water currents. Animals must fly (birds and bats), float on logs, or be carried in by humans. Birds are usually the first visitors, bringing with them hitchhiking insects and plant seeds in their digestive tracts. Bats are the only mammals to reach many islands without human help.

Island plants and animals evolve together, affected by difficult conditions; soil is often poor and food limited. Harsh environments and isolation contribute to the formation of new and unique species; some of the strangest creatures on Earth are endemic (found nowhere else) to particular islands. Most of the world's flightless birds developed on islands, where there originally were no large land predators. Island ecosystems are sensitive to disturbances, whether from natural causes such as severe storms, or human activities such as construction, agriculture, logging, and introduced species.

Introduced species (exotics), both accidental and deliberate, are a serious problem. Rats and feral animals (domestic animals that have gone wild) can devastate island ecologies. Pigs, cats, rats, and goats are particularly devastating—goats devour vegetation, cats eat birds and small animals, and rats and pigs eat anything. Introduced plants may overgrow native ones. Exotics also bring diseases to which native plants and animals have no resistance. Humans have tried to deal with exotics, with mixed results. For example, the mongoose was intentionally brought to Fiji to control accidentally introduced rats. No one considered that rats are active at night and mongooses during the day. The mongoose did not control the rats, but they did eat seven native Fijian bird species to extinction.

Another strange example occurred in Hawaii. A Hawaiian bee crawls headfirst into native, barrel-shaped flowers, gathers the nectar, and then backs out. A plant that was introduced by landscapers attracted bees, but the flowers were smaller than the native plants. Once a bee crawled in, it became stuck like a cork in a bottle. There are thousands of these plants, each with hundreds of flowers stoppered with dead bees.

Many tropical and temperate islands have coastal wetlands and mangrove swamps growing at the edge of the sea.

BIOLOGICAL MASS MURDER

The brown tree snake vividly illustrates the dangers of introducing an exotic species to an island ecosystem. The brown tree snake, a native of Australia, was accidentally introduced to Guam after World War II. It reproduced in incredible numbers and reached the highest density of any snake population on Earth, with up to sixteen to twenty thousand snakes per square mile. In the late 1970's biologists noticed that birds were disappearing from Guam. Of the fourteen bird species endemic to the island, at least nine had become extinct by the 1990's. Many small animal species, as well as chickens raised by the island's inhabitants, also disappeared. The snakes harm humans as well; they bite viciously and cause frequent power outages by climbing on power lines. Millions of dollars have been spent on unsuccessful attempts to control the brown tree snake.

Mangroves are low-growing, salt-tolerant trees that form dense tangles that are virtually impenetrable to humans. Wetlands and mangrove swamps are important breeding grounds for many types of fish and crabs, and also trap sediment, stabilize shorelines, and protect coastlines from storms. Humans often fill in the wetlands and cut down the mangroves, causing coastal erosion and the loss of food fish.

Fiji flowers
Page 1917

FIJI ISLANDS. The Fiji Islands are mostly volcanic in origin and lie in the South Pacific Ocean between longitudes 175 degrees east and 178 degrees west and 15 degrees and 22 degrees south latitudes, about 1,300 miles (2,100 km.) north of Auckland, New Zealand. Some parts of the islands receive up to 13 feet (4 meters) of rain per year, while other parts remain dry. A range of volcanic peaks divides the islands; the highest, Mount Tomanivi (formerly Mount Victoria), is 1,322 meters (4,341 feet). These differences in weather and elevation create a variety of habitats—dense rain forests, grassy savanna, and mangrove swamps—and a large diversity of species.

Human disruption on Fiji has been moderate. About half the total area is still forested, and less than one-fourth of the land is suitable for agriculture. Trees include mahogany, pine, pandanus, coconut palms, mangoes, guava, and figs. Banyan figs are difficult to cut down and are responsible for some of the lack of forest clearing. The figs are an important food for many birds and animals. Other rain forest plants include orchids, ferns, and epiphytes (plants that grow upon other plants).

There are nearly fifteen hundred endemic Fijian plant species, including ten species of palm tree on the island of Viti Levu. Endemic animals include birds such as lorikeets (parrots that eat flowers or nectar), the Fiji goshawk, spectacularly colored pigeons and parrots, and a pigeon that barks like a dog. The Vanikoro broadbill, which holds its mossy nest together with spider webs, is one of the few native birds that has adapted to forest clearing. It is commonly seen in town gardens and suburbs.

Other creatures native to Fiji are snakes, including a rare, tiny cobra, two species of frog, and several species of geckoes and skinks (small lizards). The Crested Iguana was not discovered until 1978 and lives only on the island of Yaduataba. Yaduataba is now a preserve, and the Crested Iguana is more likely to survive since feral goats were removed from the island.

Grassy savannas are found higher on the volcanic slopes and in the dry zones. They are often planted with coconut palms and taro, a plant with potato-like roots that is grown on many Pacific Islands.

There are twelve reserve areas in the Fijian islands, but several are being logged and provide little sanctuary to native plants and animals. The government is interested in increased logging of mahogany and pine. The Fiji Pine Commission hopes to remove pressure from native forest trees such as mahogany by encouraging the development of pine forests. Pines grow quickly and could form a sustainable logging industry, unlike the valuable but slow-growing mahogany trees. Increased world interest in herbal remedies has created a market for Fiji's traditional crop, kava root, and for ginger processing.

The University of the South Pacific is located in Fiji and is a source of serious research into South Pacific species. Tourism is important to Fiji's economy and, with management, could be a source of income to Fijians while still preserving native wildlife.

NEW GUINEA. The world's largest tropical island, New Guinea is located north of Australia and just south of the equator. It is tectonic in origin, with large changes in elevation and many different habitats. Because of its size and varied terrain, New Guinea has a greater variety of habitats than any similar-sized land area in the world. In fact, New Guinea is so rugged that it is one of the least explored or developed places on Earth. It provides the best remaining example of the types of organisms that can develop in island isolation.

New Guinea habitats include cold tundra, tropical rain forests, grassy savannas, coastal zones, montane rain forests, cloud forests, and bogs. There are at least twenty thousand species of flowering plants, including more than twenty-five hundred species of orchids, and hundreds of birds and animals. Many New Guinea species are unusual. Endemic Klinki pines are the tallest tropical trees in the world, reaching 295 feet (90 meters) tall.

Native birds range from the beautiful to the bizarre. There are several species of birds of paradise, some of the most beautiful birds in the world. They have brilliant colors or long, wiry feathers with metallic-looking feather disks that they wave and tremble to attract mates. The bower bird builds large, complicated structures and decorates them with colorful flowers, feathers, or trash, and even uses berry juice as paint. The megapode tunnels into the earth near volcanic hot springs with huge, powerful feet. It lays its eggs in the warm tunnel so that it does not have to sit on them.

New Guinea has several parrots, including the endangered Pesquet's parrot, whose face is completely bald so it can stick its head into fruit without getting sticky feathers. Lorikeets are colorful, nectar-eating parrots. New Guinea is also home to the flightless cassowary, a large bird up to 6.6 feet (2 meters) tall and weighing up to 130 pounds (60 kilograms). Other bird species include feathery crowned pigeons, kingfishers (twenty-two species), ducks, herons, hawks, and egrets.

As in Australia, primates and large mammals never arrived in New Guinea. Marsupials (animals with pouches) took their ecological places. There are several species of tree-living kangaroos. The basic kangaroo shape is modified in the tree species; they have larger forearms and smaller hind legs. Other marsupials include striped and feather-tailed possums, ringtails, and land wallabies that look like small, dainty kangaroos.

Other odd New Guinea animals are the echidnas, perhaps the most primitive mammal in the world. Echidnas lay eggs and are related to the duck-billed platypus. There are several echidna species; the largest is the giant spiny anteater, which has long spines, dense fur, thick claws, and a long, slender snout. Despite its name, it eats mostly earthworms, which it reels into its mouth using spines on its tongue.

New Guinea has many types of fruit bat. One large species, the flying fox, roosts in colonies. The largest roost is in a tree directly in front of the main police station in the town of Madang. Thousands of bats roosting overhead cause significant problems in street cleaning and for pedestrians without hats.

Reptiles and amphibians on New Guinea consist of snakes, lizards, frogs, and toads. The Salvadori monitor lizard is the longest in the world, growing up to 16 feet (5 meters) long, most of which is tail. Crocodiles live in many rivers and are endangered from hunting and demand for their hides. Some locals have begun crocodile ranches, where they breed and raise the crocodiles for meat and hides without damaging wild populations. Snakes include adders and pythons (eight species),

Madang's flying fox tree. (Tom McKnight/Joan Clemons)

and the deadly taipan and Papuan black snakes. There are many species of frogs, including several odd rain forest species that no longer have a tadpole stage.

New Guinea's insects include the largest moth in the world and the largest butterfly, the Queen Alexandra's birdwing. This species is endangered due to collecting and loss of habitat, but some New Guineans run butterfly ranches. They raise the insects, sell them to collectors and museums, and still preserve the species. There are also giant millipedes, stick insects 12 inches (30 centimeters) long, and a fly with its eyes on stalks. Several species of flies have antlers on their heads, which they use to fight in defense of egg-laying territory.

Many forests host "ant-plants," warty looking epiphytes that have hollow mazes inside their tissues. Ants live in the maze, safe from predators. The ants provide nutrition for the plant in the form of droppings, scraps of food, and dead ants.

Even though New Guinea is rugged and isolated, human impact is increasing. The population is rising, which means that more forests are being cut and grasslands plowed for agriculture, roads, and development. Humans have brought in food plants such as the sago palm, which can be cultivated in areas where more traditional crops will not survive. They also cultivate pandanus trees, several varieties of fruiting vine, breadfruit, fungi, tubers, sugarcane, bananas, taro, and yams. Gold, silver, and copper have been discovered, which encourages destructive mining.

It has proven difficult to develop New Guinea economically without destroying the unique life of the island. It is hoped that lessons learned on other islands, such as Guam and New Zealand, may be applied to New Guinea. The government has tried incentives to keep wild areas wild, such as encouraging ecologically friendly businesses like crocodile and butterfly farms and ecotourism. The National Park reserve that includes Mount Jaya is the only place in the world where it is possible to visit a glacier and a coral reef in the same park.

NEW ZEALAND. Located off the eastern edge of Australia, New Zealand has a fairly moderate climate that comes from conflicting warm, humid Pacific and colder Antarctic weather. It is similar to New Guinea, with rugged terrain, high mountains, and habitats from grassy open plains to dense forests, wet areas to near-deserts. Unlike New Guinea, however, New Zealand has been occupied and developed by humans for hundreds of years. Before large-scale agriculture, about half of New Zealand was covered with forests and one-third with grassland communities. Now, half is pasture for grazing and a quarter is forest, mostly introduced species. Much of the remaining native forest is maintained as national parks and reserves. Pasture land usually consists of a single species of grass and does not support the wide variety of bird and animal life of the original grassland communities.

It is sometimes said that the dominant mammal in New Zealand is the sheep. Sheep are vital to the economy but have caused problems for native animals; more than six hundred native species are threatened and several are extinct, including 43 percent of New Zealand's frogs and more than 40 percent of its native birds.

Like New Guinea and Australia, New Zealand did not originally have any large mammals or carnivores. Fourteen flightless or weak-flying birds developed there. The native Maori people hunted the large, flightless moa to extinction before the Europeans arrived, one of the rare instances in recent history when humans not from a Western culture were responsible for a species' extinction.

New Zealand's flightless kiwi has become a national symbol. (New Zealand Tourism Board)

Flightless birds that still survive in New Zealand are the kiwi and the kakapo parrot. The introduction of cats, dogs, rats, and pigs has severely endangered both species, and at the end of the twentieth century, there were fewer than seventy kakapo left. All had been moved to predator-free, offshore islands. The kiwi is New Zealand's state bird and efforts are being made to save it as well. Two species of another flightless bird, the penguin, breed on the south and east coasts. There are more than two hundred species of flying birds, at least forty of them introduced, including tropic birds, gulls, hawks, harriers, skuas, spoonbills, and pheasants.

The only original endemic mammals were two species of bats. In the last two hundred years, many exotic marsupials and mammals have appeared, including rabbits, rats, mice, weasels, otters, cats, pigs, cattle, deer, goats, and sheep. Domestic cattle, sheep, and pigs are economically important.

Amphibians and reptiles are interesting but not numerous. Among them is a frog that retains its tail as an adult and one that bypasses the tadpole stage. Some frog species have been introduced, but have had little impact. Reptiles include geckoes, skinks, and the extremely primitive, lizard-like tuatara.

Continued on page 1919

One of the most active volcanoes in the Pacific Islands is Kilauea on the big island of Hawaii. Reaching an elevation of only 4,009 feet (1,247 meters), Kilauea is not tall for a volcano; however, it has an enormous sunken caldera. (Clyde L. Rasmussen)

Hills in the central part of Fiji's main island, Viti Levu. Fiji, Papua New Guinea, the Solomon Islands, Vanuatu, and New Caledonia are all mountainous countries. (Tom McKnight/Joan Clemons)

Waterfalls in Samoa. (Clyde L. Rasmussen)

CLIMATE REGIONS OF AUSTRALIA

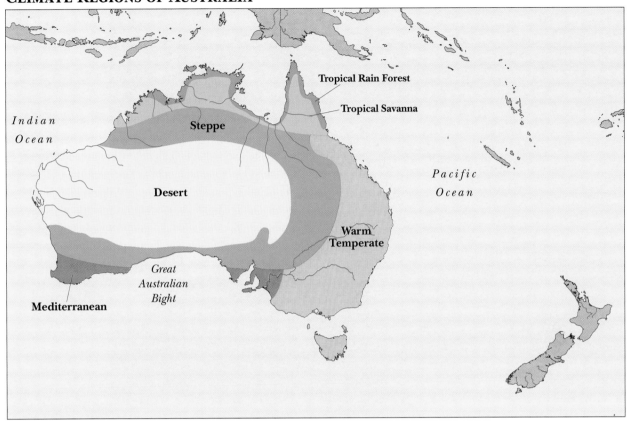

Indian
Ocean

Tropical Rain Forest

Tropical Savanna

Steppe

Pacific
Ocean

Desert

**Warm
Temperate**

*Great
Australian
Bight*

Mediterranean

Australia's wet and dry zones can be clearly seen on this photograph of the continent taken from space. (Corbis)

Lightning strike near Australia's most famous landform, Uluru (Ayers Rock). (American Stock Photography)

The Snowy Mountains are part of the Australian Alps, the only part of the continent that receives snowfall regularly. (Tom McKnight/Joan Clemons)

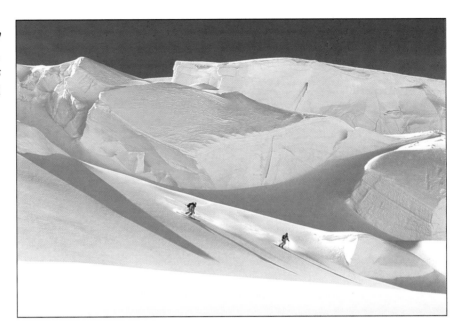

Tasman Glacier in New Zealand's Southern Alps, which retain their snow caps year round. (New Zealand Tourism Board)

SELECTED RESOURCES OF ANTARCTICA

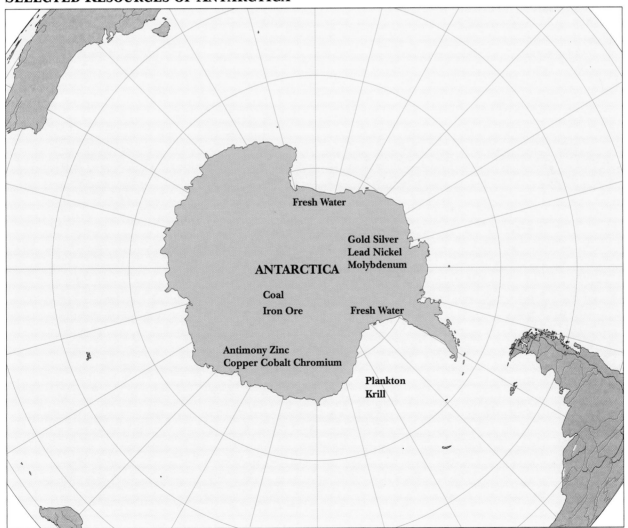

Fresh Water

Gold Silver
Lead Nickel
Molybdenum

ANTARCTICA

Coal

Iron Ore

Fresh Water

Antimony Zinc
Copper Cobalt Chromium

Plankton
Krill

SELECTED RESOURCES OF AUSTRALIA

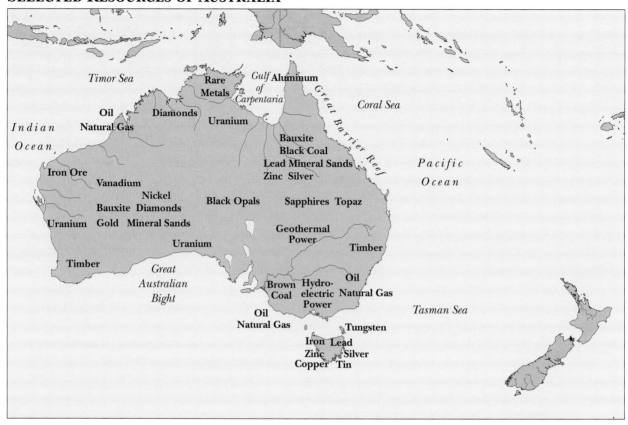

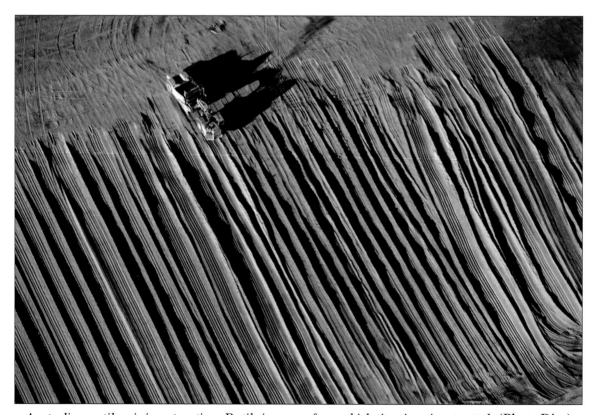

Australian rutile mining operation. Rutile is an ore from which titanium is extracted. (PhotoDisc)

Nicholson River in Queensland. Australia is dry except for the tropical north. True rivers are few, and their combined discharge is equivalent to merely a quarter that of North America's Mississippi River. (Tom McKnight/Joan Clemons)

Corrugated iron roofing is a comparative luxury in Western Samoa, which has limited mineral resources. (Clyde L. Rasmussen)

Depleted phosphate field on Nauru. (Tom McKnight/Joan Clemons)

Scientist with the U.S. Antarctic Program tags a seal at Antarctica's McMurdo Sound, as part of a study of the continent's seal population. (AP/Wide World Photos)

Australia has more than five hundred varieties of eucalyptus, ranging from tropical species in the north to alpine species in the southern mountains. The trees are one of Australia's most important exports and can now be found throughout the world. (Digital Stock)

Paperbark trees, a variety unique to Australia, in southern Victoria's Wilson's Promontory. The bark of these trees can be stripped off in sheets for many uses, including packing, roofing, caulking. (Corbis)

The Glass House Mountains in Queensland, Australia's greenest region. (Tom McKnight/Joan Clemons)

HABITATS AND SELECTED VERTEBRATES OF AUSTRALIA

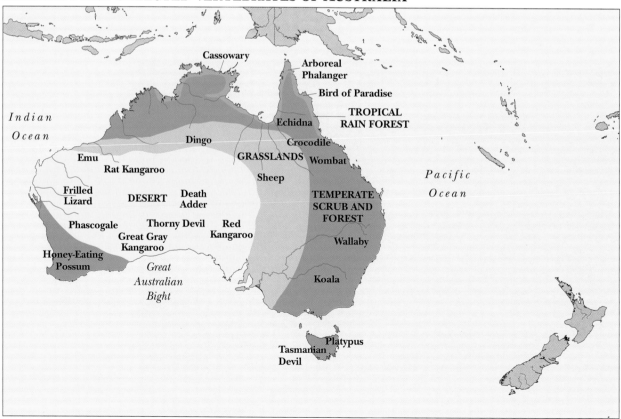

There is probably no animal in the world more closely identified with a single country than the kangaroo is with Australia. Including the closely related wallaby, Australia has more than sixty species of kangaroos. (Corbis)

Another animal closely identified with Australia is the koala. Similar in appearance to toy "teddy bears," koalas are often called "koala bears"; however, they are marsupials, not members of the bear family. (Corbis)

The rainbow lorikeet is one of the most colorful and commonly seen varieties of parrot in Australia. (American Stock Photography)

Sharks off the Sunshine Coast of Queensland, Australia, go into a feeding frenzy over a school of small fish. Sharks are abundant along most of Australia's coasts. (AP/Wide World Photos)

Papaya trees. A tropical fruit widely grown in the Pacific Islands, the papaya was introduced from South America, where it appears to have originated in Peru. (PhotoDisc)

Pollination of a passion fruit blossom with a brush on Fiji. (Clyde L. Rasmussen)

The Hibiscus Parade in Suva, Fiji, celebrates the country's colorful flora. (Clyde L. Rasmussen)

Fijian pine plantation. To reduce pressure on native trees, such as mahogany, the Fiji Pine Commission encourages the development of new forests of pine trees, which grow quickly. (Tom McKnight/Joan Clemons)

Hawaiian taro fields. (PhotoDisc)

NEW ZEALAND'S NATIONAL PARKS

New Zealand's strikingly beautiful and diverse landscape contains thirteen national parks: four on North Island and nine on South Island. These parks, comprising 30 percent of New Zealand's land area, are set aside to preserve spectacular scenery, rare and endangered flora and fauna, and archeological sites. These parks offer various outdoor activities, such as golfing, walking, mountaineering and climbing, snow sports, exploring archeological and mining sites and old volcanic landforms, geyser watching, swimming, diving, sailing, and camping.

Many parks contain features of historic and spiritual significance to the Maori. In 1887 the Maori chiefs of the Tuwharetoa tribe dedicated their ancestral North Island volcanic peaks of Tongariro, Ruapehu, and Nguaruhoe to all people of New Zealand. This area, named Tongariro National Park, is the country's first—and the world's fourth—national park. It is one of two World Heritage sites within the country. The other site, on South Island, includes parts of Westland, Fiordland, Mount Cook, and Mount Aspiring National Parks.

Invertebrate species include such oddities as a giant carnivorous land snail. There are more than four thousand species of beetles, two thousand species of flies, and fifteen hundred species of butterflies and moths. In a reversal of the usual ecological concerns, some native insects are destroying introduced pasture grasses.

CORAL ATOLLS. The Federated States of Micronesia consists mainly of small atolls. Coral atolls are found only in tropical latitudes because coral (small, colonial animals) grows only in warm water. Coral reefs support a tremendous variety of fish, crabs, and mollusks. Atolls tend to have porous, infertile soil and to be very low in elevation; the inhabited state of Tokelau, three small islands located at 9 degrees south latitude, longitude 172 degrees west, has a maximum elevation of 16 feet (5 meters). Due to the low profile, poor soil, and occasional scouring by typhoons, flora are mostly limited to hardy root crops and fast-growing trees such as coconut and pandanus. Other vegetation may include native and introduced species such as papaya, banana, arrowroot, taro, lime, bread-fruit, and pumpkin. Fauna usually consists of lizards, rodents, crabs, and other small creatures. Pigs, ducks, and chickens are raised for food, and dogs and cats are kept as pets.

Human disturbances on coral atolls often have been particularly violent; several nuclear test bombs were exploded on Bikini Atoll and other islands in the 1940's and 1950's. Kwajalein, the largest atoll in the world, is used by the U.S. military for intercontinental ballistic missile target practice. Johnston Atoll, about 820 miles (1,320 km.) southwest of Honolulu, Hawaii, is a U.S. military base and storage facility for radioactive and toxic substances. It is also designated as a protected area and bird-breeding ground.

FUTURE PROSPECTS. Island ecologies are unique and fragile. Some, like those in Guam and New Zealand, can never be returned to their original state, but with extensive wildlife management, many native species can be saved from extinction. Ironically, people in the developed world who visit zoos see more native Pacific island species than those who live on those

Papaya trees Page 1916

islands. Some endemic species have been wiped out or had their habitat destroyed, so zoos are the last refuge for many creatures.

New Guinea, Fiji, and many smaller islands are in earlier stages of modern development and wildlife destruction can still be controlled. Conservationists sometimes do not realize that islands are not small, geographical zoos; people live there and want to improve their lives. Development cannot be stopped, but it can be managed so that the humans can improve their standard of living as they wish, and the original, amazing island dwellers can still survive.

Kelly Howard

FOR FURTHER STUDY

Adams, Douglas, and Mark Carwardine. *Last Chance to See.* New York: Ballantine Books, 1990.

Doubilet, David. "Lord Howe Island: Australian Haven in a Distant Sea." *National Geographic* 4 (October, 1991): 126-146.

Eliot, John L. "Bikini's Nuclear Graveyard." *National Geographic* 6 (June, 1992): 70-83.

Jaffe, Mark. *And No Birds Sing: The Story of an Ecological Disaster in a Tropical Paradise.* New York: Simon & Schuster, 1994.

INFORMATION ON THE WORLD WIDE WEB

The Lonely Planet Web site features information on the plants and animals of the Pacific Islands, categorized under the Environment link within each individual country's site. (www.lonelyplanet.com.au/dest/)

HUMAN GEOGRAPHY

PEOPLE

AUSTRALIA

At the end of the twentieth century, Australia had about 19 million people, the smallest population of any continent except Antarctica. Although it is about the same size as the continental United States, Australia has only about one-fourteenth the number of inhabitants. The size of the population is the result of two major processes: migration from outside of the country and natural increase.

MIGRATION. Australia is a multiethnic country. Its population, like those of the United States and Canada, is composed of descendants of the original native peoples plus migrants from many other regions of the world. Even the indigenous Aborigines were immigrants long ago. About 75 percent of Australia's people are of British ancestry, reflecting colonial ties to the United Kingdom. The number of migrants from other regions—especially Asia—is increasing as Australia weaves closer bonds with its Pacific Rim neighbors.

The first Australians, ancestors of the peoples now known as Aborigines, came to the continent at least 60,000 years ago and perhaps as early as 120,000 years ago. Apparently, they traveled from Southeast Asia through the Indonesian islands during periods of lower sea levels. In the Pleistocene geologic epoch, much of the earth's water was locked in ice caps, which reduced sea levels by 600 feet (180 meters) or more below current depths. The shallow straits between New Guinea and Australia were often dry during this period, and the seas that separated the continent from Indonesia were narrower than they are now. These conditions reduced Australia's isolation and allowed humans to enter its pristine environments for the first time.

*Aboriginal hunter
Page 1969*

It is not known how many of these early settlers arrived in northern Australia or how they traveled. They may have paddled simple rafts or canoes. Much of the evidence of their earliest settlement is presumed to be submerged on the drowned continental shelf. In any event, their descendants gradually spread over the entire continent, even reaching Tasmania before it became an island isolated by rising sea levels.

Aborigines probably distributed themselves in patterns somewhat resembling the modern population, with larger numbers along the coastlines and in the wetter environments of the east, south, and north, and fewer in the arid interior. The central interior may have been settled as recently as ten thousand years ago. Aboriginal tribes learned to use the varied plant and animal resources of Australia to support their hunting and gathering economies.

By the time Europeans reached Australia, the Aboriginal population was probably about 500,000, although estimates range from 300,000 to as high as 1 million.

These estimates are based on archaeological remains and evidence of food supplies, but no one knows exactly how many people descended from those initial immigrants. The arrival of European colonists proved devastating to the Aborigines. Their numbers shrank rapidly as they suffered from warfare, diseases for which they possessed no immunity, and disruption of their traditional cultures and economies. Until the mid-twentieth century, Aboriginal people were denied citizenship rights and many other Australians believed that they were a dying race. In the 1990's, however, people of Aboriginal descent were about 1.5 percent of the Australian population, or at least 300,000 people.

CONVICT COLONIES. The first British settlers in Australia were mostly deported convicts and their guards. The English judicial system typically sent prisoners to serve their sentences in the colonies instead of building expensive prisons in the British Isles. North America stopped accepting British prisoners after the American Revolution, so a new penal colony was needed. The east coast of Australia, explored by Captain James Cook in 1770, was selected by the British government for this purpose.

The present city of Sydney was the site of the initial prison camp established by the First Fleet in 1788. From that year until 1858, over 160,000 convicts were transported to Australia. Most were English, but Scottish, Welsh, and Irish prisoners also arrived; roughly 20 percent were women. The convicts were usually sentenced to serve seven- to fourteen-year terms for crimes such as robbery, burglary, or fraud. Prison colonies were established in Tasmania, Queensland, Victoria, and Western Australia, as well as in New South Wales. When their terms expired, most of the convicts stayed in Australia as emancipated settlers.

The convicts were joined by a trickle of free settlers who wanted to take advantage of agricultural and business opportunities in the new colonies. The British government began to pay the costs of passage for some migrants, mainly single women seeking marriage partners and skilled workers needed in specific industries. A few thousand Germans arrived in the 1830's and 1840's, fleeing political upheaval in their homeland. By 1850 the total European population of Australia was about half a million. These people clustered in the growing port towns of Sydney, Melbourne, Hobart, Brisbane, Adelaide, and Perth, and in nearby agricultural areas, displacing the Aborigines who had once lived along the coastlines.

OTHER SETTLERS. From 1850 to 1860, Australia's population doubled from about 500,000 to 1 million, as a result of the discovery of gold in the colonies of Victoria and New South Wales. Fortune seekers arrived from the British Isles, other European countries, the United States, and China. Although some miners returned to their homelands at the end of the gold rush decade, most stayed to take up new

---

AUSTRALIA'S CONVICT HERITAGE

The fact that nearly a third of Australia lies within the hot tropics gave Great Britain's late-eighteenth century leaders the idea that Australia would be a suitable place to punish criminal convicts. As British jails overflowed with prisoners, many convicts were sent to Australia, and criminals came to dread being "transported" there.

occupations in the booming cities and towns. Since most of the new migrants were relatively unskilled male laborers, the British government continued to pay moving costs for young women and skilled workers who wished to make the long journey to Australia. By assisting potential brides and small business owners, the government helped create a more balanced colonial economy and society.

Chinese gold miners formed the first large group of Asian migrants to Australia. By 1860 there were at least forty thousand Chinese in the Victorian gold fields. Discrimination against the Chinese was legalized through state laws that prevented non-Europeans from becoming citizens, thus effectively barring them from property ownership and professional occupations. Despite these restrictions and the anti-Asian Immigration Restriction Act of 1901, Chinese communities persisted in Melbourne, Sydney, Brisbane, and Perth.

The other major non-European migration in the nineteenth century was the movement of South Pacific islanders called Kanakas into Queensland. Young men were recruited from Vanuatu, the Solomon Islands, and other western Pacific Islands to work for low wages in the sugar and cotton plantations of the tropical Queensland coast. Humanitarian groups and labor unions protested that this arrangement was little better than slavery; others deplored the fact that a large number of nonwhites had been admitted to Australia. Importation of Kanaka laborers was prohibited in 1901, and most were sent back to their homelands by 1905.

TWENTIETH CENTURY MIGRATIONS. Australia became an independent state within the British Commonwealth in 1901. Isolated by distance from Great Britain and fearing the growing power of Asian countries, the new Australian federal government developed a White Australia policy aimed at excluding non-European immigrants. This policy was implemented by the Immigration Restriction Act of 1901, which gave the government the ability to prohibit "undesirable" migrants without specifying which groups were to be rejected or how this goal would be accomplished. In practice, Asian migrants usually could be rejected by an English literacy test. This law prevented Asian migration until the 1970's.

Although migration from the British Isles continued, the twentieth century brought people from other homelands as well. Political and economic turmoil caused by World War I created a major surge of newcomers. At least 200,000 migrants, including former British soldiers and other Europeans, received assisted passages to Australia in the aftermath of World War I. In 1938 Australia agreed to accept fifteen thousand refugees from Nazi persecution, many of them Jewish. These humane acts marked the opening of a new era of migration from Europe.

After World War II ended in 1945, about 250,000 European displaced persons moved to Australia. In the 1950's and 1960's, the refugees were joined by thousands of people from the less-prosperous Mediterranean countries, which suffered from high unemployment and lack of economic opportunities. Groups from countries such as Italy, Greece, the former Yugoslavia, and Lebanon created ethnic neighborhoods that have become important features of the cultural landscape of Melbourne, Sydney, and other cities.

The number of Asian migrants increased in the last quarter of the twentieth century. Australia's involvement in the Vietnam War resulted in a strong flow of refugees from Vietnam and Cambodia in the 1970's and 1980's. When Australia discarded the Immigration Restriction Act

AUSTRALIA'S IMMIGRATION POLICIES

The White Australia Policy and the Immigration Restriction Act were based on attitudes of racial superiority that were common in Australia, as well as in Europe and North America, during the late nineteenth and early twentieth centuries. These policies also reflected concern about Japan's growing economic and military power and China's large, land-hungry population. In 1901 many Australians believed that their new country must "populate or perish." Their fear was that if there were not enough British or other European settlers to occupy the entire continent, they would risk losing it to the rising Asian forces. In the second half of the twentieth century, however, Australia realized that its closest neighbors were Asian-Pacific countries, not Great Britain and Europe. Trade, investment, and tourism now tightly link Australia to Japan and other Pacific Rim states. Anti-Asian immigration policies were largely abandoned by the Australian government in the 1970's.

Current immigration policies focus on individual migrants' qualifications, such as their educational level and specific skills, rather than their country of origin. Family reunification and refugee status also are considered. Ongoing debate about migration policies centers on environmental, economic, and political concerns.

and reoriented its economic ties to Asia, migrants began to arrive from Malaysia, the Philippines, Hong Kong, India, and China, among other sources. About 4 percent of the people living in Australia at the end of the twentieth century had been born in Asia. With the exception of Vietnamese and Cambodian war refugees, large numbers of the Asian migrants were well-educated people with professional or skilled occupations. As a result of twentieth century migrations, New Australians—those with non-British ancestry—make up about 25 percent of the Australian population.

NATURAL INCREASE. Although a simple timeline shows that the population has grown steadily since Europeans arrived in the region, the rate of increase has varied substantially. Natural increase is the surplus of births over deaths in an existing population. In general, both migration and natural increase rates helped Australia grow during periods of economic prosperity and social stability. Birth rates rose after both world wars, for example, as returning soldiers married and the peacetime economy stabilized. In periods of war and economic depression, however, population growth leveled off. For a few short periods, the population actually declined. Marriage rates and birth rates plummeted during the world wars and the major depressions of the 1890's and 1930's, when few could afford to start a family. Since both depressions also prevented potential migrants from reaching Australia and caused some people to seek jobs in other countries, the population declined slightly during these decades.

AUSTRALIA'S POPULATION FUTURE. At the turn of the twenty-first century, Australia's rate of natural increase averaged about seven per thousand per year. Assuming that this rate stays about the same and immigration levels also do not change, the Australian Bureau of Statistics estimates that another million people will be added to the population every six years for the next few decades.

Although rates of natural increase are comparable to those of other developed nations, Australia historically has not been able to attract as many migrants as North and South America. Isolated by vast distances and expensive transportation from potential migrants, Australia's economic opportunities generally could not compete with those in other regions. In the 1990's, however, Australia offered a stable democratic society with opportunities to participate in the global economy. Australia's citizens must decide how many people are enough.

Susan P. Reynolds

FOR FURTHER STUDY

Breeden, Stanley. "The First Australians." *National Geographic* (February, 1988): 267-294.

Camm, J. C. R., and John McQuilton, eds. *Australians: A Historical Atlas.* Broadway, New South Wales: Fairfax, Syme & Weldon Associates, 1987.

Everingham, John. "Children of the First Fleet." *National Geographic* (February, 1988): 233-245.

Heathcote, Ronald L., ed. *Australia.* 2d ed. New York: John Wiley & Sons, 1994.

Hughes, Robert. *The Fatal Shore.* New York: Alfred A. Knopf, 1987.

Kohen, James. *Aboriginal Environmental Impacts.* Sydney: University of New South Wales Press, 1995.

McKnight, Tom L. *Oceania: The Geography of Australia, New Zealand, and the Pacific Islands.* Englewood Cliffs, N.J.: Prentice Hall, 1995.

INFORMATION ON THE WORLD WIDE WEB

Up-to-date statistical information and current articles about the Australian population can be found at the Australian Bureau of Statistics site. (www.abs.gov.au)

PACIFIC ISLANDS

The Pacific is the world's largest ocean, covering about 64 million square miles (165 million sq. km.) between Singapore and Panama—nearly 40 percent of the earth's surface. While most of the Pacific is empty of land, it does have a large number of islands stretching from Southeast Asia to the coast of South America.

PREHISTORY. Several hundred million years ago, the world's continents were linked together in one landmass that geologists have called Pangaea. After the Ice Age, rising waters separated the land into two sections, Laurasia in the north and Gondwanaland in the south. Water spaces between these new continents were narrow, making travel from one land to the other possible.

The Pacific is probably the last place on the earth to be inhabited by humans. It is also the last major region of the world, except for the North and South Poles, to be

THOR HEYERDAHL ON THE PEOPLING OF POLYNESIA

Norwegian ethnologist Thor Heyerdahl developed a theory that Polynesia may have been settled by South American Indians from Bolivia. He reasoned that most of the European voyagers took routes from east to west. He believed west-to-east travel would have been too difficult against the prevailing winds and currents. Heyerdahl also reasoned that the first settlers did not come from Indonesia because Sanskrit words, found in Indonesian languages, were absent from Polynesian languages. There are, however, some similarities between the Polynesian languages and the Inca language. Heyerdahl also pointed out that the sweet potato, native to South America, was also found in the South Pacific. Heyerdahl believed that the original settlers traveled from Asia to North America through the Bering Strait, down to South America, then across to Polynesia. In 1947, to prove his theory, Heyerdahl and a crew constructed a balsa raft called the Kon-Tiki and set sail from Peru, South America. They sailed 101 days, following winds and currents until they crash-landed on the atoll of Raroia in the Tuamotus, thus proving that South American Indians could have reached Polynesia by this route.

Thor Heyerdahl. (Library of Congress)

explored and settled by Europeans. The majority of islands in the South Pacific are grouped together under the name Oceania. The three groups within Oceania are Melanesia ("black islands"), Micronesia ("tiny islands"), and Polynesia ("many islands").

THE VOYAGE. Prevailing winds and currents in the South Pacific follow east-to-west patterns. Therefore, voyagers from Southeast Asia to the Pacific Islands would have had to sail hundreds, even thousands, of miles against the currents to their new homes. The immigrants had no navigational tools and depended solely upon skills they learned from their ancestors. They followed the Sun, clouds, the Moon and stars, the waves and winds, and flights of migratory birds. It is probable that some vessels drifted off course during cloudy days or storms.

The canoes the voyagers traveled in

were made of hollowed-out tree trunks. The sides were built up with planks and lashed together with coconut fibers. They were made watertight with vegetable gum or a mix of charcoal and earth. To stabilize the vessel, a smaller canoe often was connected to the side by a wooden boom. This canoe was called an outrigger. Some double canoes had small shelters built over the connections, which the travelers used for protection during longer voyages. These vessels were paddled by oars or powered by triangular sails.

MELANESIA. Situated northeast of Australia, the island group known as Melanesia was settled as early as fifty thousand years ago by Austronesian tribes who left their homeland of Southeast Asia, traveling south and east in dugout canoes. These hunters and gatherers were short, with dark skin and frizzy hair. They are the direct ancestors of the Aborigines of Australia, the highland people of Papua New Guinea, and Negritos still living in the interior of the Philippines and Malaysia.

About five thousand years ago, another wave of immigrants left Southeast Asia. These people were a mixture of Mongoloid and Caucasian, known as Proto-Malay. Their language was different than that of the Austronesians. Proto-Malays had light brown skin, broad faces, and black hair. Later groups of Proto-Malay sailed from Southeast Asia directly to western Micronesia.

Eight thousand years ago, more settlers arrived. These people, Oceanic Negroids, were of a different racial background than the first group. They drove the Negritos into the mountains, mingled with other races, and became known as Papuans. Present-day Negritos, known as Highlanders, still live as their Stone Age ancestors did thousands of years ago. Oceanic Negroids intermixed with the existing populations and eventually traveled north and east into Micronesia.

MICRONESIA. At about the same time the Proto-Malay were migrating to Melanesia, another group from Southeast Asia headed for the islands of Micronesia. Predominately farmers, the immigrants found life on these atolls—small islands composed of coral reefs—very different from what they were used to. They had to change their methods of farming, losing old skills but learning new ones. They became expert boat builders and navigators and developed their outrigger canoes into the fastest and most maneuverable long-distance vessels in the Pacific.

Migration from one island group to another was slow, usually being spread over several generations. After a group had settled on an island for some length of time, a new sailing party would continue eastward to the next group of islands. This migration accounts for the similarity in languages, cultures, traditions, and appearance of the peoples of the Pacific. Some islanders stayed at home, intermarrying with Melanesians and other Asian travelers.

POLYNESIA. The largest island group of the region, Polynesia forms a triangle bounded by Hawaii in the north, New Zealand in the southwest, and Easter Island (Rapa Nui) in the southeast. It is believed to be the last region to have been settled. The first Polynesians were tall, with lighter hair than Micronesians and Melanesians. They were more advanced culturally and technologically than the Negritos. Since most Polynesians speak closely related languages, it is believed they must have come from one direction in a short period of time, possibly through Micronesia or Melanesia, or both. Polynesians eventually traveled farther east to New Zealand.

Uninhabited longer than any major landmass, New Zealand is the southernmost point of the Polynesian triangle and

Papua New Guineans Page 1968

consists of three major islands: North, South and Stewart. The first human inhabitants were Polynesian. The first phase of migrants, who arrived approximately twelve hundred years ago, can be identified by their archeological remains and are known as Archaic Maori. The second phase, Classic Maori, is probably the culture encountered by European explorers. British explorer Captain James Cook noted the similarity in the languages of New Zealand Maori and Polynesians. It is not yet clear how the first phase evolved into the second. It is believed that the first Maori may have reached New Zealand by accident, being blown off course on fishing expeditions.

A self-sufficient people, the Maori easily adapted to the temperate climate of their new home. They had no concept of culture, nationhood, or race. They were a tribal people, protective of their ancestry, often living in the same place from birth to death. Their culture was the same throughout the islands, with slight regional differences. Languages spoken on the North Island differed in dialect from that spoken on South Island. By the end of the eighteenth century, the Maori had to make room for new immigrants: explorers, whalers, escaped convicts, and traders. The British began their colonization of the islands in the 1830's.

LANGUAGES AND CULTURES. Language, folklore, and culture were, and still are, individual to each region. This indicates that immigrants probably did not originate from the same race. Migrations were probably made as a result of changes on their home islands, including changes in environment, economics, or war. Languages spoken in Melanesia, Micronesia, and Polynesia all come from one basic language group, the Austronesian family. Melanesia alone has more than twelve hundred different languages. In Micronesia, the people in the west speak differently than those in the east. Languages from eastern Micronesia have similarities to those in eastern Melanesia. Polynesia is the only region whose languages, nearly thirty, are alike enough that one islander can understand what another from a different area is saying.

EUROPEAN EXPLORERS. Additional migrations to the South Pacific were initiated by Europeans, beginning with the Spanish and Portuguese in the sixteenth century, followed by the Dutch in the seventeenth century and the English and French in the

---

THE PEOPLING OF EASTER ISLAND

Easter Island lies 2,400 miles (3,862 km.) from Chile and 1,500 miles (2,414 km.) from the nearest inhabited island. It was discovered by Dutch explorer Jacob Roggeveen on Easter Sunday, April 15, 1722. It is not known exactly how the first inhabitants reached Easter Island, but it is generally agreed that people of Polynesian stock arrived on the island from the central Pacific. When Europeans first arrived in 1722, the sparse population of the island was visibly of Polynesian origin. The inhabitants of Easter Island carved huge stone statues, weighing more than fifty tons and standing as tall as 40 feet (12 meters) on stone platforms, that line the shore with their backs to the sea. Some of the statues have "hats." Although Roggeveen noted that the islanders often bowed to these statues, he did not ask them how they had managed to move these massive monuments.

Early Polynesian settlers on Easter Island carved hundreds of stone figures that stand between ten and twenty feet (three to six meters) high and weigh as much as fifty tons. Exactly who built the statues and why remains a mystery. (PhotoDisc)

eighteenth century. The explorers were followed by whalers and traders, missionaries, planters and merchants, soldiers and sailors, and slavers. With the appearance of European explorers, the populations of the islands were threatened by diseases and social and political issues that were introduced. By the early nineteenth century, missionaries were spreading through the area converting a proud people who were now regarded as savages. Respect for the Polynesian culture was gone. Bans were put on dancing and singing, and European-style dress was enforced.

Maryanne Barsotti

FOR FURTHER STUDY

Bellwood, Peter. *The Polynesians: Prehistory of an Island People.* London: Thames and Hudson, 1978.

Kane, Robert S. *South Pacific A to Z.* Garden City, N.Y.: Doubleday, 1966.

King, Michael. *New Zealand.* Auckland: Hodder and Stoughton, 1987.

Margolis, Susana. *Adventuring in the South Pacific, the Sierra Club Travel Guide.* San Francisco: Sierra Club Books, 1988.

Rowe, James W. *New Zealand.* New York: Praeger, 1968.

INFORMATION ON THE WORLD WIDE WEB

The Web site of the Pacific Islands Development Program of the East-West Center for Pacific Islands Studies at the University of Hawaii at Manoa links to dozens of useful Pacific Island sites. (pidp.ewc.hawaii.edu/PIReport/news_links.htm)

POPULATION DISTRIBUTION

AUSTRALIA

The vast majority of Australia's population of 19 million people is concentrated in a core region that stretches along the eastern and southeastern coastline of the continent. From Cairns in northern Queensland through the states of New South Wales and Victoria and beyond to Adelaide in the state of South Australia, this core region contains the largest cities and is the industrial and agricultural heartland of the country. Much smaller secondary concentrations of population lie in Western Australia around the city of Perth and on the northern and southern coasts of the island state of Tasmania. Beyond these core regions, a scattering of small communities holds the rest of the Australian people.

PHYSICAL AND HISTORICAL FACTORS. The map of population distribution clearly reveals the peripheral location of Australia's settlement. This spatial pattern reflects the constraints of the physical environment. The eastern plains and highlands, including Tasmania, contain the best agricultural lands and receive sufficient rainfall year-round for crop production.

The western slopes of the Great Dividing Range in New South Wales and Victoria are drier, but provide enough moisture for grain farming. Along the boundary between these two states, the Murray River basin offers irrigated lands for specialty crops. The southern and western margins of the continent around Adelaide and Perth also have good soils and a Mediterranean-type climate with adequate winter rainfall. The agricultural population of these regions is fairly dense. Beyond these areas, the arid interior is suitable mainly for grazing sheep and cattle on huge pastures and the population is sparse. The driest areas are virtually uninhabited, because they lack enough surface water and vegetation for even a grazing economy.

Other natural resources, especially minerals, attract people to specific locations. Beginning in the gold rush days of the 1850's, the settlement frontier advanced into the harsher environments of the Australian interior in response to new mineral discoveries. Rich deposits of silver, copper, lead, and zinc brought miners to places such as Broken Hill, New South Wales, and Mount Isa, Queensland. Recent developments are even more remote from the population core: The bauxite mines at Weipa in northern Queensland and the Hamersley Range iron mines in Western Australia are good examples. Modern mechanized mining requires few workers, and the extreme climates of these newest resource regions are not attractive to the average Australian. Thus, these mining towns likely will remain relatively small.

Each of the largest cities was the focus of early colonial settlement in its region. The initial settlements were located on the coast to facilitate transportation and communication with Great Britain and the other Australian colonies. These small port towns grew by consolidating government functions, trade, industry, and services, and developed into Australia's major cities. Sydney, for example, was the first convict settlement and from the beginning was the administrative capital of New South Wales. Its beautiful bay offered deep water to accommodate ships, and railroads were built there to bring agricultural products and natural resources to the port. Once Sydney established a large enough population base, it attracted manufacturing industries and consumer services. The first British settlement in Australia, Sydney has always remained the largest.

The national capital city, Canberra, is the only exception to the rule that all large Australian cities are located on the coast. Canberra was established after the individual Australian colonies federated as an independent state within the British Commonwealth in 1901. The new city was deliberately situated in the Eastern Highlands midway between Sydney and its major rival Melbourne, capital of the state of Victoria. Canberra represents a geographic compromise between the two largest cities, each of which had hoped to become the national capital.

URBANIZATION. Australia is a highly urbanized society. About 85 percent of the population is urban and more than 40 percent live in Sydney and Melbourne, the two largest metropolitan centers. In several states, the majority of people live in the capital city and its suburbs. For example, about 60 percent of the

New South Wales population lives in Sydney and 68 percent of Victorians live in the Melbourne metropolitan area. About 73 percent of South Australians cluster in Adelaide, while Perth and its suburbs contain 72 percent of Western Australia's inhabitants.

Sydney
Page 2042

As in North America and other economically developed countries, Australia's cities attract those who are searching for new opportunities. Urban manufacturing and service businesses, universities and cultural organizations, and entertainment facilities offer jobs and leisure activities. Former rural residents and new immigrants alike are drawn to join those who were born and raised in the cities. Recent migrants, especially those from non-English speaking homelands, tend to cluster in ethnic neighborhoods. Approximately 70 percent of the Aboriginal population also lives in urban settings.

Within the larger cities, sprawling residential areas surround the skyscraper-studded central business districts. Single-

---

CLIMATE AND POPULATION DISTRIBUTION

The first British immigrants who settled in Australia during the late eighteenth and early nineteenth centuries had no idea how dry their new land was. When Captain James Cook first reached Australia during the 1770's, he landed at Botany Bay on the temperate and comparatively moist east coast. As his voyage of discovery continued northward, Cook crossed the Tropic of Capricorn, which neatly divides the northern and southern portions of the continent, and found a region where rainfall was abundant.

It was not until after the British began settling the region that the continent's dry interior was penetrated by explorers, some of whom perished in the harsh desert interior. After that time, climate played a major role in determining the pattern of the continent's population distribution. The vast majority of Australia's people now live in coastal cities in the temperate midlatitudes, particularly in the southeast.

AUSTRALIAN STATE AND CITY POPULATIONS IN 1999

State	Population (millions)	Capital City	Population (millions)
New South Wales	6.2	Sydney	3.7
Victoria	4.7	Melbourne	3.2
Queensland	3.4	Brisbane	1.6
Western Australia	1.9	Perth	1.4
South Australia	1.5	Adelaide	1.1
Tasmania	0.5	Hobart	0.2
Australian Capital Territory	0.3	Canberra	0.3
Northern Territory	0.2	Darwin	0.1

tired persons. The expansion of international tourism has also created resort settlements on Great Barrier Reef islands, in the Red Center near Uluru (Ayers Rock), and in other remote places.

Susan P. Reynolds

FOR FURTHER STUDY

Camm, J. C. R., and John McQuilton, eds. *Australians: A Historical Atlas*. Broadway, New South Wales: Fairfax, Syme & Weldon, 1987.

Docherty, James C. *Historical Dictionary of Australia*. Landham, Md.: Scarecrow Press, 1999.

Heathcote, R. L. *Australia*. 2d ed. New York: John Wiley & Sons, 1994.

Lines, William J. *Taming the Great South Land*. Berkeley: University of California Press, 1991.

McKnight, Tom L. *Oceania: The Geography of Australia, New Zealand, and the Pacific Islands*. Englewood Cliffs, N.J.: Prentice-Hall, 1995.

Terrill, Ross. "Australia at 200." *National Geographic* (February, 1988): 181-211.

family houses and apartment buildings are linked by multilane highways and served by shopping malls in a suburban landscape that resembles the cities of the western United States.

RURAL POPULATION. About 15 percent of the Australian population lives in small towns and rural areas. Most farmers live on individual farmsteads at some distance from their closest neighbors; livestock grazers often live on huge pastoral stations (ranches) that may be hundreds of miles from the nearest large city. Approximately 30 percent of the Aboriginal population are rural dwellers. Some Aboriginal people live and work on livestock stations, while a few maintain their traditional hunting and gathering lifestyles in isolated regions of the Outback.

Although many agricultural districts face declining numbers as economic reorganization continues, some small towns and rural areas attract new residents. Growth areas include pleasant towns within commuting distance of urban jobs and coastal beach communities that draw re-

INFORMATION ON THE WORLD WIDE WEB

The Web site of the Australian Bureau of Statistics Information, Australia's official statistical organization, features a variety of statistics on the Australian population. (www.abs.gov.au)

PACIFIC ISLANDS

The Pacific Islands region, including New Zealand, has 12.7 million people, which is roughly equivalent to the population of Illinois. The obvious difference is that this region's population is distributed on islands that are spread out over a vast area of ocean. Hawaii and New Zealand have highly urbanized populations and advanced economies. Most of the remaining islands have large rural populations, because many of their inhabitants depend on farming, fishing, and, to a lesser extent, mining for their livelihoods.

On less-developed islands, rising population and loss of soil fertility and forestland in rural areas are spurring a migration from the countryside to urban areas. Consequently, the population of urban areas is growing faster than rural areas, urban housing and health and transportation services are not keeping pace with the rate of population growth, and squatter populations have become permanent fixtures around the edges of many cities and large towns. Migration to the United States (especially Hawaii and California), Canada, Australia, and New Zealand serves as a safety-valve to lessen the impact of overpopulation of many islands.

There are two true metropolitan centers: Honolulu, Hawaii, with a population of about 850,000, and Auckland, New Zealand, with about 1.2 million people. New Zealand has seven other cities with populations exceeding 100,000: Wellington, Canterbury, Manukau, Northshore, Waitakere, Dunedin, and Hamilton. Other cities with populations of more than 100,000 include Port Moresby in Papua New Guinea (250,000), Suva in Fiji (166,000), Noumea in New Caledonia (112,000), and Papeete in French Polynesia (120,000).

MELANESIA. This subregion has 6.5 million inhabitants, about one-half the total population of the Pacific Islands. Three-fourths of the population is in Papua New Guinea. Seventy-eight percent of the population is rural, one of the highest proportions of rural population in the world.

Fiji (population, 823,400) has an area 1.5 times the size of Washington, D.C. Its capital is Suva. Most of the land (86 percent) and people (92 percent) are on the two largest islands—Viti Levu and Vanua Levu. Cities grew rapidly on these two islands at the end of the twentieth century. Forty-six percent of Fiji's population has become urbanized. Population pressure is moderate, as Fiji's economy is relatively advanced and its annual growth rate is 1.1 percent, one of the lowest in the Pacific Islands.

New Caledonia (population, 200,500) has an area slightly smaller than that of New Jersey. The capital, Noumea, is the principal center on the island. Seventy percent of its population is urbanized. New Caledonia Island, the largest oceanic island in the Pacific basin, is home to a majority of the population. In recent years, the migration of rural peoples to urban places has been so high that the total rural population decreased 3.3 percent.

Papua New Guinea (population, 4.8 million) has an area slightly larger than California. It is the most populous nation in the Pacific Islands. The capital, Port Moresby, located on the southern coast, is one of the fastest growing urban centers in

*Honolulu
Pages
1968, 2033*

*Port
Moresby
Page 1971*

the region. The highest proportion of population (36.7 percent) is in the five central highland provinces, the second-highest is in the northern coastal region (27.4 percent), followed by the southern coastal region (20 percent), and finally the islands region (15.7 percent).

The Solomon Islands (population, 470,000) has an area slightly smaller than Maryland. The capital, Honiara, is located on the island of Guadalcanal and has a population of 53,000. Only 17 percent of the inhabitants live in cities, although the annual growth of the urban population (6.35 percent) was been one of the highest in the Pacific Islands in the 1990's.

Vanuatu (population, 192,800) has an area slightly larger than Connecticut. Nineteen percent of the population is ur-banized. The main urban center is Vila (population, 23,000) on the island of Efate. A scarce supply of water and defor-estation are forcing rural people to move to cities. Consequently, Vanuatu has a high urban growth rate (3.6 percent).

POLYNESIA. This subregion's 5.7 million inhabitants account for 44 percent of the total population of the Pacific Islands. Most of the people of Polynesia live in New Zealand and Hawaii. Together, these countries account for 87 percent of this subregion's total population and 94 percent of the urban population.

Most of the people in American Samoa (population, 65,500) live on the island of Tutuila, where the capital, Pago Pago, (population, 12,000) is located. There is a high rate of urban growth—4.7 percent

Young Guadalcanal islanders. (Tom McKnight/Joan Clemons)

Main street in Tonga's capital and chief city, Nuku'alofa. (Tom McKnight/Joan Clemons)

annually, with 50 percent of the population urbanized. Population pressures have been reduced somewhat, as Samoans have migrated in considerable numbers to Hawaii and California.

The Cook Islands (population, 20,400) has an area 1.3 times the size of Washington, D.C. Fifty-nine percent of the population is urbanized. Most of the people live on the island of Raratonga, where the capital, Avaru (population, 16,000), is located. Large numbers of Cook Islanders have migrated to New Zealand.

Easter Island has an area three-fourths the size of Washington, D.C. About 3,000 people live on the island, nearly all in the town of Hanga Roa. The island has one of the lowest population densities in Poly-

nesia. Nevertheless, there is some out-migration. About seven hundred Easter Islanders—known as Rapa Nuis—live in Chile, three hundred in French Polynesia, and fifty in the United States.

French Polynesia (population, 246,200) has an area slightly less than one-third the size of Connecticut. Fifty-four percent of the people live in cities. The island of Tahiti makes up about one-fourth the total land area and is home to about two-thirds of the total population. Tahiti includes the capital city of Papeete, with a population of 120,000.

Hawaii (population, 1.2 million) is organized in five counties: Honolulu, Hawaii, Kauai, Maui, and Kalawao. Honolulu, the state capital, is the largest city (population, 872,000), with three-fourths of the state's population. Honolulu County's population density is fifty times greater than the next most populous county, and the highest population density for a single island in the entire Pacific Islands region.

New Zealand (population, 3.7 million) is the second-most populous country in the Pacific Islands. Eighty-five percent of its population is urbanized. More than three-fourths of all New Zealanders live on North Island, primarily in the Aukland region. Due to its historical ties to other Pacific Islands, New Zealand is an important destination of emigrants from Samoa, the Cook Islands, Tonga, Niue, Fiji, and Tokelau.

Niue (population, twenty-one hundred) consists of one island 1.5 times the size of Washington, D.C. Alofi, the capital, has a thousand residents. At the end of the twentieth century, the island was losing population because of migration of Niueans to New Zealand.

Apia
Page 1971

The Pitcairn Islands have an area twice the size of Washington, D.C. The entire population of about four dozen people lives in the settlement of Adamstown. This sparse population, which has been stable for years, depends on a small tourist trade, the sale of limited edition post cards and stamps, and honey production.

Most of the population of Samoa (235,300) lives on the islands of Savai'I and Upolu. Apia, the capital, is the largest town (population, 33,000). Twenty-one percent of the population is urbanized. The 2.3 percent annual growth rate would be higher were it not for a steady flow of emigrants to New Zealand and the United States.

Tokelau has an area seventeen times the size of the Mall in Washington, D.C. The population of fifteen hundred has been decreasing slightly as a result of emigration to New Zealand.

Tonga (population, 110,000) has an area four times the size of Washington,

LAND AREAS AND POPULATION DENSITIES OF PACIFIC ISLAND COUNTRIES, MID-1999 ESTIMATES

Country	Population	Area in sq. mi.	Persons/sq. mi.
Fiji	832,494	7,052	118.05
Kiribati	91,985	277	332.08
Marshall Islands	68,126	70	973.23
Micronesia	133,144	271	491.31
Nauru	11,845	8	1,480.63
New Zealand	3,819,762	103,710	36.83
Palau	18,766	177	106.02
Papua New Guinea	4,926,984	178,212	27.65
Samoa	179,466	1,104	162.56
Solomon Islands	466,194	10,982	42.45
Tonga	102,321	289	354.05
Tuvalu	10,838	10	1,083.80
Vanuatu	189,618	5,697	33.28

Source: U.S. Census Bureau, International Data Base and *The World Factbook, 1998.*

D.C. Thirty-five percent of the population is urbanized. Approximately two-thirds of the people live on the main island of Tongatapu, where the capital, Nuku'alofa (population, 40,000), is located. A low annual population growth rate (0.8 percent) is due in part to a steady emigration of Tongans to New Zealand and Australia.

Tuvalu (population, 10,800) has an area one-tenth the size of Washington, D.C. Forty-six percent of the population is urbanized. Its capital, Funafuti, has 4,000 residents. The annual population growth rate is fairly low (1.6 percent).

Wallis and Futuna (15,300) has an area 1.5 times the size of Washington, D.C. The principal town, Mata-Utu, has a thousand residents. A low population growth rate (1.1 percent) is partly caused by the fact that, as citizens of France, its inhabitants can easily migrate to France to find employment.

MICRONESIA. This subregion has 225,400 inhabitants. All the islands in this region are small and consequently the population density (persons per unit area) is more than ten times greater here than in Melanesia and Polynesia. The percentage of rural population (59 percent) is similar to many countries in Africa and Latin America. Population pressures are relieved somewhat because citizens of most of these islands can travel to the United States to seek employment.

Guam (population, 155,000) has an area three times the size of Washington, D.C. About 40 percent of the population is urbanized. Agana, the capital, has 4,000 residents. The island is the site of a large U.S. Air Force base, and more than one-third of the island's population is from the U.S. mainland, principally military personnel and dependents.

The Republic of Kiribati (population, 87,000) has an area four times the size of Washington, D.C. Thirty-seven percent of

Kiribatians live in cities, most in the city of Tarawa (population, 28,000), located on the island of Tarawa. The government of Kiribati planned to move its surplus population from Tarawa Island to Kiritimati Island, but it was decided that such a move would devastate the ecosystem of the latter.

The Republic of the Marshall Islands (population, 68,100) has an area the size of Washington, D.C. Sixty-nine percent of the people live in cities. Majuro Island (population, twenty-eight hundred) and Kwajalein atoll (population, ninety-three hundred) are important population centers. Majuro has one of the highest population densities in the Pacific Islands.

The Federated States of Micronesia (population, 133,100) has an area four times the size of Washington, D.C. Twenty-seven percent of this country's population is urbanized. The capital city of Kolonia, located in the State of Pohnpei, has 34,000 residents. Approximately half the population is in the state of Chuuk. About 15,000 Micronesians reside in the United States.

The Republic of Nauru (population, 11,000) consists of just one island, which is about one-tenth the size of Washington, D.C. Nearly all its work force is employed in phosphate mines. Farming is impossible, because most of the island is a wasteland due to intensive mining and the limited water supply.

The Commonwealth of the Northern Mariana Islands (population, 72,000) has an area 2.5 times the size of Washington, D.C. Most of the people live on Saipan, Rota, and Tinian. Fifty-three percent of the total population lives in urban areas. Saipan, the largest city, has 16,000 residents. This country has the Pacific Islands' highest rate of annual population increase (4.9 percent) and percentage increase of urban population (5.7 percent).

The Republic of Palau (population, 19,000) has an area 2.5 times the size of

Washington, D.C. Palau has the largest percentage of urban population (71 percent) in Micronesia. The population is concentrated on two islands: Babelthuap, the largest island and future site of the capital, and Koror, the old capital.

Wake Island has an area eleven times the size of the Mall in Washington, D.C. There is no indigenous population; it is a United States military and commercial base.

FUTURE PROJECTIONS. Population growth and urbanization in this region are expected to continue unabated. Between 1996 and 2030, the urban population, excluding Hawaii and New Zealand, is projected to increase from 32 percent to 69 percent. By 2050, the total population is expected to be 70 percent higher than in the year 2000. The greatest increases are forecast for the Republic of the Marshall Islands (411 percent), the Solomon Islands (146 percent), the Northern Mariana Islands (125 percent), Papua New Guinea (108 percent), and American Samoa (96 percent).

Richard A. Crooker

FOR FURTHER STUDY

Conniff, Richard. "Easter Island Unveiled." *National Geographic* (March, 1993): 54-79.

Jackson, Keith. *Historical Dictionary of New Zealand.* Landham, Md.: Scarecrow Press, 1996.

McKnight, Tom L. *Oceania: The Geography of Australia, New Zealand, and the Pacific Islands.* Englewood Cliffs, N.J.: Prentice Hall, 1995.

Rawlings, Gregory E. "Foundations of Urbanization: Port Vila Town and Pango Village, Vanuatu." *Oceania* 70, no. 1 (September, 1999).

Salter, Christopher, et al. *Essentials of World Regional Geography.* 2d ed. New York: Harcourt Brace, 1998.

Turner, Ann. *Historical Dictionary of Papua New Guinea.* Landham, Md.: Scarecrow Press, 1994.

Vaughn, Roger. "The Two Worlds of Fiji." *National Geographic* (October, 1995): 114-137.

Wuerch, William L., and Dirk Anthony Ballendorf. *Historical Dictionary of Guam and Micronesia.* Landham, Md.: Scarecrow Press, 1994.

INFORMATION ON THE WORLD WIDE WEB

Pyramids representing population figures and projections for the Pacific Island countries and territories for 1997, 2025, and 2050 can be seen at the U.S. Census Bureau International Data Base Web site. Nearly all of these pyramids foretell rapid population growth. For example, a comparison of the population pyramids for American Samoa shows that the 1997 pyramid has more people in the younger-than-fifteen group than in any older age group. The 2025 and 2050 pyramids show that, as this large group moves through its reproductive years (ages 15 to 39), larger numbers of people will be added to American Samoa's population. (www.census.gov/ipc/www/idbpyr.html)

CULTURE REGIONS

AUSTRALIA

Most Australians live in the coastal regions. The center part of the continent is largely desert unable to support many people, although there are cattle and sheep stations in the so-called Outback. Eastern Australia, from Cairns in Queensland to Adelaide in South Australia, is more heavily populated than the west coast. The southern coast west of Adelaide has few residents. Although the north coast has a concentration of residents in and around Darwin, this coast also is sparsely populated.

New South Wales has one-third of the country's population, with more than 6 million residents. Victoria has about 4.5 million residents, and Queensland, north of New South Wales, has just over 3 million people. Western Australia has about 1.7 million residents. South Australia has 1.5 million people. Tasmania has fewer than half a million. The Northern Territory has a population of about 190,000, most of them concentrated in the capital, Darwin.

REGIONALITY. Various regions of the United States are typified by speech patterns, cuisine, music, and other such characteristics, but such is not the case in Australia. Australian dialect differences are largely based on socioeconomic status and educational level rather than location. A university graduate from rural Georgia or coastal South Carolina usually has different speech patterns from a university graduate from Maine or Massachusetts. In Australia, university graduates from Sydney or Melbourne have speech patterns similar to those of university graduates from Perth or Darwin.

Dialect variations would be most noticeable between a university graduate and, for example, a factory worker or a garage mechanic, but factory workers or garage mechanics in Sydney would have speech patterns almost identical to those of their counterparts in Kalgoorlie or Alice Springs. Cuisine from one end of Australia to the other is quite similar, as are musical and cultural tastes and offerings.

EARLIEST INHABITANTS. When the first Europeans reached Australia in 1788, the country was inhabited by Aborigines, who are thought to have lived in the area for more than fifty thousand years. Cave paintings discovered throughout mainland Australia and in the island state of Tasmania are more than thirty thousand years old.

Although estimates vary, most scholars conclude that about 300,000 Aborigines lived on the continent when the first Europeans arrived. They were divided into tribes and clans (extended families). Some 650 groups were formed by these people, who spoke about 250 languages, many mutually intelligible to people from different tribes or clans. Currently, about 50 of these indigenous languages survive.

Aboriginal hunter Page 1969

Road in the Outback of Queensland. (Corbis)

Early European immigrants drove the Aborigines from their property and demeaned them because they were considered primitive, although they had sophisticated art forms and were notable for their conservation measures. These included the controlled burning of brush in the Outback to enrich the soil and to provide grasses to feed livestock in the unforgiving environment. Their reverence for nature was similar to that of the Anasazi in the southwestern United States.

Driven from their land, the Aborigines lurked for almost two centuries on the fringes of society, an impoverished group that, in some instances, was assimilated into mainstream Australian society through intermarriage. Those with Aboriginal roots often sought to obscure their backgrounds, denying Aboriginal connections. The 1991 census recorded 257,333 Aborigines, although this number had increased by nearly one hundred thousand by 2000 when more Aborigines, who had been reluctant to acknowledge their origins, began to admit their Aboriginal heritage.

Legislation in 1967 and afterward acknowledged Aboriginal property claims. Although they and the Torres Strait islanders off Australia's northeastern tip comprise 1.6 percent of Australia's population, they now hold claim to 9.6 percent of the land, most of it in Western Australia, North Australia, and South Australia, where the largest concentrations of modern Aborigines live. Substantial numbers of Aborigines can be found in all of Australia's major cities.

POPULATION SHORTAGE. From the time of its earliest European settlement, Australia had a shortage of people. Originally colonized by prisoners from Great

The Aborigines were hunters and gatherers who lived a nomadic existence. Aboriginal tribes lived throughout Australia, with the largest concentrations in the coastal regions, particularly in the north and east. The Outback, mostly desert, could support few people. Hunting in the Outback was much less productive than it was closer to the coast, whose oceans were important sources of food. Fruits, vegetables, and nuts were more plentiful in the coastal regions.

MULTICULTURALISM IN AUSTRALIA

Australia's high rate of immigration, mainly from Europe and Asia, has the potential to change voting patterns. Asian immigration, particularly, has been used by right-wing groups to arouse nativist resentment, as in the racially tinged late-1990's One Nation movement that flourished briefly in Queensland. Most Australian political parties welcome all races, affirming multiculturalism and reconciliation with Australia's often-oppressed Aboriginal population. The growing Aboriginal demands for land rights and cultural recognition are expected to continue as a dominant issue for Australia in the twenty-first century.

Britain's overcrowded jails, Australia at first had a Caucasian population in which men outnumbered women by about six to one. Although the transportation of criminals to New South Wales and Tasmania ended officially in the 1840's, it resumed in Western Australia in 1850 and continued for eighteen years.

By 1868, 137,000 men but only 25,000 women had been transported to Australia, 80 percent of both sexes having been incarcerated in Britain for crimes against property—theft, larceny, burglary—rather than crimes against persons. Most of the convicts worked for free settlers who had voluntarily relocated in Australia in search of a better life there. These convicts usually had a seven-year work obligation, after which they were freed. As unemployment and poverty engulfed Britain between 1830 and 1850, the British government agreed to pay the passage of those who wished to emigrate to Australia.

With the discovery of gold in Victoria during the 1850's, many Asians flocked into the area. About forty thousand Chinese lived in eastern Australia during the 1880's. Melanesians were imported as field workers, but in 1904, three years after the formation of the first Australian parliament, the Melanesians were expelled to their native countries. A considerable anti-Asian bias was apparent among Australians.

MODERN IMMIGRATION PATTERNS. At the beginning of World War II in 1939, 98 percent of Australia's seven million people were of British origin. Between the end of that war and 1970, some three million people immigrated to Australia from Britain, Italy, Greece, Germany, the Netherlands, and the Middle East. The White Australian Policy, which precluded Asians from immigrating, was repealed in 1973, after which many refugees from Vietnam, Laos, and Cambodia settled permanently in the country. By 1999 the country was 92 percent Caucasian and 7 percent Asian.

The official aim of the Australian government is to build a multicultural society in which those from other cultures will be integrated but not assimilated. In other words, people from other cultures are discouraged from abandoning the cultures from which they came. As a result, ethnic neighborhoods have grown up in all of Australia's cities as well as in many of its small towns.

A census in 1996 revealed that 240 different languages, about 50 of which are Aboriginal, are currently spoken in Australian homes. After English, the most common languages are, in descending order, Italian, Greek, Cantonese, Arabic, and Vietnamese. The fastest-growing language groups are Mandarin Chinese, Vietnamese, and Cantonese. The languages declining the most are Dutch, German, Italian, and Greek. These figures indicate the direction in which population growth through immigration is taking place.

R. Baird Shuman

FOR FURTHER STUDY

Darien-Smith, Kate. *Exploration into Australia.* Parsippany, N.J.: New Discovery Books, 1996.

Docherty, James C. *Historical Dictionary of Australia.* Landham, Md.: Scarecrow Press, 1999.

Griffiths, Diane. *Australia.* Milwaukee: Gareth Stevens, 1999.

Heathcote, Ronald L., ed. *Australia.* 2d ed. New York: John Wiley & Sons, 1994.

Heinrichs, Ann. *Australia.* New York: Children's Press, 1998.

Hughes, Robert. *The Fatal Shore: The Epic of Australia's Founding.* New York: Alfred A. Knopf, 1987.

Lourandos, Harry. *Continent of Hunter-Gatherers: New Perspectives in Australian Prehistory.* New York: Cambridge University Press, 1997.

PACIFIC ISLANDS

The Pacific Islands traditionally are divided into three cultural and geographic areas: Melanesia, Micronesia, and Polynesia. Melanesia, which means "black islands," contains the larger, hilly, mountainous islands, including New Guinea, the Solomon Islands, New Caledonia, Vanuatu, and Fiji. Micronesia, which means "tiny islands," comprises more than two thousand small islands, many of which are atolls formed from coral reefs that rise just a few feet above sea level. These islands include Palau, the Mariana Islands, Guam, Kiribati, the Caroline Islands, the Marshall Islands, Nauru, and the Gilbert Islands. Polynesia, which means "many islands," is the largest of these geographical areas, covering a triangular area defined by Hawaii, New Zealand, and Easter Island. It includes Midway, the Cook Islands, Western and American Samoa, Tonga, the Society Islands, and Pitcairn.

The people who populate the Pacific Islands are believed to have arrived from southeastern Asia in a series of migratory waves. However, the pattern of their distribution across the islands and their subsequent development into such highly differentiated groups as the dark-skinned Melanesians, Asiatic-featured Micronesians, and lighter-skinned Polynesians is unknown. Many experts believe that the newcomers gradually spread across the Pacific Islands, traveling from west to east using prevailing winds and currents. After settling in separated and physically distant islands, they gradually came to differ in appearance and culture. The three cultural and geographical groupings were evident when the first Europeans arrived in the sixteenth century and are described in the writings of European explorers in the eighteenth and nineteenth centuries. These explorers noted that the regions had distinct religions, languages, and customs. Europeans brought their own way of living, which many islanders, particularly those who live in the larger cities, have adopted.

NEW ZEALAND AND HAWAII. Two of the larger islands—New Zealand, an independent nation, and Hawaii, part of the United States—are highly developed economies and reflect strong European influences. New Zealand was populated originally by people who arrived by canoe from eastern Polynesia. These people became known as the Maori. They fished, hunted, farmed, and engaged in warfare. Individuals specialized in arts such as creating poetry, tattooing, and carving wood, bone, and stone. Their religion had a number of nature-based gods, as well as spirits that performed magical spells and punished those who broke taboos. Many religious concepts, including taboos and personal prestige, were similar to other Polynesian beliefs.

The Maori fiercely resisted settlement by Europeans, engaging in a number of wars after being colonized by the British in 1840. The wars and European diseases reduced the numbers of the Maori from about 120,000 in 1769 to 42,000 in 1896. By 1996 the number of Maori had grown to 500,000, about 14 percent of New Zealand's population. Many Maori in rural areas maintain their traditions; however, a large number in urban areas have become assimilated to the predominant, British-derived culture.

The Hawaiians, like the Maori, are a minority presence on their native lands. The first Europeans arrived in the Hawaiian Islands in the late eighteenth century. In the nineteenth century, the islands developed a plantation economy, and thousands of Japanese and Filipino immigrants came seeking work. According to the 1990 census, about one-eighth of Hawaii's population consisted of native Hawaiians, 22 per-

cent were of Japanese origin, and 33 percent were white. Although most Pacific Islanders live in rural areas, about 89 percent of all Hawaii residents live in urban areas. Native Hawaiians retain some traditional practices, but the culture in Hawaii is basically American, with considerable Asian influence. The predominant religion in Hawaii is Christianity, although Buddhism also has a large following. The native Hawaiian religion was a form of nature worship, which was abolished by Kamehameha II in 1819.

MELANESIA. The Melanesians are short and dark-skinned with broad noses, and many have black, woolly hair. Culturally, Melanesians exhibit a wide diversity: those who dwell along the beaches tend to be less traditional because of prolonged contact with other cultures; those who live inland in relative isolation have retained their traditions. A definite Polynesian influence marks the culture of Fiji and the outlying islands to the northwest. Many languages are spoken in Melanesia, with 740 spoken in Papua New Guinea.

Many islanders (although not those in New Caledonia or Fiji) use Pidgin English (Neo-Melanesian), a combination of native and English words, as their common language. Although Christianity is the main religion in many of the Pacific Islands, in the Melanesian islands of New Guinea, the Solomons, and Vanuatu, many island religions—predominantly animistic beliefs combining magic, sorcery, and ancestor worship—still survive, and many islanders continue to believe in magic and witchcraft. Cannibalism, once practiced in a few Pacific Islands, is thought to persist only in remote areas of New Guinea.

Although considerable variation exists between groups, Melanesian traditional society relies on kinship systems, usually

Buddhist temple Page 1969

Papua New Guineans Page 1968

FIJI: AN UNEASY MIX

In the late 1990's, the Fiji Islands were home to about 802,600 people, spread out over more than 330 islands covering 7,095 square miles (18,375 sq. km.). About 39 percent of the population lived in urban areas, including the capital, Suva.

Native Fijians, who comprise about 51 percent of the population, are ethnically Melanesian but culturally are more similar to the Polynesians. The next largest group of people, 44 percent of the population, is Indian. From 1879, five years after Fiji became a British colony, until 1916, the British brought more than sixty thousand Indians to work as indentured laborers on the sugarcane and cotton plantations. After their five years of servitude were up, about 60 percent of the Indians remained in Fiji, farming leased land or opening shops in urban areas. The remaining 5 percent of Fiji's population consists of Europeans, Chinese, other Pacific Islanders, and people of mixed ethnicity. The population of the Fiji Islands is 53 percent Christian (Methodist and Roman Catholic), 39 percent Hindu, and 8 percent Muslim. Fijians are primarily Christian, and Indians are Hindu or Muslim. The official language is English, although ethnic Fijians also speak Fijian and Indians speak Hindi.

The Fijians tend to discriminate against Indians, whose sheer numbers threaten the Fijians' traditional way of life. The Indians' economic success in sugarcane farming and other key industries also produces tension between the two groups. Racial clashes between Fijians and Indians first erupted in 1959 and broke out again in 1970, just before Fiji gained its independence from Great Britain. From 1970 to 1987 Fiji was part of the Commonwealth, ruled by Prime Minister Ratu Sir Kamisese Mara. Mara lost the elections of April, 1987, to a coalition of Fijians and Indians. A perception that the new government was dominated by Indians led to racial violence and two military coups by Lieutenant Colonel Sitiveni Ligamamada Rabuka in 1987, after which Rabuka declared Fiji to be a republic.

Fiji's 1990 constitution increased native Fijian representation in the government, mandated that the prime minister be ethnic Fijian, and gave hereditary clan chiefs a role in the government. In 1997 the government eliminated preferential treatment for Fijians. In May, 1999, Mahendra Chaudhry, an ethnic Indian, became prime minister. However, the rift between the Fijians and Indians had not healed. In May of 2000, Fiji businessman George Speight took Chaudhry and his entire cabinet hostage, demanding indigenous Fijian control of the country. Speight released the hostages after fifty-six days and later was charged with treason. A new government excluding Indians from positions of power was installed, with Ratu Josefa Iloilo as president and Laisenia Qarase as prime minister. A quick solution to the ethnic and cultural conflict between the indigenous and Indian Fijians seemed unlikely.

with clan membership dependent on descent from some common ancestor. Traditional society has been described as classless because power and status are not inherited or attained by membership in a group, but must be earned by the individual. To gain a position of leadership (to be a "big man"), the Melanesian must accumulate wealth or acquire a skill such as oratory. Traditional arts include the production of bark cloth, basket weaving, and pottery.

MICRONESIA. In comparison with Melanesians, Micronesians are somewhat fairer-skinned and are taller, with wavy or woolly hair. Those with Asiatic features such as high cheekbones tend to have straight hair. Micronesians speak about thirteen languages, including English, French, and Japanese, the languages of their colonizers. Micronesians traditionally believed in the stability of society and culture. Living in small communities on small islands, they valued harmony and good manners, preferring to settle disagreements by negotiating rather than fighting. Micronesians often lived in extended family groups, separate from other families, and often on the lagoon side of the atolls, making fishing and canoeing easier. Low-island cultures (Marshalls, Gilberts) tended to venture farther away from shore, while high-island (Marianas, Palau) residents tended to stay near their own islands. Islands with higher levels of social stratification included Yap, Palau, the Marshalls, and the Gilberts.

The native polytheistic religions of Micronesia continued to be practiced until the mid-twentieth century on Yap and parts of the Carolines; however, Christianity largely supplanted these beliefs. Micronesian traditional culture has been influenced greatly by European colonizers; several traditional crafts, such as weaving and pottery, have disappeared. Other traditional arts and crafts are matwork, tattooing, shell ornaments, body painting, and the recital of poetry and tales. However, the only island with substantial numbers of non-Micronesians is Guam, part of the United States since 1898. Despite the presence of many Americans, the native Chamorros still have considerable political power.

POLYNESIA. Of the Pacific Islanders, Polynesians are the tallest and have the lightest skin and straight or wavy hair. The Tongans, Hawaiians, and Samoans tend to be large-boned and heavier. Because of intermarriages with Europeans and Asians, many Polynesians have characteristics typical of those groups. Polynesians speak about twenty languages, most of which are related.

English is the official language of Hawaii, Samoa, and Tonga, as well as those islands controlled by English-speaking nations. Polynesians are more homogeneous in custom than the Melanesians or Micronesians. Traditionally, Polynesians were gardeners and fishermen whose lifestyles were remarkably in tune with the ocean environment. Polynesian languages contain many words for winds, currents, stars, and directions, all useful for life on and near the ocean.

Traditional Polynesian culture was conservative, dedicated to preserving its complicated social etiquette and rituals. Polynesians defined a person's relation to society and nature, creating elaborate mythologies and genealogies. Society was arranged by hierarchical, branching descent groups based on kinship. The main lines in the hierarchy were believed to be closest to the gods. Alternatively, societies were arranged around a direct descent line from a mythological ancestor. These descent lines handed down titles that gave their holder societal positions such as chief. Polynesians lived in extended family groupings, and their kinship patterns made distinctions among the grandparents', parents', one's own, and children's generations, as might be expected in a highly stratified society.

Traditional Polynesian religion was polytheistic, with sometimes malevolent gods that required worship through sacrifices, feasting, sexual acts, chants, and various elaborate rituals. Animals, people, and even inanimate objects were endowed with *mana*, a supernatural power that had to be guarded so that it would not be diminished through various acts. For example, stepping over a person's head would destroy the *mana* of that person. This belief created many prohibitions (*tapu*), violation of which meant harsh and violent punishment, even death. Lesser violations received spiritual punishment such as illness.

Polynesians also believed in magic; people practiced rituals designed to guarantee success in various endeavors or to bring bad luck upon others, sometimes visiting practitioners of magic. Although many indigenous religious beliefs have faded and been replaced by Christianity, many Polynesians still believe in magic. Introduction of Europeans and European culture to Polynesia brought disease and social and political instability to the islands. Missionaries also altered and destroyed cultures, including that of the Marquesas. Modern-day Polynesia is a sometimes uneasy combination of European and indigenous culture.

Rowena Wildin

FOR FURTHER STUDY

Campbell, I. C. *A History of the Pacific Islands.* Berkeley: University of California Press, 1990.

Howe, K. R. *Nature, Culture, and History: The "Knowing" of Oceania.* Honolulu: University of Hawaii Press, 2000.

Lal, Brij V., and Kate Fortune, eds. *Encyclopedia of the Pacific Islands.* Honolulu: University of Hawaii Press, 2000.

Nile, Richard, and Christian Clerk. *Cultural Atlas of Australia, New Zealand, and the South Pacific.* New York: Facts on File, 1996.

Nunn, Patrick D. *Oceanic Islands.* The Natural Environment series. Cambridge, Mass.: Blackwell, 1994.

Nunn, Patrick D., William Aalbersberg, and Asesela D. Ravuvu, eds. *Climate and Agriculture in the Pacific Islands: Future Perspectives.* Suva, Fiji: Institute of Pacific Studies, 1993.

Rapaport, Moshe, ed. *The Pacific Islands: Environment and Society.* Honolulu: Bess Press, 1999.

EXPLORATION

*Map
Page 1970*

The aboriginal peoples were not only the first residents of Australia, but also its first explorers. They crossed into Australia when there was still a land bridge connecting Australia with the Eurasian landmass. The Aborigines then branched out over every area of the continent. They established complex systems of communication—the "songlines"—that helped map the continent. Similarly, most of Polynesia was settled by voyagers plunging eastward and, in the case of the Maoris who settled New Zealand, southward. They paddled in great canoe (*waka*) after great canoe in search of new lands.

In classical European culture, ancient geographers such as Ptolemy had postulated the existence of a great southern landmass to counterbalance the known areas of land in the northern hemisphere. These ideas of a Great Southern Land (*terra australis* in Latin, thus eventually "Australia") were revived after Christopher Columbus and Ferdinand Magellan empirically proved the roundness of the world in the fifteenth and sixteenth centuries.

Captain Pedro Fernandez de Quiros, a Portuguese navigator who captained a Spanish ship, is thought to be the first European to sight the Australian mainland, but he did not set foot ashore. Fernandez wanted to establish a Spanish empire in the South Pacific. He thought New Guinea was the Great Southern Land, but his lieutenant, Luis Vaz de Torres, established that it was not by discovering the strait to the south of New Guinea. This body of water is now called Torres Strait.

In 1642 Dutch navigator Abel Tasman became the first explorer to sail entirely around Australia. Ironically, during the entire voyage he never actually sighted the continent. However, his expedition did glimpse a small island to the south of the continent that was later called Tasmania in Tasman's honor. Another Dutch expedition headed by Willem Schouten had sailed east of Fiji in 1616.

William Dampier, a crew member of an English expedition that briefly touched the Australian coast in 1688, returned there eleven years later as captain of his own ship. Dampier had little formal education, but he had instinctive scientific curiosity. His expeditions made accurate geographical observation a top priority in future Pacific voyaging. Dampier became the first Englishman to set foot in Australia, landing on the north coast. Although equipment damage to his ship prevented Dampier from exploring the east coast of Australia, his narrative of his travels, published in 1703, helped spur interest in further South Pacific exploration.

British explorer Captain James Cook brought Australasia fully within the orbit of Western exploration. An outwardly unspectacular man, Cook commanded ships built for the rough North Sea currents off his native Yorkshire, sailing them tens of thousands of miles away from home. In a short ten-year sequence, from 1769 to 1779, Cook vastly expanded Europe's knowledge of the globe.

AUSTRALIA. By Cook's time, the motives for geographical expeditions had become less economic and more scientific in nature. This was to the benefit of South Pacific exploration, because the trading possibilities in these areas were less attractive than in other areas of the globe. Nevertheless, there were extraordinary possibilities for the gain of scientific knowledge, both of these regions and the globe itself.

Cook's expedition included a botanical scientist, Joseph Banks, who named many of the new species he encountered, classifying them within the systems recently developed as a result of the European Enlightenment. Banks was so enthusiastic about the expedition that he helped finance it, contributing a considerable amount of his own funds to assist in sponsoring the voyage. Another scientist on board, Daniel Carl Solander, had actually studied under Carl Linnaeus, who had established the classifications of genuses and species still used for animals and plants today.

Cook himself was not a trained scientist (although he was knowledgeable about astronomy) and in fact had a more imaginative cast of mind than his colleagues. However, his voyages were the first in which exploration ceased to be primarily a search for spoils and instead became a search for knowledge. Cook's expeditions not only brought back geographic data, but also made advances in geographic practice. Cook perfected precise calculations of longitude, which overcame the final barrier to reliable mapping of what were, to Europeans, distant, unknown areas. Cook's explorations marked what has been termed "the closing of the global circle." Before Cook's travels, there were still mysterious, unexplored places on Earth. After his voyages, every significant inhabited portion of the world had been mapped and surveyed, and only hidden corners remained for future explorers to discover.

This scientific orientation made it no accident that, when the *Endeavour* landed near what is now Sydney in 1770, the inlet the ship came upon was named Botany Bay after the many notable plant specimens Banks observed and classified along shore. Botany Bay is one of the few places on Earth named after a scientific field. The British followed up Cook's expedition in 1788 by sending a fleetload of convicts (transported prisoners) to a place near Botany Bay that was to become known as Sydney Harbor

At nearly the same time, a French expedition headed by Jean-François La Perouse had reached Australia. Its goal was

---

LUDWIG LEICHHARDT AND THE EXPLORATION OF AUSTRALIA

The German explorer Ludwig Leichhardt came to Australia in 1841, his scientific curiosity stirred by the exotic land and its strange flora, fauna, and geology. He achieved celebrity when he crossed from Brisbane, in Queensland, over thousands of miles of barren land to discover the Burdekin River and reach the area of the present-day Northern Territory. In his next, ill-fated, expedition, Leichhardt attempted to cross the entire Australian continent, but he and his entire party disappeared without a trace. Their remains have never been found. Leichhardt's earlier success had made him famous, but his failure turned him into an Australian legend. An echo of Leichhardt's story is found in Patrick White's novel *Voss* (1957), which is considered the single greatest work of Australian fiction. The novel raised the tale of the doomed explorer in the desolate continent to the status of myth.

to research the feasibility of whale and fur trading in the South Pacific. A relief voyage headed by Bruni d'Entrecasteaux was later sent out to look for La Perouse, who, with his entire expedition, mysteriously vanished. La Perouse's expedition occurred contemporaneously with the French Revolution and at the height of the influence of the French Enlightenment. It has always fascinated Australians.

Along with the much earlier voyage of Captain Pedro Fernandez de Quiros, it seemed to be an alternative, non-British genesis for European Australia. The Spanish and French voyages were never followed up by actual colonization. The British expedition, led by Arthur Philip, appeared to be just a solution to prison overcrowding, and the loss of another site for the relocation of prisoners after the successful American rebellion. Australia, however, quickly developed into a fullfledged British colony. Australia was now not just a point on the globe to be explored, but a land to be settled.

INTO THE INTERIOR. The first quartercentury of European settlement of Australia was confined to the coastline, whose lush vegetation and superb harbors offered little challenge to the continent's new residents. Soon, however, they realized that an entire continent was before them. In 1813 Gregory Blaxland became the first European to probe beyond the Blue Mountains, breaking out of the confines between the mountains and the Pacific coast and plunging into the interior. This opened up much of the long but, in terms of water resources, sparse MurrayDarling river system to exploration by men such as Charles Sturt.

The fringes of this inland area proved hospitable to agriculture and, especially, cattle and sheep grazing. It soon became clear that most of the Australian interior was barren and contained, at best, only

mineral resources. Settlement could not continue along the same lines as in the lands near Botany Bay.

The goal then became to find what was at the center of Australia, as the coasts had by now been well charted. The goal once again became scientific and geographic, this time tinged with a kind of romantic quest for knowledge and great deeds. As with the eighteenth century explorers, the trekkers across nineteenth century Australia, whatever their formal education, were intensely knowledgeable about the landscape, and what they did not know they sought to learn. The seat of exploration now became Adelaide in South Australia, and efforts were made to find a giant inland lake or a sizable river in the center of the continent, some form of oasis in the inhospitable, arid land. Instead, all the explorer Edward John Eyre found was the Nullarbor Plain, whose name is Latin for "no trees."

Although explorers of Australia showed great courage, their stories do not have the heroic ring associated with explorers of North America such as Vasco Nuñez de Balboa or Henry Hudson. In fact, some of the most prominent figures in Australian exploration lore are men who failed, such as Ludwig Leichhardt, who died trying to traverse the continent, or Robert Burke and William Wills, who tried to fulfill Leichhardt's vain quest. Burke and Wills had little geographical knowledge or wilderness know-how, and died of hunger, not having neared their goal.

One of the reasons adduced for Burke and Wills' failure was their lack of Aboriginal guides. Although the Aborigines were often victimized by the explorations, they also played a crucial role in aiding and guiding the European-led expeditions. The Aborigines not only knew the lay of the land but also how to survive upon it. Without Aboriginal help, many of the

Explorer Russell G. Frazier examines an unusual ice formation during an expedition in 1941. (AP/Wide World Photos)

most famous explorations of the Australian interior, particularly the passage beyond the Blue Mountains, would never have been viable.

NEW ZEALAND. New Zealand first was sighted by Europeans in 1642, when a part of its coast was observed by Tasman in his two ships, the *Heemskerk* and the *Zeehaen*. Tasman named the islands after the Dutch province of Zeeland; the Maori name for the country is *Aotearoa*, meaning Land of the Long White Cloud. Tasman's crew did not land, but they did engage a group of Maori in battle at sea, in which four of Tasman's men were killed.

The events that led to New Zealand's permanent European settlement began on October 7, 1769, when Cook and his crew arrived at what they later named Poverty Bay. The crew of the *Endeavour* was thrilled to see such a sizable landmass after a long voyage filled with only specks of islands, but they soon realized that New Zealand was not the Great Southern Land. The crew remained in the area through March, 1770, and circumnavigated both the North and South Islands, making accurate charts and establishing that the islands were not peninsular outgrowths of an interior landmass. The hungry crew often waded ashore to raid for the tasty sweet potato (*kumara*), which led to several skirmishes with angry Maori. Expeditions after Cook's were largely mounted by whalers; along with a wave of British missionaries, the whalers laid the foundations, in the early nineteenth century, for New Zealand's European settlement.

OTHER PACIFIC ISLANDS. The first Pacific island group to gain a foothold on Western consciousness was Tahiti, or, as the early explorers spelled it, Otaheite. When Captain Cook landed there in the *Endeavour* in April, 1769, he initiated an era of cultural contact that would see Polynesian and Melanesian people become conscious of the wider globe. Cook was well received by the Tahitians and dealt judiciously with them.

Cook's main agenda there was neither economic nor military, but scientific: The Royal Society (a scientific group in Great Britain) had commanded him to observe the transit of Venus on June 3, 1769, and the British Admiralty (navy department) had advised him to watch for any promising areas of land he might encounter on his voyage. (It was for the astronomical purpose to Cook's voyage that one of the U.S. space shuttles was named *Endeavour*). On this and his two subsequent voyages, Cook sailed around numerous Polynesian islands. He made informed Pacific navigation possible. Englishman John Harrison's invention of the chronometer, a mode of measuring longitude, was crucial to Cook in this task. When native peoples, apparently as a joke, stole Cook's chronometer on one island he visited, it was a moment of great crisis. Fortunately, the instrument was returned. Also important was Cook's solution to the problem of shipboard disease. He encouraged his sailors to eat fruit, which kept them healthy.

Cook made friends with a chief called "Tioony" on Tonga. Therefore, he called that island group the Friendly Islands. Cook's interaction with the native island peoples did not always go so smoothly,

however. Cook himself was killed by Hawaiians in 1779, in circumstances still hotly debated among historians. Also, his expedition spread disease that often decimated indigenous communities.

As with the Aborigines in Australia and the Maoris in New Zealand, the Pacific Islanders were subjugated and displaced by the European colonists. Sometimes the cultural interaction was happier. When one of Cook's subordinates, William Bligh, led his own Pacific expedition on the ship HMS *Bounty* in 1789, his men mutinied. This was the famous "Mutiny on the *Bounty.*" The mutineers married Tahitian women and set up their own domain on remote Pitcairn Island.

Cook affected geography as much as any other individual since Columbus. By showing that the Southern Hemisphere did not have the same amount of land mass as the Northern Hemisphere, he paved the way for accurate measurement of the world.

ANTARCTICA. The exploration of Antarctica—the earth's only uninhabited continent—does not include the scenes of cultural encounter that made exploration in

---

ANTARCTIC EXPLORATION IN THE INTERNATIONAL GEOPHYSICAL YEAR

In 1958 British scholar Sir Vivian Fuchs led the first successful overland crossing of Antarctica. Fuchs's expedition took place in the context of the International Geophysical Year, a worldwide research effort extending through 1957 and 1958, which determined the mineral composition of Antarctica and surveyed the thickness of the Antarctic ice cap. This international cooperation led to the Antarctic Treaty in 1961. This treaty, renewed in 1991, deferred all national claims to Antarctica and in effect made the continent into a giant world research station.

other areas so dramatic. Indeed, one might say that the exploration of Antarctica is still continuing. As in other areas still unknown in the eighteenth century, Cook was the pioneering figure. Cook had established that neither Australia nor New Zealand was the Great Southern Land for which explorers had been searching for the past two centuries, and that the only remaining possibility was the uttermost south. Cook's voyage on the ship *Resolution* in 1772 was the first human expedition known to cross the Antarctic Circle. Its progress was, unsurprisingly, blocked by ice. Cook was the first known explorer to set foot on the sub-Antarctic South Sandwich Islands; although he turned back north, he was able to verify that any southern continent would be completely icebound.

In 1821 U.S. explorer John Davis became the first human being known to have set foot on Antarctica. Two years later, British explorer James Weddell sailed into a large bay in the outer fringes of West Antarctica, which was named the Weddell Sea in his honor. Unspurred by any hunger for resources beyond offshore whaling and sealing, further nautical explorations continued at a leisurely pace until a Norwegian expedition brought people to the continent again in 1895. Once it was determined that humans could survive on Antarctica and that the South Pole rested on this giant landmass, the main goal of exploration was to reach the Pole.

Members of Robert F. Scott's (center) ill-fated 1912 expedition. (AP/Wide World Photos)

From 1908 to 1912, the famous expeditions to the South Pole of Norwegian Roald Amundsen and British explorers Ernest Shackleton and Robert Falcon Scott took place. Shackleton narrowly failed to reach the South Pole as a result of a shortage of supplies. Scott fell short once but reached it later on his second attempt. However, he and all his party perished on the journey. Amundsen became the first to reach the South Pole in 1911. Although there were initially hopes that mineral deposits would be found in the area, the race to the pole became its own reward

When the Norwegian Borge Ousland became the first person to travel across all of Antarctica alone in January, 1997, it was but the latest landmark in Antarctic exploration. The continent today serves as a base for research into weather, oceanography, and especially fossil research, as the ice preserved prehistoric remains not found on other continents. The most exciting area of Antarctic research is astrophysics. Many believe conditions in Antarctica are the closest to what can be expected if humans seek to settle permanently in outer space.

Nicholas Birns

Statue honoring Sir Ernest Shackleton at the Royal Geographical Society in London. (Ray Sumner)

FOR FURTHER STUDY

Asimov, Isaac. *The Ends of the Earth.* New York: Weybright and Talley, 1975.

Beaglehole, John C. *The Exploration of the Pacific.* Stanford, Calif.: Stanford University Press, 1966.

Carter, Paul. *The Road to Botany Bay.* New York: Knopf, 1988.

Fausett, David. *Writing the New World: Imaginary Voyages and Utopias of the Great Southern Land.* Syracuse, N.Y.: Syracuse University Press, 1993.

Hough, Richard. *Captain James Cook.* New York: Norton, 1997.

Moorehead, Alan. *The Fatal Impact.* London: Hamish Hamilton, 1966.

Obeyesekere, Gananath. *The Apotheosis of Captain Cook: European Mythmaking in the Pacific.* Princeton, N.J.: Princeton University Press, 1997.

Pyne, Stephen. *The Ice.* Seattle: University of Washington Press, 1998.

INFORMATION ON THE WORLD WIDE WEB

The Web site of the Polynesian Cultural Center provides general information about Polynesia. (www.polynesia.com)

URBANIZATION

AUSTRALIA

*Map
Page 1970*

To many people, including Australians themselves, the typical "Aussie" is a strong, lanky, suntanned person from the Outback, wearing a broad-brimmed hat and speaking slowly, with a distinctive accent and a dry sense of humor—a "Crocodile Dundee" figure. His world is thought to be one of kangaroos, horses, and sheep traveling on dusty and deserted plains. In reality, Australians have been city dwellers throughout most of the history of European settlement of the country, and Australia has long been one of the world's most urbanized populations.

IMMIGRATION HISTORY. The history of immigration to Australia explains this pattern of settlement. After the American Revolution, the British needed a place to send their criminals and turned their attention to the southern continent discovered and mapped by Captain James Cook in 1770. A new penal colony was established in New South Wales, at Botany Bay, in 1788. Thus, immigrants to Australia were initially convicts, or prisoners, sent into exile as punishment for their crimes. A small number of penal settlements soon were located around the coast of the continent. These grew into the colonial centers that are today the capital cities of Australia's states.

Some free settlers also came from Britain to the Australian colonies to take up land, but their numbers were small, and they wanted to become pastoralists, rather than agriculturalists. Not until 1830 were there more free settlers than convicts in Australia. The discovery of gold in Victoria in 1851 attracted thousands of miners from around the world and led to the establishment of inland towns, which persist today as Bendigo, Ballarat, and Castlemaine.

Later gold discoveries in other colonies led to population increases in New South Wales, Queensland, and Western Australia. Unsuccessful miners often stayed in Australia and established businesses. Overall, immigrants to Australia came to the cities and towns. In contrast, in the United States the majority of immigrants in the eighteenth and nineteenth centuries wanted to be farmers. At the time of World War I, more than 50 percent of the U.S. population still lived in rural areas, while only 40 percent of Australians lived in rural areas then. The percentage continued to decline throughout the twentieth century in both countries: in 1998, 14 percent of Australians and 25 percent of people in the United States lived in rural areas.

MODERN POPULATION TRENDS. The pattern of population distribution in Australia in the year 2000 reflected environmental constraints as well as history. The driest parts of the continent are almost empty; the arid 50 percent of the continent in the center contains only 0.3 percent of Australia's population. The well-watered temperate parts have a moderate population density; the coastal areas have high-density urban settlements. The largest population concentration is in the southeastern part, in the more temperate regions. East of a line drawn from Adelaide to Brisbane, 90 percent of Australian residents are found, and 84 percent of the people are crowded into a densely populated 1 percent of the area of Australia. The southwest corner, around Perth, has the other significant population concentration.

In the year 2000 Australia had a population of nineteen million people. New South Wales was the most populous state, with more than six million people, followed by Victoria with more than four million. Queensland's population is increasing most rapidly, due to interstate migration. The population of Western Australia also increased rapidly after the 1980's; in contrast, the population of Tasmania is decreasing through out-migration to the mainland.

Australia remains one of the world's most urbanized countries. Forty percent of all Australians live in either Sydney or Melbourne, which, despite ranking sixty-sixth and eighty-seventh respectively in comparative world city population size, are cosmopolitan cities. Three other Australian capital cities have a population of more than one million—Brisbane, Perth, and Adelaide. Four more urban areas have a population greater than 200,000—the conurbations of Canberra-Queanbeyan and Gold Coast-Tweed Heads and the cities of Newcastle and Wollongong. All of these are coastal cities. Australia's largest inland towns are Albury-Wodonga, Toowoomba, Ballarat, and Bendigo, with populations of about seventy thousand each. Suburban life is typical in Australia,

with Sydney and Melbourne each having more than one million privately occupied dwellings.

Two-thirds of Australians live in either one of the six capital cities, the national capital, Canberra, or the administrative center of Darwin. This makes the comparative size of cities in Australia noteworthy; the typical rank-size pattern of a primate city, some middle-sized cities, and many smaller towns does not apply. The state capitals contain the greatest proportion of each state's population. In South Australia, Western Australia, and Victoria, almost three-quarters of the people live in the capital city.

In Queensland, the Northern Territory, and Tasmania, fewer than 50 percent of the people live in the capital city. This dominance of the capital cities is a demonstration of primacy, reflecting both the his-

AUSTRALIA'S LARGEST CITIES IN 1997

City	Population (in millions)
Sydney	3,934.7
Melbourne	3,321.7
Brisbane	1,548.3
Adelaide	1,083.1
Perth	1,319.0
Newcastle	468.9
Gold Coast-Tweed	367.7
Canberra-Queanbeyan	347.1
Wollongong	258.1
Hobart	195.5
Sunshine Coast	162.1
Geelong	153.1
Townsville	123.6
Cairns	109.5

Source: Australia Now: A Statistical Profile, Australia Bureau of Statistics.

Nineteenth century office buildings in Brisbane that were originally townhouses for wealthy professionals. (Ray Sumner)

tory and the relative location of the cities. Those states with a more dispersed population also have a less centrally located capital city. Queensland is the best example: its capital, Brisbane, is located in the far southeast of the state. Such a location can lead to separatist movements initiated by people in areas remote from the seat of government, which has happened several times in Queensland.

Immigration led to the growth of Australian cities, and recent immigration has changed the ethnic profile of Australian cities. In the last quarter of the twentieth century, there was a significant change in the source countries of Australian immigrants. In the 1960's, the main countries of origin were the United Kingdom and Ire-

land, which accounted for just over half of all immigrants, followed by Greece, Italy, Yugoslavia, Malta, and Germany. In the 1990's, the major source countries were New Zealand, with over half of all immigrants, the United Kingdom, Ireland, China, Vietnam, Hong Kong, and the Philippines. Numbers of immigrants to Australia are not large compared with the United States, but they are significant in Australia's small population. Between 1992 and 1997, 1.2 million people arrived in Australia intending to stay for one year or more.

Major Cities. Sydney is located in one of the world's most beautiful settings, around a huge protected harbor, so that the inner parts of the city slope down to

Sydney Page 2042

the water. The Sydney Opera House was designed with sail-like roof shells to reflect the water-loving characteristic of the town's people. The site at Sydney Cove was chosen in 1788 for the first penal settlement, so there was some controversy when Australians decided to celebrate the Bicentennial in 1988, since other colonies were settled later. The indigenous people, the Aborigines, also noted that they had little reason to celebrate the event. Sydney was selected as the site for the Olympic Games of 2000.

Melbourne began as an unofficial settlement to serve pastoralists in 1853. Gold discoveries inland from Melbourne led to the rapid growth of a rich and beautiful city, full of impressive Victorian-period buildings and large public parks. Melbourne is the most English of Australia's cities in appearance. It was larger than Sydney during the latter half of the nineteenth century and was Australia's capital city until Canberra was built. The Olympic Games were held in Melbourne in 1956—the first time the event took place in the Southern Hemisphere.

Brisbane was first settled in 1824 as the penal outpost of Moreton Bay, a place of savage punishment for hardened criminals. Free settlement was permitted in 1841, and in 1859 the separate colony of Queensland was created. Brisbane was located in a hilly area upstream from the mouth of the Brisbane River. The subtropical climate of Brisbane gives it a different character from Australia's other state capitals, and wooden houses raised on rough wooden piers called stumps are an interesting feature.

Brisbane Page 2031

Hillside residences in Hobart, Tasmania. (Tom McKnight/Joan Clemons)

AUSTRALIA'S POETIC TOWN NAMES

Mark Twain spent several months in Australia in 1895-1896 and was enchanted with the names of Australian towns—many of which were adapted from Aborigine words. He called these names "good words for poetry. Among the best I have ever seen," and used sixty-six of them to write the poem that follows.

His favorite name was "Woolloomooloo," which he called "the most musical and gurgly." He made no pretense of the poem's having any meaning other than the beauty of its words, but it can stand as a commentary on Australia's climate. (Some of these names are actually from New Zealand.)

A SWELTERING DAY IN AUSTRALIA

(To be read soft and low, with the lights turned down.)

The Bombola faints in the hot Bowral tree,
Where fierce Mullengudgery's smothering fires
Far from the breezes of Coolgardie
Burn ghastly and blue as the day expires;

And Murriwillumba complaineth in song
For the garlanded bowers of Woolloomooloo,
And the Ballarat Fly and the lone Wollongong
They dream of the gardens of Jamberoo;

The wallabi sighs for the Murrumbidgee,
For the velvety sod of the Munno Parah,
Where the waters of healing from Muloowurtie
Flow dim in the gloaming by Yaranyackah;

The Koppio sorrows for lost Wolloway,
And sigheth in secret for Murrurundi,
The Whangaroa wombat lamenteth the day
That made him an exile from Jerrilderie;

The Teawamute Tumut from Wirrega's glade,
The Nangkita swallow, the Wallaroo swan,
They long for the peace of the Timaru shade
And thy balmy soft airs, O sweet Mittagong!

The Kooringa buffalo pants in the sun,
The Kondoparinga lies gaping for breath,
The Kongorong Comaum to the shadow has won
But the Goomeroo sinks in the slumber of dead

In the weltering hell of the Moorooroo plain
The Yatala Wangary withers and dies,
And the Worrow Wanilla, demented with pain,
To the Woolgoolga woodlands despairingly flies;

Sweet Nangwarry's desolate, Coonamble wails,
And Tungkillo Kuitpo in sables is drest,
For the Whangarei winds fall asleep in the sails
And the Booleroo life-breeze is dead in the west.

Myponga, Kapunda, O slumber no more!
Yankalilla, Parawirra, be warned!
There's death in the air! Killanoola, wherefore
Shall the prayer of Penola be scorned?

Cootamundra, and Takee, and Wakatipu,
Toowoomba, Kaikoura are lost!
From Oukaparinga to far Oamaru
All burn in this hell holocaust!

Parramatta and Binnum are gone to their rest
In the vale of Tapanni Taroom,
Kawakawa, Deniliquin—all that was best
In the earth are but graves and a tomb!

Narrandera mourns, Cameroo answers not
When the roll of the scathless we cry:
Tongariro, Goondiwindi, Woolundunga, the spot
Is mute and forlorn where ye lie.

Source: Mark Twain, *Following the Equator* (1897), chapter 36.

Adelaide was founded in 1836. The man behind this city was Edward Gibbon Wakefield, a severe critic of convict colonies, who envisioned a community of small farmers who purchased relatively expensive land; the proceeds were to be used to bring laborers from overcrowded England. The location and elegant design of the city were the work of the surveyor-general Colonel Light. Prosperity did not ensue, however, as settlers stayed in the town rather than beginning farming. Adelaide is still a beautiful city, as well as a manufacturing center.

Perth is one of the most isolated cities in the world. It was founded in 1829 as a free settlement known as the Swan River Colony, but it fared so badly that in 1846, the governor requested that it become a penal settlement. Despite opposition from the eastern colonies, almost one thousand convicts, all men, were sent to Western Australia from 1850 to 1868. In 1890 Western Australia became a self-governing colony, and gold discoveries at Coolgardie and Kalgoorlie brought new prosperity and a rapid population increase. Perth has grown most rapidly since the 1980's, partly as a result of prosperity from mining in Western Australia.

Hobart was settled in 1803 as a penal colony. It prospered as a free settlement, as agriculture and mining created new wealth, but in the late twentieth century it declined in comparative importance. It is the center for Antarctic research, being the closest city to that continent.

Darwin, the administrative center of the Northern Territory, relies heavily on government employment. Its port is well located for trade with Asia. It was the only Australian city bombed by the Japanese during World War II.

Canberra, the national capital of Australia, is located within the Australian Capital Territory. Part of the agreement that led to the union of the former colonies into the Commonwealth of Australia was the construction of a new capital city, located in New South Wales. After the site was chosen, an international competition was held to select the architect. Walter Burley Griffin, an American who had worked for Frank Lloyd Wright, won, and construction was completed in 1927. Canberra remains a well-planned city with many important modern buildings, including the High Court of Australia, the National Library, National Art Gallery, National War Museum, and the impressive new Parliament House.

Alice Springs is a small town of fewer than thirty thousand residents, but is located close to the center of the continent and is visited by many tourists. It is close to Uluru (Ayers Rock), a well-known landform, and is a center of Aboriginal art.

Cairns is located on the northeast coast of Queensland. A city of more than 100,000 residents, it is an important port and popular with tourists because of its tropical climate and its proximity to such attractions as the Great Barrier Reef, rain forests, beaches, and Outback experiences.

Ray Sumner

*Perth
Page 2039*

FOR FURTHER STUDY

Bolitho, Harold, and Chris Wallace-Crabbe, eds. *Approaching Australia: Papers from the Harvard Australian Studies Symposium.* Cambridge, Mass.: Harvard University Press, 1998.

Cannon, Michael. *Life in the Cities.* Melbourne, Australia: Nelson, 1975.

Frost, Lionel. *New Urban Frontier, The Urbanisation and City-Building in Australasia and the American West.* Kensington: University of New South Wales Press, 1991.

Modjeska, Drusilla, ed. *Inner Cities: Australian Women's Memory of Place.* Ringwood, Australia: Penguin, 1989.

Morris, Jan. *Sydney.* London: Viking, 1992.

Sandercock, Leonie. *Property, Politics, and Urban Planning: A History of Australian City Planning, 1890-1990.* New Brunswick, N.J.: Transaction, 1990.

Smith, Roff Martin. *Australia: The National Geographic Traveler.* Washington, D.C.: National Geographic Society, 1999.

Troy, Patrick, ed. *Australian Cities: Issues, Strategies and Policies for Urban Australia in the 1990's.* New Brunswick, N.J.: Cambridge University Press, 1995.

Ward, Russel. *The Australian Legend.* Melbourne, Australia: Oxford University Press, 1978.

PACIFIC ISLANDS

The Pacific Islands, also known as Oceania, include approximately thirty thousand islands. They can be divided into three distinct groups: Melanesia, Micronesia, and Polynesia. The Pacific Ocean has more islands than all other oceans put together, most located in the southwestern quadrant of the Pacific Ocean. It is estimated that when the first Europeans landed in the area during the sixteenth century, more than three million people lived there. Anthropologists believe that the region has been inhabited for fifty thousand years and that the first inhabitants came from Southeast Asia.

In the nineteenth century, the Pacific Islands began to become truly integrated into the world economy. By the 1970's, the world was shrinking at an accelerated pace and the Pacific Island countries and territories were having to cope with increasing urban, social, and economic problems that had not affected them before. Urban growth has increased air, water, and land pollution in the Pacific Islands.

The Pacific Island countries and territories are small and isolated in the vast Pacific Ocean. Most rely on agriculture, mining, and tourism for economic survival. In 1999 it was reported that each year the Pacific population increased by more than 150,000 people. Because of a high fertility rate, the population was growing younger. The population density varied throughout the islands: In New Caledonia, the density was 4 persons per square mile (10.4 per sq. km.), while Nauru had a density of 200 persons per square mile (524 per sq. km.) in 1998. It appears that family planning programs and economic conditions have not slowed down the growth of population. Since the 1970's, there has been an increase in the number of islanders who live in towns or cities. For some of the poorer islands, the increase in the urban population led to poor sanitation, scarcity of land for adequate housing, underemployment, and the breakup of the family structure.

MELANESIA. While some islands have an area that is at least a few thousand square miles, many islands are no more than small mounds of rock or sand. Melanesia, which includes Fiji, New Caledonia, Papua New Guinea, the Solomon Islands, and Vanuatu, had a population in the year 2000 of approximately 6.5 million. It was projected that Melanesia would double its population in only thirty years, with an annual growth rate of approximately 2.3 percent. More than two-thirds of Melanesia's population live in Papua New Guinea, which had a population of almost 4.8 million in 2000.

In the year 2000 the overall urban population in Melanesia had reached 21 percent. While the Solomon Islands at 13 percent, Papua New Guinea at 15 percent, and Vanuatu at 21 percent had relatively small urban populations percentage-wise, Fiji at 46 percent and New Caledonia at 71 percent had comparatively large urban populations. The capital of Fiji is Suva, located on the island of Viti Levu; in 1990 it had a population of 200,000. The city was overwhelmed by the amount of solid waste created by urban growth. New Caledonia's urban population grew at an annual rate of 2.7 percent. It is an overseas territory of France and is made up of the island of New Caledonia, where most of the population lives, and several outlying islands. The capital of New Caledonia, Noumea, had a population of 76,293 in 1996.

The urban population in Papua New Guinea was only 15 percent in the year 2000. Its capital, Port Moresby, had a population of almost 250,000 in 1994. While the percentage may be low for the urban population in Papua New Guinea, the annual urban growth rate in 2000 was rather robust at 4.1 percent. On the large islands of Melanesia, such as Papua New Guinea, people began leaving the interior highlands in order to settle in the coastal areas where the cities were. As expectations were not met, some urban settlers became frustrated with urban life and vented their dissatisfaction through destructive patterns of behavior. Social problems such as drug abuse and alcoholism increased in Port Moresby.

The highest annual urban growth rate in the Pacific Islands was in the Solomon Islands, with a rate of 6.2 percent. While only 13 percent of the population was urban in the year 2000, that percentage was expected to increase dramatically because of the high annual rate. The capital of the Solomon Islands is Honiara, located on the island of Guadalcanal; in 1990 it had a population of more than 35,000.

Vanuatu, formerly known as the New Hebrides, had a rural population that made up 79 percent of its total in 2000. It also had a high annual urban growth rate (4.3 percent), which would lead to more citizens moving to its few cities. The capital of Vanuatu, Port-Vila, had a population of 31,800 in 1996. Islands with rapidly growing urban areas faced the pressing issues of providing adequate housing, a safe water supply, proper sanitation, and steady employment.

MICRONESIA. Including the Federated States of Micronesia, Guam, Kiribati, the Marshall Islands, Nauru, the Northern Mariana Islands, and Palau, Micronesia had a population in 2000 of approximately 516,100. The population was expected to grow to 616,600 by 2010 and double in thirty years. The overall percentage for the Micronesian urban population in 2000 was 48 percent—more than twice that of Melanesia. The Federated States of Micronesia, comprising 607 islands, had a relatively low urban population at 27 percent, with an annual urban growth rate of only 0.4 percent. Located on the island of Pohnpei, the capital of the Federated States of Micronesia is Palikir. While there are no separate population figures available on Palikir, Pohnpei had a total population of 33,372 in 1994.

Guam is a territory of the United States. Because of its strategic importance, U.S. air force and naval personnel occupy part of the island. The urban population on Guam reached 38 percent in 2000. Kiribati, formerly known as the Gilbert Islands, had an estimated total population of 90,700 in 2000. The urban population was 37 percent, with an annual urban growth rate of 2.2 percent.

Port
Moresby
Page 1971

The Kiribati capital, Tarawa, had a population in 1990 of more than 25,000. During the 1990's, an urban development plan was instituted to alleviate overcrowding. Under this plan, some of Kiribati's outlying atolls were chosen for resettlement. The Marshall Islands became independent in 1986. With a population of approximately 68,000 in the year 2000, their urban population was 65 percent. The capital of the Marshall Islands is Majuro; in 1997 its population was 28,000.

In the year 2000 Nauru was the only Pacific Island country with a 100 percent urban population. It also had the highest average household size (ten) in the region. In 1983 Nauru's population was 8,100. By 2000 the population had grown to more than 11,000.

The Northern Mariana Islands had the next highest percentage of urban dwellers of any Pacific Island country or territory, with 90 percent in 2000. In 1995 the percentage of urban dwellers had been 53.6 percent. The Northern Mariana Islands ranked second in the region to the Solomon Islands, with an annual urban growth rate of 5.6 percent. In 1994 Palau became an independent republic. With a 2000 population of little more than 19,000, its urban population had grown to 71 percent. The annual urban growth rate was 2.9 percent.

The number of urban Pacific Islanders having an adequate sewage system is small. In the Marshall Islands, surface pollution was widespread in the 1990's because of faulty septic tanks, pit latrines, and household waste.

POLYNESIA. Including American Samoa, the Cook Islands, French Polynesia, Niue, Pitcairn Island, Samoa, Tokelau, Tonga, Tuvalu, and Wallis and Futuna, Polynesia had a 2000 population of 613,100. The population was expected to increase to 681,300 by 2010 and double in fifty-eight years.

American Samoa is a territory of the United States. With a population of approximately 65,000 in mid-2000, the urban population hovered around 50 percent. The annual urban growth rate was 4.6 percent. The capital of American Samoa is Pago Pago, located on the island of Tutuila, which had a population of 3,519 in 1990. American Samoa's economy was not large enough to adequately support its native population, and thousands of American Samoans have emigrated to the United States. In 1990 approximately 85,000 American Samoans were living in the United States.

Both the Cook Islands and French Polynesia had urban populations above 52 percent in 2000. The Cook Islands had a "self-governing in free association" relationship with New Zealand. Because of this relationship, many Cook Island citizens emigrated to New Zealand in search of a better life. French Polynesia is an overseas territory of France. Tahiti, one of the most important tourist locations in the South Pacific, is part of French Polynesia. The capital of French Polynesia, Papeete, is located on Tahiti. Because of the influx of people moving to Papeete, poor shantytowns sprouted up on the outskirts of the city. Tuvalu was the only other French Polynesian country or territory to have an urban population above 40 percent in 2000. It also had the highest annual urban growth rate (4.8 percent) in all of Polynesia.

While technically not part of Polynesia, Hawaii has close ties to the region. Hawaii's native population originally came from Polynesia. The fiftieth state of the United States, Hawaii has a high standard of living. The capital of the state is Honolulu, located on the island of Oahu. Hawaii's largest city, in 1998 Honolulu had a population of approximately 400,000, and a metropolitan area population of more than 850,000. Honolulu is one of the primary destinations for tourists from the United States mainland and a primary destination for Polynesians looking to resettle.

NEW ZEALAND. New Zealand has an advanced economy. In the year 2000 the population was more than 3.8 million, with 85 percent living in urban centers. New Zealand's population was estimated to grow to 4.2 million in 2010. The annual urban growth rate was a modest 1.4 percent in 2000. Pacific Islanders made up 5.6 percent of the total population. Beginning in the 1950's, Pacific Islanders came from the Cook Islands, Fiji, Samoa, and Tonga. Compared to the problems associated with urban growth in the other Pacific Island countries or territories, New Zealand seemed to offer greater possibilities for advancement. However, unemployment remained high among the Pacific Islanders who settled there. In 1993 New Zealand had nine cities with populations of more than 100,000. The capital of New Zealand, Wellington, had a population of 150,000 in the city proper and more than 320,000 in the metropolitan area.

CONCLUSION. Because land space is so limited in the Pacific Islands, population density in urban areas can be high. Pacific Island cities are faced with such issues as urban waste, economic growth, and expanding squatter encampments. In the twenty-first century, Pacific Island government institutions both local and national will need to work with more traditional native leadership to make the growth of urban centers less chaotic. Effective urban planning, appropriate government oversight, and vigorous public feedback can help to make the transition from life in rural villages to swirling urban cities more efficient and less traumatic for all Pacific Islanders.

Jeffry Jensen

Honolulu Pages 1968, 2033

FOR FURTHER STUDY

Colbert, Evelyn S. *The Pacific Islands: Paths to the Present.* Boulder, Colo.: Westview Press, 1997.

Denoon, Donald, et al., eds. *The Cambridge History of the Pacific Islanders.* New York: Cambridge University Press, 1997.

Henderson, Andrea Kovacs, project ed. *Asia and Oceania.* Vol. 4 in *Worldmark Encyclopedia of the Nations.* 9th ed. Detroit: Gale Research, 1998.

Rallu, Jean Louis. "Recent Trends in International Migration and Economic Development in the South Pacific." *Asia-Pacific Population Journal* 11, no. 2 (1996): 23-46.

Rapaport, Moshe, ed. *The Pacific Islands: Environment and Society.* Honolulu, Hawaii: Bess Press, 1999.

Stanley, David. *South Pacific Handbook.* Emeryville, Calif.: Avalon Travel, 2000.

Zurick, David N. "Preserving Paradise." *Geographical Review* 85, no. 2 (April, 1995): 157-165.

Wellington Page 2046

POLITICAL GEOGRAPHY

The vast Pacific Ocean encompasses a huge variety of landforms, from the continent of Australia to tiny coral atolls. The main geographic divisions are Australia, New Zealand, and the Pacific Islands. The Pacific's many countries exist under a variety of governmental systems—from kingships to democratic republics.

AUSTRALIA. Australia is a federation, with six states—Queensland, Western Australia, South Australia, New South Wales, Victoria, Tasmania—and two territories—Northern Territory and Australian Capital Territory. One underappreciated aspect of Australian politics is how decentralized the country is. Each state has its own premier, who is a figure of national scope, although state politicians rarely go on to assume significant roles in the federal government. The federal Australian parliament reflects this decentralization. Australia's federal system is similar to that of the United States, with two crucial differences.

In Australia's parliamentary system, the head of government (the prime minister on the federal level, the premier on the state level) comes out of the legislature and must command a legislative majority. The lower chamber, the House of Representatives, is determined by population. As in the United States, each state has the same number of senators, in the case of Australia, twelve. To amend the constitution, a majority of the states, that is, four out of six, must consent. This gives even the smaller states a substantial veto power over the national agenda.

Australia's history has been notably peaceful, with few of the sectional rivalries found in the United States or Canada. Recent analysts, however, have noted a fundamental division between New South Wales and Victoria, on the one hand, and Queensland, Southern Australia, Western Australia, and Tasmania on the other. The first two states are the headquarters of what is perceived as "the Eastern Establishment." The Eastern Establishment is urbane and sophisticated, based on a service economy, culturally permissive, and in tune with international trends. However, it is generally favorable to a free-market economic approach and to ideas of globalization. The other four states are agricultural and socially conservative.

Even the individual states have internal divisions. Within Sydney, the nation's largest city, two political worlds exist. The cultural elite that identify with the global information society tend to live in the eastern portions of the inner city or in beachfront suburbs such as Manly. The "battlers," those who have to fight to maintain a steady wage and a place in society, live in the less-upscale western suburbs. They are often members of labor unions and maintain the strong presence organized labor traditionally has had in Australian politics. In U.S. terms, the cultural elite would be liberal on social issues and conservative on economics, the battlers the reverse. These divisions defy the party distinctions in Australia between Labor and Liberal/Coalition.

Continued on page 1983

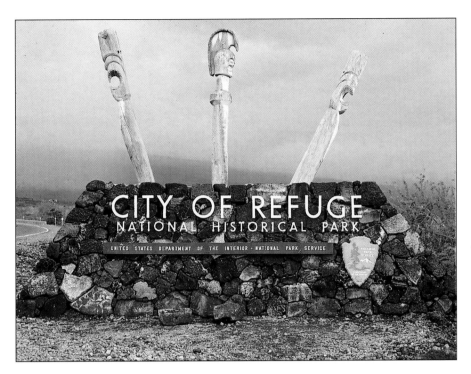

During the reign of Hawaii's early kings, the City of Refuge on the big island of Hawaii was a place where convicted criminals could flee to find sanctuary from punishment. (Clyde L. Rasmussen)

Produce market in Fiji run by Indians. A large component of Fiji's population is made up of Indians, who were originally brought to the islands as laborers by the British during the colonial era. (Tom McKnight/Joan Clemons)

Papua New Guineans dressed for a traditional musical festival. (Tom McKnight/Joan Clemons)

Honolulu, the capital of Hawaii, is home to three-fourths of the state's people, and its island, Oahu, has the highest population density in the entire Pacific Islands region. (PhotoDisc)

Aboriginal man hunting. The native Australians known as Aboriginals lived throughout Australia, with the largest concentrations in the coastal regions, particularly in the north and east. Early European immigrants drove them from their lands and demeaned them as "primitive." (Corbis)

Buddhist temple on the island of Oahu. East Asians began emigrating to Hawaii in the nineteenth century to work on plantations, and now a large proportion of Hawaii's residents are Asians and Asian Americans. (Corbis)

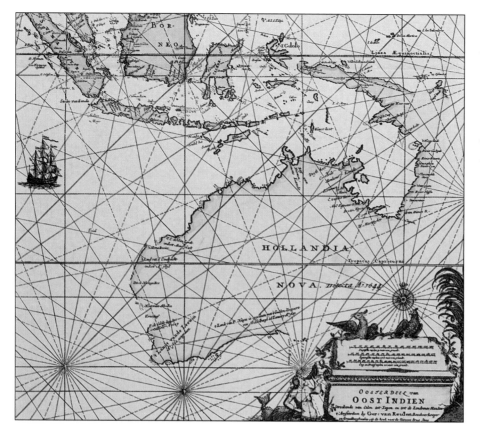

When this map of western Australia was made around the early eighteenth century, Europeans had no idea of the full size of the continent or of its relationship to nearby islands. (Corbis)

MAJOR URBAN CENTERS IN AUSTRALIA

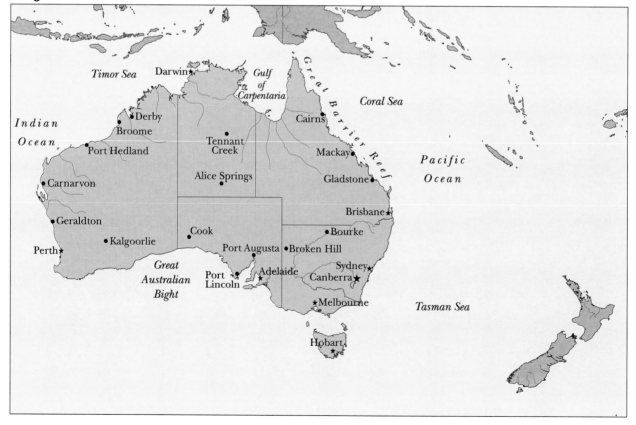

Apia, the capital of Samoa, from the air in 1970. Apia is the largest town in Samoa with a late 1990's population of only 33,000. (Clyde L. Rasmussen)

Port Moresby, the capital of Papua New Guinea, is one of the largest and the fastest-growing cities among the Pacific Islands. (Tom McKnight/Joan Clemons)

The Fangataufa atoll, one of the islands in French Polynesia where France created an international controversy by conducting nuclear weapons testing during the mid-1990's. (AP/Wide World Photos)

SELECTED AGRICULTURAL PRODUCTS OF AUSTRALIA

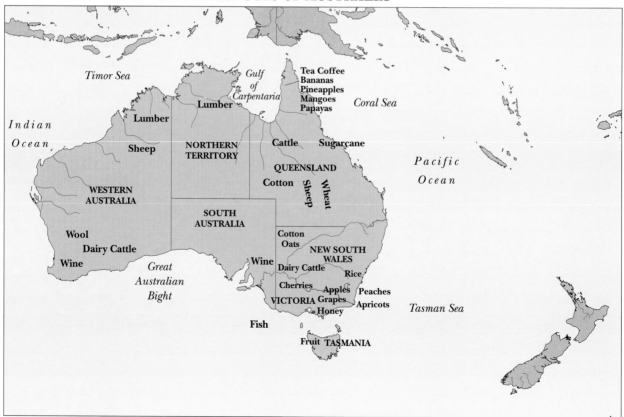

Sheep farm by Palliser Bay on the southern end of New Zealand's North Island. Livestock outnumber people by a factor of about twenty-three to one in New Zealand. About half the country is in permanent pasture, and sheep account for most of the livestock. (New Zealand Tourism Board)

Australian farmer with wool. (Corbis)

Grape harvest in South Australia. Australia grows grapes for eating and raisin production, but grapes grown for wine production are more important, especially in South Australia's Barossa Valley, New South Wales's Hunter Valley, and Western Australia's Margaret River area. (Corbis)

Pineapple field. Hawaii is one of the world's leading producers of pineapples—a fruit that requires heavy irrigation. (PhotoDisc)

Taro field. One of the oldest cultivated plants in the Pacific Islands, taro was once a staple food of island people. The starchy, edible rhizome can be cultivated by clearing or partially clearing patches in the tropical rain forest and planting the taro in moist ground. Taro can be used in land reclamation by building mud ridges or mounds in swampy ponds between beach ramparts and the foothills. (PhotoDisc)

Farms line the Sigatoka River on Fiji's Viti Levu. (Tom McKnight/Joan Clemons)

Coconut plantation in Tonga. (Tom McKnight/Joan Clemons)

Docks used to load phosphate on Nauru. (Tom McKnight/Joan Clemons)

Western Australian highway. (Digital Stock)

A remote train station in South Australia. (Tom McKnight/Joan Clemons)

In the nineteenth century camels were brought to Australia from Asia because they were expected to make good pack animals in the arid Outback. After that experiment was abandoned, most of the camels were set free. Hundreds of thousands of their descendants now roam the Outback. (Tom McKnight/Joan Clemons)

Train station at Dunedin, the second-largest city on New Zealand's South Island. (Clyde L. Rasmussen)

Produce market in Papua New Guinea's chief city, Port Moresby. (Tom McKnight/Joan Clemons)

One of three deep space tracking stations in the world is located in Australia's Tinbinbilla Nature Reserve, near Canberra. The station uses a dish antenna 230 feet (70 meters) high to communicate with astronauts orbiting the earth in U.S. spacecraft. (Digital Stock)

Residents of Port Moresby, Papua New Guinea, gather to listen to a radio broadcast on a political crisis in 1997. As in other parts of the developing world, many Pacific Islanders depend on radio to get most of their news. (AP/Wide World Photos)

The spring after which Alice Springs is named. (Tom McKnight/Joan Clemons)

Snowy Mountain Project pipelines and sluice gates, near Khancoban in New South Wales. (Tom McKnight/Joan Clemons)

Akaka Falls. Located near the Hamakua coast of the big island of Hawaii, these falls are the tallest in the Hawaiian Islands, at 442 feet (135 meters). (Clyde L. Rasmussen)

Australia's old parliament building in Canberra. (Tom McKnight/Joan Clemons)

Australia is formally a monarchy. The king or queen of Great Britain is Australia's head of state. A powerful movement launched in the 1990's for Australia to become a republic proved unsuccessful in a referendum on November 6, 1999, receiving only 45 percent of the vote. Many observers felt this was because the model for a republic on the ballot did not provide for the direct election of the president (who would replace the queen and her representative, the governor-general, as head of state). A more democratic model for the presidency might have garnered approval for a republic. In the year 2000 Queen Elizabeth II was still Queen of Australia.

AUSTRALIA'S ADMINISTRATIVE DIVISIONS

When considering the names of Australian regions, one must be careful not to confuse phrases such as "southern Australia" with actual place names. The country is administratively divided into six states and two territories. One of these states is called "South Australia," and it occupies the center portion of the continent's southern coast, immediately west of two other states, New South Wales and Victoria. Western Australia, the largest state, covers most of the west half of the continent. Occupying most of northeastern Australia is Queensland. The Northern Territory occupies the central part of the northern coast. Tasmania, the sixth state, is an island directly south of Victoria. Australia's capital city, Canberra, is located in the Australian Capital Territory—much the way the U.S. capital, Washington, is in the District of Columbia.

Australia is known worldwide as the originator of the secret ballot, often termed the Australian ballot. Voting is compulsory in Australia, with only a small minority of "informal" votes (those who have not come out to the polls or have not followed the electoral rules) being disqualified.

NEW ZEALAND. New Zealand's parliamentary system, modeled on Great Britain's, was once considered an ideal form of the Westminster system. In this system, each member of parliament was elected as a representative from his or her own constituency, and elections were governed by the first-past-the-post principle, by which the party that won the most seats formed the government. In 1995 New Zealand switched to a mixed member proportional system. This allocated slightly less than half of the seats solely on the basis of what percentage of the overall votes the party had won. The remainder continued to be allotted by the vote for candidates in individual districts.

The Labor Party, traditionally socialist, underwent a radical reversal in the mid-1980's in favor of free markets and deregulation. The National Party, traditionally conservative, has become more open to the viewpoints of women and minorities. The party produced New Zealand's first woman prime minister, Jenny Shipley, in 1997; when Shipley was defeated in 1999, she was replaced by another woman, her Labor opponent, Helen Clark.

New Zealand is a unitary, not a federal, state. Although there are nine districts and three special city areas, regions do not have the influence there they do in Australia or the United States. The legislature is unicameral (having only one house). A group with a distinct electoral role are the Maori, New Zealand's pre-European inhabitants. Under both old and new electoral systems, there were parliamentary seats reserved for the Maori, who are growing in political influence. Many Maoris have left their traditional lands to work in large urban centers such as Auckland and Wellington; these cities also host many new immigrants from Europe and Polynesia. This characterization is mainly true of North Island; South Island, with fewer Maori and immigrants and a more rural economy, tends to be more conservative politically.

Like Australia, New Zealand has retained the constitutional role of the British monarchy. There has been less of a republican movement in New Zealand than in Australia. This is partially because of the role of the Crown in signing the treaty of Waitangi, the 1840 document that is the foundation for the relationship between Maoris and Pakehas (European New Zealanders). Although the Maoris dispute several provisions of the treaty, they are seeking to work within the existing framework. Until the issue of Maori rights is fully settled, the prospects for radical constitutional change in New Zealand seem unlikely.

THE PACIFIC ISLANDS. The Pacific Islands, inhabited largely by Polynesians and Melanesians, have not seen the dictatorships that have often characterized newly independent countries in Africa and mainland Asia. The Pacific Island region was decolonized later than the rest of the non-European world, and the European colonial powers were able to learn from the mistakes made earlier in previously decolonized countries. The strong influence of Christian missionaries was another element conducive to democracy. Many Pacific Island states have small populations that lend themselves more easily to consensus.

Papua New Guinea, for example, has seen several changes of government since its independence from Australia in 1975,

Wellington
Page 2046

but they have all been democratic ones. In each case, one party has lost an election or parliamentary support and another party has stepped in to take its place, without the constitution or the political regime changing. Although Papua New Guinea is plagued by poverty, illiteracy, and a strong secessionist movement on the island of Bougainville, it has managed to maintain a level of political stability without resorting to authoritarian rule.

Most Pacific nations are republics, operating with a president and a legislature of one or two chambers. Several, however, are constitutional monarchies. These include nations with native monarchs, such as Samoa (formerly Western Samoa) and especially Tonga, where the king or queen is as active a ruler as occurs anywhere in

the world, other than in the Arab countries. Other countries, such as Papua New Guinea, have retained the British monarch as formal head of state. Fiji, which disestablished the monarchy during its 1987 coup, briefly considered bringing the monarchy back in the late 1990's, although this plan was rejected as unworkable. The Union Jack in the corner of Fiji's flag still testifies to how much Fijians value their British connections.

In many island countries, traditional chiefs (*alii* or *ariki*) still retain substantial power. In some they have a formal constitutional role, usually comprising an upper or advisory chamber; in others they exercise informal power. There have been many complaints about the concentration of power in the chiefly ranks, which in-

Royal palace of Tonga's monarchs, in Nuku'alofa. (Tom McKnight/Joan Clemons)

fringes upon the ideals of liberal democracy found in these states' constitutions. However, often the chiefs serve as mediators of potentially difficult social problems.

Since Pacific Island nations are usually composed of archipelagoes containing several small islands, the usual administrative subdivision is by island, although subdivisions also occur within islands and by grouping a number of islands. Only on the large island of New Guinea are there sizable regional subdivisions of the sort typical of most countries.

The United States has been a direct influence on governmental forms in the Pacific Islands as much as anywhere in the world, because Micronesia and the Marshall Islands were under U.S. trusteeship from 1945 to 1991 and Palau from 1945 to 1994. Upon independence, the three countries all adopted constitutions similar to the U.S. model, with minor variations. American Samoa, Guam, and the Northern Marianas remain under United States control with internal self-government.

As of the year 2000 France was the only European power fully maintaining its colonial presence in the Pacific. Although Tahiti and New Caledonia were represented in the French parliament, there was considerable discontent among the native peoples of those lands. French nuclear testing is a source of great concern in the Pacific region. This is not only because of the political overtones of continued European presence but also the ecological danger nuclear explosions pose to an already fragile natural environment. Regional organizations such as the South Pacific Forum, including all states in the area, have sharply condemned nuclear testing.

The Pacific Island states, with their low populations and limited natural resources, tend not to receive much attention in the world media or to exercise great influence in international debates. Considering the obstacles in their way, their political achievement has been notable.

Nicholas Birns

Nuclear testing site Page 1972

FOR FURTHER STUDY

Lal, Brij V. *Broken Waves: A History of Fiji in the Twentieth Century*. Honolulu: University of Hawaii Press, 1992.

Melleuish, Gregory. *The Packaging of Australia*. Sydney: University of New South Wales Press, 1997.

Morrow, Patrick. *Post-Colonial Essays on South Pacific Literature*. Lewiston, N.Y.: Edwin Mellen Press, 1998.

Mulgan, Richard. "Democracy In Retreat? Assessing New Zealand's Political Experiments." *New Zealand Studies* 8, no. 2 (September, 1998): 12-21.

Nile, Richard, with Christian Clerk. *Cultural Atlas of Australia, New Zealand, and the South Pacific*. New York: Facts on File, 1996.

Rickard, John. *Australia: A Cultural History*. New York: Longman, 1988.

Sinclair, Keith. *A History of New Zealand*. Harmondsworth, England: Penguin, 1969.

Theroux, Paul. *The Happy Isles of Oceania: Paddling the Pacific*. New York: Putnam, 1992.

INFORMATION ON THE WORLD WIDE WEB

The governments of Australia (www.aph.gov.au), New Zealand (www.parliament.govt.nz), and Fiji (www.fiji.gov.fj) all maintain informative Web sites about politics and government.

ECONOMIC GEOGRAPHY

AGRICULTURE

AUSTRALIA

Map Page 1972

Agriculture is an important part of Australia's economy. Australia's exports were overwhelmingly agricultural products until the 1960's, when mining and manufacturing grew in importance. Agricultural production continues to increase, but so do other sectors of the economy, including the service sector, so that agriculture accounted for only 3 percent of Australia's gross domestic product by the late 1990's. In 1997, 403,000 people were employed in agriculture in Australia—about 4 percent of the population. This is a higher percentage than in the United States, where 2 percent of the population is employed in agriculture.

Agriculture occupies 60 percent of the land area of Australia, but much of this is used for open-range cattle grazing, especially in huge areas of the states of Queensland and Western Australia. Only 5 percent of Australia's agricultural land is used for growing crops. Western Australia and New South Wales have the greatest areas of cropland. The small area suitable for growing commercial crops is limited mainly by climate, since Australia is the world's driest continent.

As a general guide, annual rainfall of 20 inches (500 millimeters) is necessary to grow crops successfully without irrigation; less than half of Australia receives this amount, and the rainfall is often variable or unreliable. Years of drought may be followed by severe flooding. High temperatures throughout most of Australia also mean high evaporation rates, so rainfall figures alone are not a good guide to agriculture.

Australian soils usually require the application of fertilizer to grow crops successfully. The wet tropical north of Australia is suitable for cattle raising, with sugarcane growing on the east coast. The cooler southern parts are suited to wheat growing and sheep raising. Dairy production is found in selected cool, wet regions. Irrigation has opened up large areas of drier land to agriculture, especially for fruit growing, but salinization has become a major problem in some areas, especially near the mouth of the Murray River.

Major agricultural exports from Australia are wool, beef and other meat, wheat, and sugar. Other important agricultural exports are dairy products, fruits, cotton, rice, and flowers.

WHEAT. Long the most important crop of Australia, wheat is produced in the Wheat Belt, a crescent of land just west of the Eastern Highlands, or Great Dividing Range, which extends from central Queensland through New South Wales to Victoria, as well as in the south of South Australia and southwest Western Australia. This is also the most important region of sheep raising, so it is sometimes called the Wheat-Sheep Belt. More than 120,000

Australian sheep. Australia produces about one-quarter of the world's wool, but Australian wool is high-quality fleece from Merino sheep, so that 70 percent of the world's fine wool comes from Australia. (Corbis)

farms in Australia grow grains, and wheat is the principal crop on some 25,000 farms. The average Australian wheat farm is family owned and has an area of 3,700 acres (1,500 hectares). Crops are rotated, usually because of low soil fertility.

Australian wheat is planted during the winter, which is much milder than winter on the prairies of North America. Harvesting begins in September in the warm state of Queensland and moves south to Victoria and Western Australia by January. Australian wheat is high in quality and low in moisture, so it is easy to mill. Wheat crops are frequently affected by drought; another problem is markets, since Australia competes with the United States in selling wheat.

When the British first came to Australia, the convicts planted wheat on a government farm in what is now inner Sydney. They had difficulty growing wheat because of poor soils, unfamiliar climate, and inexperience, causing fear of widespread hunger. As settlement spread beyond the coastal plain and into the interior, wheat production rose dramatically. The rapid increase in population after the gold discoveries of the 1850's also led to increased demand for wheat. Australia began exporting wheat in 1845 and is now the world's fourth-largest exporter of wheat.

WOOL. Australia produces around one-quarter of the world's wool, but Australian wool is high-quality fleece from Merino sheep, so that 70 percent of the world's

Wool
Page 1973

fine wool comes from Australia. Merino wool is used to make clothing such as suits.

The Merino breed of sheep originated in Spain. The first Merino sheep were imported to Australia in 1794 by John Macarthur, an officer in the New South Wales Corps who became a rich landowner in that colony. The flat grassy plains and temperate dry climate of inland New South Wales were a favorable environment for sheep raising. Merino sheep were bred to produce new kinds of animals, or "strains," with the emphasis on high production of fine woollen fleece. New South Wales today has one-third of Australia's sheep. Wool is produced from the New England Tableland to the Goulbourn area. Western Australia is the second-largest wool-producing state. An average Australian fleece can weigh 10 pounds (4.5 kilograms).

Wool was Australia's main export in the earliest days of British colonization. It is exported as greasy wool, meaning the wool is not cleaned or treated. Sheep and cattle farms are called "stations" in Australia. The sheep were shorn each year by teams of men who traveled from one station to another. The work was physically demanding, especially before electric shears were adopted. The Australian Labor party traces its origins to disputes between shearers and station owners in central Queensland, which led to widespread strikes in the 1890's.

In 1970 there were 180 million sheep in Australia. By 2000, that number had fallen to about 120 million, or about six per human Australian. Great Britain was the traditional market for Australian wool until the 1960's, but Japan later became the main buyer. Wool ranks fourth in terms of value of agricultural commodities produced in Australia.

BEEF AND OTHER MEAT. Cattle are raised for beef throughout Australia, but predominantly in the tropical north. Australia has more than twenty-six million cattle; Queensland has the largest number, more than ten million head of cattle. Large herds are kept on the unimproved

Sheep shearing. (Corbis)

native grasses, although in southern states, improved pastures and fodder crops are more common in the cattle industry. There is some feedlot production in the south of New South Wales and in Victoria, in the grain-growing areas. The pastoral industries are subject to great losses through both drought and flooding. Japan is the largest customer for Australian beef, with the United States second. One promising late twentieth century trend was the export of live cattle to Middle Eastern countries.

Poultry ranks second in Australian meat production, followed by pork, mutton, lamb, and veal. An interesting new type of agriculture in northern Australia is crocodile farming. The creatures are raised for both meat and skins.

DAIRY PRODUCTS. Dairying is Australia's third-most important type of agriculture, after wheat and beef. Australia has more than three million dairy cattle. Dairy cows are kept throughout the cooler and more closely settled areas of Australia, in a belt extending south around the east coast to Adelaide in South Australia; the southwest of Western Australia also has dairy herds. The state of Victoria produces 60 percent of Australia's milk. A dairy area of interest is the Atherton Tableland in north Queensland, where elevation enables the industry to exist in the Tropics. The milk from the Atherton Tableland is taken by road-tanker to Townsville, which is claimed to be the world's longest milk-run. Australia produces more than 2.1 million gallons (8 million liters) of milk

While the Australian market is well supplied with fresh milk and dairy products, exports are also important. Some 45 percent of the fresh milk is processed for export as dried milk powder and cheese; butter is also exported. Australia is the world's third-largest exporter of dairy products, after the European Union and New Zea-

Grape harvest Page 1974

land. Japan and countries in Southeast Asia are major importers of Australian dairy products.

SUGAR. Sugarcane is grown in a series of small regions along the tropical coast of Queensland, extending slightly across the border into northern New South Wales. A warm, wet climate is required for successful cultivation of sugarcane, so it is confined to parts of the coastal plain with good deep soils and reliable rainfall. Australia is the world's third-largest exporter of sugar. Sugar is grown on more than six thousand small, individually owned farms. Until the 1960's, cane was cut by hand. Now, it is harvested mechanically and taken by light rail to a nearby mill. There are twenty-five mills in Queensland and three in New South Wales.

The Australian sugar industry is an interesting case study in attitudes of Europeans. In the nineteenth century, men were brought from the islands of Melanesia to work in the sugar fields, as it was believed that no white person could survive physical work in a tropical climate. These workers were called "kanakas," and they were almost slaves of the plantation managers. The practice was stopped in 1901, when Queensland became part of the new Commonwealth of Australia. Italians then were encouraged to migrate to Queensland to do the hard work. Many sugar farms today are owned by families of Italian descent.

FRUIT. Fruit growing has a long history in Australia, and is strongly influenced by climatic considerations. In Queensland, tropical fruits such as bananas, pineapples, mangoes, and papaya (called pawpaw in Australia) are cultivated. In the cooler south, apples, peaches, apricots, cherries, and grapes are grown.

Grapes are grown for eating and dried as raisins, but more important is wine production, especially in the Barossa Valley (South Australia), Hunter Valley (New

South Wales), Margaret River area (Western Australia), and the Murrumbidgee Irrigation Area and Riverina. John Macarthur, the founder of the Australian wool industry, also established the first commercial vineyard, in New South Wales; later European settlers planted vineyards in Victoria and South Australia. In the 1960's, modern plantings and production methods were introduced. Australia has 242,060 acres (98,000 hectares) of vineyards and more than one thousand wineries. Wine is an important export for Australia, with the European Union purchasing 60 percent of wine exported.

OTHER AGRICULTURAL PRODUCTS. Cotton is grown in drier interior parts of northern New South Wales and in part of central Queensland. Cotton is usually grown in conjunction with sheep farming, on family farms. Indonesia is the major customer for Australian cotton. Rice has been grown commercially in Australia since 1924, using irrigation. New South Wales is the main producer, where the Murrumbidgee Irrigation Area dominates rice production. Australia exports most of its rice crop and in 1999 was the world's eighth-largest exporter of rice. Oats are grown where the climate is too cool and too moist for wheat. In Australia, this means in the interior southeast with a small area in Western Australia. This state and New South Wales are the biggest producers of oats, which is used mainly for fodder.

Other agricultural products of Australia include barley; grain sorghum; corn,

Mechanical sugarcane harvester. (Ray Sumner)

Hydroponic gardens in which lettuce and salad greens are grown in chemically treated water for Australian restaurants. (Ray Sumner)

called maize in Australia; vegetables, including potatoes, peas, tomatoes, and beans; oil seeds such as sunflower; soybeans; and tea and coffee in northern Queensland. Australia is a major producer of honey, with more than eight hundred commercial apiarists. Blossoms of the eucalyptus tree produce distinctive-tasting honey, which is sold mainly to European Union countries.

Australian agriculture suffered when the United Kingdom joined the European Union in 1972, and new markets had to be found for agricultural and other products. Globalization of trade continues to affect many industries, while distance from world markets together with high labor costs hamper Australian agricultural exports.

Ray Sumner

FOR FURTHER STUDY

Buckley, K. D., and Ted Wheelwright. *No Paradise for Workers: Capitalism and the Common People in Australia, 1788-1914.* New York: Oxford University Press, 1988.

Dyster, Barrie, and David Meredith. *Australia in the International Economy in the Twentieth Century.* Cambridge, England: Cambridge University Press, 1990.

Gibson, Ross. *South of the West: Postcolonialism and the Narrative Construction of Australia.* Bloomington: Indiana University Press, 1992.

Keast, Allen, R. L. Crocker, and C. S. Christian, eds. *Biogeography and Ecology in Australia.* The Hague, Netherlands: W. Junk, 1959.

Lines, William J. *Taming the Great South Land: A History of the Conquest of Nature in Australia.* 2d ed. Athens: University of Georgia Press, 1999.

Malcolm, Bill, Peter Sale, and Adrian R. Egan. *Agriculture in Australia: An Introduction.* Oxford University Press, 1996.

INFORMATION ON THE WORLD WIDE WEB

A good site for detailed Australian agricultural information is that of the United Nations' Food and Agriculture Organization (FAO), which features a searchable database organized by individual country. (www.fao.org)

PACIFIC ISLANDS

Agricultural practices in the Pacific Islands have an unsettled history, and they share some common problems. Many of these islands are separated from one another by hundreds to thousands of miles. Typhoons, storms, drought, and volcanic activity can cause havoc to their agriculture. Even the rise of sea level can devastate some of these islands. Throughout history, attempts by foreigners to encourage commercial agriculture through monoculture have threatened fragile island environments.

Large-scale land clearing and the use of fertilizers and pesticides have caused erosion, contamination of soils and lagoons, loss of important trees, and depletion of precious soils. Introducing new crops to these island communities can result in the loss of native crops, harm to native species, and the elimination of traditional mixed farming methods. The Pacific Islands have unique and fragile ecosystems, many of which are endangered by modern agricultural practices.

The islands can be divided into two main types: the high islands, which are generally volcanic islands, and the atolls or low islands. Volcanic lava weathers rapidly and provides reasonably fertile soil for cultivation, whereas atolls are low-lying coral reefs, which generally have an inadequate supply of freshwater and poor soils. Coconuts, which can ripen throughout the year and can grow on poor soil, are one of the few crops that thrive on the low islands. Coconuts are an important source of nutritious food and are easy to store. The meat of the coconut can be dried into a product called copra, which is pressed to make multipurpose oils and cream for cosmetics.

Islands show great variations in the amounts of rainfall they receive, the steepness of their slopes, and the variety of plant life that can grow. Great differences in rainfall and vegetation can exist on different sides or parts of the same island. For example, one side of the island of Hawaii has one of the driest deserts on Earth,

Taro fields
Pages
1918, 1975

whereas a few miles away on the other side of the island, a tropical rain forest exists.

MELANESIAN ISLANDS. These fairly large islands are located to the northeast of Australia. They are quite damp, have a hot climate, and display a mountainous terrain that is covered with dense vegetation. Papua New Guinea is the largest island in Melanesia, slightly larger in size than California. It has a mountainous interior with rolling foothills that are surrounded by lowlands along the coastal areas. Its highest point is Mount Wilhelm, which rises to 14,795 feet (4,509 meters). Arable lands make up only one-tenth of a percent of its land, and permanent crops occupy 1 percent of the land. Crops often need to be terraced in areas having steep slopes and extreme vegetation. Irrigation water is often brought to the crops through bamboo pipes. Approximately 64 percent of the labor force is involved in subsistence agriculture. Agricultural products grown include coffee, cocoa, coconuts, palm kernels, tea, rubber, fruit, sweet potatoes, vegetables, poultry, and pork. Palm oil, coffee, and cocoa are exported. In 1997 droughts brought on by the El Niño weather cycle caused extreme damage to coffee, cocoa, and coconut production.

Vanuatu, which includes eighty islands in the South Pacific, covers a total area a bit larger than the state of Connecticut. Its mostly mountainous terrain provides only minimal arable land. Approximately 2 percent of the land is arable, and another 2 percent is used for pasture. About two-thirds of the population is involved in sub-

Cattle grazing under coconut trees on Vanuatu. (Tom McKnight/Joan Clemons)

LEADING AGRICULTURAL PRODUCTS OF PACIFIC ISLAND NATIONS

Country	Products	Percent of Arable Land
Fiji	Sugarcane, coconuts, cassava, rice, sweet potatoes, bananas, cattle, pigs, horses, goats, fish	10
Micronesia	Black pepper, tropical fruits and vegetables, coconuts, cassava, sweet potatoes, pigs, chicken	—
New Zealand	Wheat, barley, potatoes, pulses, fruits, vegetables, wool, meat, dairy products, fish	9
Palau	Coconuts, copra, cassava, sweet potatoes	—
Papua New Guinea	Coffee, tea, cocoa, coconuts, palm kernels, tea, rubber, sweet potatoes, fruit, vegetables, poultry, pork	—
The Philippines	Rice, coconuts, corn, sugarcane, bananas, pineapples, mangoes, pork, eggs, beef, fish	19
Polynesia	Coconuts, vegetables, fruits, vanilla, poultry, beef, dairy products	—
Solomon Islands	Coconuts, palm oil, rice, cocoa, yams, pigs, vegetables, cattle, timber, fish, beans, potatoes	1
Vanuatu	Copra, cocoa, coffee, coconut, taro, yams, fruits, vegetables, beef	2

Source: Time Almanac 2000. Boston: Infoplease, 1999.

sistence or small-scale agriculture. The main agricultural products are copra, coconuts, cocoa, yams, coffee, fruits, vegetables, fish, and beef. Copra, beef, cocoa, and coffee are exported.

New Caledonia, located east of Australia in the South Pacific Ocean, is almost the size of New Jersey. It consists of coastal plains with interior mountains that range up to 5,340 feet (1,628 meters) high. New Caledonia, which is known for its nickel resources, imports much of its food supply. A few vegetables are grown, but raising livestock is more common. Twelve percent of New Caledonia's land is in permanent pasture used for raising beef cattle.

The Fiji Islands include 332 islands, only 110 of which are inhabited. These islands are volcanic in origin, and approximately 10 percent of the land is arable and 10 percent is in permanent pasture. Approximately 67 percent of the labor force is involved in subsistence agriculture. Sugarcane is an important crop in Fiji and constitutes a major industry and 32 percent of Fiji's exports. Other agricultural products grown in Fiji are coconuts, cassava (tapioca), rice, sweet potatoes, cattle, pigs, and goats.

The Solomon Islands are a cluster of small islands that collectively cover an area almost the size of Maryland. They are located in the Solomon Sea between Papua New Guinea and Vanuatu. Some of the islands have rugged mountainous terrain, others are low coral atolls. Only 1 percent of the land is arable and 1 percent devoted to pastures. Approximately 24 percent of the working population is involved in agriculture, forestry, or fishing. Beans, cocoa,

Fiji farms Page 1975

Fiji market Page 1967

coconuts, palm kernels, rice, potatoes, fruit, and vegetables are grown on the islands. Cattle and pigs are the primary livestock raised there. Palm oil, cocoa, copra, and tuna are exported.

MICRONESIAN ISLANDS. Micronesia comprises thousands of relatively small islands located along the equator in the central Pacific Ocean and up to 120 miles (2,000 km.) north of the equator in the western Pacific Ocean. The region covers approximately 1.54 million square miles (4 million sq. km.) and is subdivided into four areas: the Kiribati group, which lies around the intersection of the equator (0 degrees latitude) and the international date line (longitude 180 degrees); the Marshall Islands, which are about 900 miles (1,500 km.) to the northwest of Kiribati; the Federated States of Micronesia, which extend westward from the Marshall Islands for another 900 miles; and Guam, a U.S. territory located within the western cluster of islands of the Federated States of Micronesia.

The Kiribati group includes the Gilbert, Line, and Phoenix Islands, which are primarily low-lying atolls encircled by extensive living reefs. Twenty of the thirty-three islands in the group are inhabited. Agriculture is mainly subsistence, with copra (dried coconut meat) being one of Kiribati's few exports. Grown on the island for local consumption are taro, breadfruit, sweet potatoes, vegetables, and coconuts. Taro is one of the oldest cultivated plants in Pacific Island history and was once a staple food of the island people. This starchy, edible rhizome can be cultivated by clearing or partially clearing a patch in the tropical rain forest and planting the taro in the moist ground.

The Marshall Islands contain two island chains of 30 atolls and 1,152 islands. The economy of the Marshall Islands is dependent upon aid from the U.S. government.

Agriculture exists as small farms that provide commercial crops of tomatoes, melons, coconuts, and breadfruit. Coconuts, cacao, taro, breadfruit, pigs and chickens are produced for local consumption.

The Federated States of Micronesia include Pohnei, the Truk Islands, the Yap Islands, and Kosrae. There are a total of 607 diverse islands, some high and mountainous, others low-lying atolls. Volcanic outcroppings are found on Kosrae, Pohnpei, and Truk. Agriculture on the islands is mainly subsistence farming. Products grown include black pepper, coconuts, tropical fruits and vegetables, cassava, and sweet potatoes. Pigs and chickens are the main livestock raised. Bananas and black pepper are exported.

Guam, the largest island in the Mariana archipelago, is of volcanic origin and surrounded by coral reefs. It has a flat coral limestone plateau that serves as a source of fresh water for the islands. In Guam, 15 percent of the land is used as permanent pasture and another 11 percent is arable. Although fruits, vegetable, copra, eggs, poultry, pork, and beef are raised on the island, much of its food is imported because the economy relies heavily on U.S. military spending and the tourist trade.

POLYNESIA. Polynesia comprises a diverse set of islands lying within a triangular area having corners at New Zealand, the Hawaiian Islands, and Easter Island. French Polynesia is at the center of the triangle, 15 degrees south latitude and longitude 140 degrees west, and includes 118 islands and atolls.

The five archipelagoes of French Polynesia include four volcanic island chains (the Society Islands, the Marquesas, the Gambiers, and the Australs) and the low-lying atolls of the Tuamotus. The mountainous volcanic islands contain quite fertile soils along their narrow coastal strips. The atolls have little soil and lack a permanent water supply. Permanent pasture covers 5 percent of French Polynesia, and 6 percent is used for permanent crops. Agricultural products raised include coconuts, vegetable, fruits, vanilla, poultry, beef, and dairy products. Coconut products and vanilla are exported. Thirteen percent of the population is involved in agriculture. On Tahiti, the largest island in French Polynesia, less than 10 percent of the land is arable. Exports include vanilla and coffee, but the main export from French Polynesia is pearls.

Samoa is a chain of seven islands lying several thousand miles to the west of Tahiti. Collectively, the islands are almost the size of Rhode Island, and they are covered with rugged mountains with a narrow coastal plain. Approximately 24 percent of the land sustains crops of bananas, taro, yams, and coconuts. Taro is a crop that can be used in land reclamation by building mud ridges or mounds in swampy ponds between the beach rampart and the foothills. Coconuts grown on the island are processed into creams and copra for export.

Tuvalu is a group of nine coral atolls located almost halfway between Hawaii and Australia. The soil is poor on these islands and there are no streams or rivers. Water for the islands is captured in catchment systems and put into storage. Islanders live by subsistence farming and fishing. Coconuts are one of the few crops that can grow in the poor soils, and coconut farming allows the islanders to export copra.

The Cook Islands comprise a combined area almost the size of Washington, D.C. Located halfway between Hawaii and New Zealand, the northern islands are primarily low coral atolls and the southern Cook Islands are hilly volcanic islands. Permanent crops occupy about 13 percent of the land; 29 percent of the labor force is involved in agriculture. The Cook Islands produce a wide diversity of crops, including pineapple, tomatoes, beans, paw paws, bananas, yams, taro, coffee, and citrus fruits. Agriculture is an important part of the economy, and copra, fresh and canned citrus fruit, and coffee are major exports.

The Hawaiian Islands are a volcanic chain of more than 130 islands, centered near 25 degrees north latitude and longitude 160 degrees west. Hawaii, with more than one million people, has the largest population in the Polynesian Island group. Lanai, one of the seven largest islands in Hawaii, is privately owned and almost all its cultivated land is planted in pineapples. There are more than fifty-five hundred farms in Hawaii, and more than forty crops are grown commercially.

Because of the absence of adequate water on some sides of the Hawaiian Islands, water is brought through aqueducts from the wet sides of the islands to the dry sides, then kept in lined reservoirs to be used for irrigation, ranching, and tourism needs. Sugarcane requires enormous amounts of water to grow, and most pineapple crops are grown under irrigation. Hawaii is the second-largest producer of macadamia nuts in the world. The islands of Hawaii, Kauai, Maui, Molokai, and Oahu produce 7.6 million pounds of green coffee a year. Hawaii is also a prime producer of pineapple, cane from sugar, greenhouse and nursery plants, and dairy products. The main exports are fruits, coffee, and nuts.

NEW ZEALAND. About the size of Colorado, New Zealand is divided into two large islands and numerous smaller islands. About 50 percent of its land is in permanent pasture. A mountainous country with large coastal plains, 9 percent of the land in New Zealand is arable and 5 percent is planted in permanent crops. Agriculture accounts for 9 percent of the gross national product and employs approximately 10 percent of the labor force.

Pineapple field Page 1974

Tonga coconut plantation Page 1976

Vineyards on New Zealand's South Island, whose Mediterranean climate makes it ideal for wine production. (Digital Stock)

In New Zealand, livestock outnumber people twenty-three to one. Wool, lamb, mutton, beef, and dairy products account for more than one-third of New Zealand's exports, and New Zealand is one of the world's top exporters of these products. New Zealand exports 90 percent of its dairy products. Other exports include cheese, fruits, and vegetables. Industry in New Zealand is primarily based on food products, including processed fruit, wines, and textiles.

Toby R. Stewart

FOR FURTHER STUDY

Gibson, Arrell Morgan. *Yankees in Paradise.* Albuquerque: University of New Mexico Press, 1993.

Harding, Thomas, ed. *Cultures of the Pacific.* New York: The Free Press, 1970.

Lee, W. Storrs. *The Islands.* New York: Holt, Rinehart and Winston, 1966.

Oliver, Douglas L. *The Pacific Islands.* Cambridge, Mass.: Harvard University Press, 1967.

Salter, Christopher, et al. *World Regional Geography.* Orlando, Fla.: Harcourt Brace, 1998.

INFORMATION ON THE WORLD WIDE WEB

A good site for detailed agricultural information is that of the United Nations' Food and Agriculture Organization (FAO), which features a searchable database organized by individual country. (www.fao.org)

INDUSTRIES

AUSTRALIA

The basis for much of Australia's industrial activity is its vast mineral industries. Few countries possess either the large number of minerals or the immense reserves of those minerals that Australia does. Sixty minerals have been produced commercially. Australia is not only self-sufficient in most minerals, but it also is a leading producer of bauxite (the raw material for aluminum), copper, iron ore, lead, zinc, nickel, diamonds, gold, silver, salt, and uranium. Minerals are important both because they provide the raw materials for many industrial processes and for the huge amounts of minerals exported annually. In the 1990's, more than 40 percent of Australia's export earnings was derived from minerals.

EARLY MINERAL INDUSTRIES. From the time the British established the first colonies in Australia, minerals have been extracted. Before 1800, coal was being exported from mines near New Castle, New South Wales. In the 1840's, copper and lead mines were established first in South Australia, then in New South Wales and Victoria. In the 1850's and 1860's, gold was discovered at diverse locations in Victoria and New South Wales. The ensuing gold rush led to a rapid increase in Australia's population. Through the years, other minerals were discovered and mined locally. By 1900 Australia was exporting large amounts of copper, lead, zinc, tin, gold, and silver.

As mineral exploration techniques were improved, other minerals were discovered in the 1950's and 1960's. Enormous deposits of coal, iron ore, and bauxite were discovered in the 1950's. The following decade, large deposits of petroleum, natural gas, nickel, and manganese were found. By the early 1990's, Australia was the world's leading exporter of coal, iron ore, and bauxite, three minerals in widespread demand.

MINERALS AND MANUFACTURING. Western Australia is Australia's leading mineral-producing state, followed by Queensland and New South Wales. Extensive mineral resources are distributed widely in other states as well. Many of the mines, smelters (plants to extract minerals from ore), and refineries (plants for purifying minerals) are located in remote, arid regions of the country, factors that contribute to the high production costs for several minerals. The mining companies must provide housing, education, health care, recreation, and other services for their workers and their families. In addition, costly roads and railroads must be built to serve the mines, smelters, and refineries.

Australia's mineral industries, along with its farms and ranches, provide many of the raw materials for its manufacturing industries. Although some manufacturing developed in the nineteenth century, substantial industrial development did not oc-

AUSTRALIA'S DIAMONDS

Northwest Australia's famous Argyle Diamond Mine opened in 1985 to exploit the abundant diamondiferous ore. By the 1990's, more than thirty million carats—about one-third of the world's diamonds—were produced by this single mine. Only about 5 percent of the mine's diamonds are of gem quality, but these include the rare pink diamond, which has a value fifty times that of white diamonds. The mine's non-gem-quality diamonds are used by industry.

cur until after 1900. During the first half of that century, manufacturing centered around the processing of minerals. This led to the development and expansion of such basic manufacturing industries as steel, aluminum, petroleum, shipbuilding, and fabricated metals.

These industries, and many others, were expanded during World War II when industrial growth was stimulated by a reduction in imports. Rapid expansion of manufacturing continued in the 1950's and 1960's as the demand for both consumer goods and products used by businesses accelerated. During those two decades, manufacturing employment rose 70 percent. By the early 1970's, more than 40 percent of Australia's gross domestic product was derived from manufacturing, and 1.2 million workers toiled in factories.

At the end of the twentieth century, Australia, like other developed countries, produced a wide range of manufactured goods. However, much manufacturing still involved processing of the country's abundant natural resources, including the production of steel, aluminum, and petroleum. Other important industries were motor vehicles, machinery, chemicals, plastics, and paper products. The food, beverage, and tobacco sector was the leading employer, however.

CHARACTERISTICS AND TRENDS. Among the long-term characteristics and trends regarding industrial activity in Australia has been its dependence on foreign investment capital. Throughout the nineteenth century, industrial development of the Australian colonies and territories was carried out by a constant infusion of British capital. In the years immediately following World War II, Australia attracted capital from several other countries, especially the United States. By the end of the twentieth century, Australia's mining industry was dominated by foreign capital; half of the industry was owned or controlled by foreign investors. By the late twentieth century, most of Australia's twenty-five largest firms, which produced more than one-third of the country's gross domestic product, were wholly or partially owned subsidiaries of major international firms headquartered outside of Australia. Japan, Great Britain, and the United States each provided about 20 percent of Australia's foreign investment at the end of the century.

Another characteristic of Australian industry is its high degree of concentration in the southeast, in particular in New South Wales and Victoria. Until recently, when there has been some dispersion of industry, about half of Australia's manufactured goods were produced in New South Wales. Even within New South Wales, industry is concentrated. The manufacturing core is an elongated strip along the eastern coast of the state, extending from Wollongong to Sydney to Maitland. Melbourne is the center of manufacturing in Victoria, although industry has spread to other nearby cities. About one-third of the nation's factory production is located in Victoria. The concentration of industry in southeastern Australia dates from the early nineteenth century. Although governments promoted the dispersal of industries to other states in the late twentieth century, such efforts met with little success.

Australian industry also is highly concentrated in the capital cities of the states and territories, while there is a scarcity of industry in other cities and towns. In New South Wales, for example, almost three-fourths of the state's manufacturing industries were located in Sydney, the state's capital, and about half of Queensland's factory production occurred in Brisbane at the close of the twentieth century. The high concentration of industry in the capital cities was partially related to the origin of the independent colonies that now compose Australia and the historical evolution of these colonies in the eighteenth and nineteenth centuries. These colonies were founded and grew independently of one another.

The capital city of each colony was the focus for its development. Transportation and communication linkages developed between the capital cities and their respective hinterlands. However, few links emerged to tie the colonies together. Moreover, for several decades after their founding, government-owned enterprises produced most of the manufactured goods within the colonies. Since the colonies were administered from the capital cities, manufacturing tended to be located there.

Another industrial trend of the late twentieth century was the sharp increase in the number of mergers (combining of two firms) and acquisitions (purchase of one firm by another). Virtually every sector of the Australian economy experienced increases in mergers and acquisitions. Sectors where mergers and acquisitions have been especially prominent include retail, finance, and manufacturing. The competitive position of many firms affected by mergers and acquisitions has been substantially improved, although some loss of manufacturing jobs may be attributed to these events. This trend is expected to continue in the twenty-first century.

Several other long-term trends were similar to those that occurred in developed countries in the last quarter of the twentieth century. Perhaps the most important of those trends, one that mirrors the United States, Canada, and several European countries, has been the decline of manufacturing. Since 1970, the large cities in New South Wales and Victoria have been negatively affected as many manufacturing plants closed. Employment in textiles, apparel, coal mining, steel, aluminum, shipbuilding, and the metal fabricating industries has declined dramatically. The reasons for this deterioration are complex, but low-cost foreign imports contributed to the decline.

As manufacturing declined after 1970, Australia's service industries gained prominence. By the year 2000 nearly 80 percent of the labor force was employed in services and more than 70 percent of the gross domestic product was derived from this sector. Major service industries included retail, finance, insurance, real estate, recreation, and information services.

TOURISM. One of the most rapidly growing tertiary sectors of the Australian economy was tourism. Domestic travel was the most important component, providing 75 percent of tourism revenues in the late 1990's. International tourism had increased in importance until the widespread East Asian economic crisis curtailed much travel in the 1990's. In the early 1990's, more than 2.5 million foreign tourists visited Australia. About one-quarter of the international visitors arrived from Japan; many others came from New Zealand, Great Britain, Ireland, and the United States. Visitors from several Southeast Asian countries sojourned in the country as well. By the early 1990's, about 500,000 workers were employed in tourism, which contributed 5.5 percent to the gross domestic product. This sector holds much promise for expansion in the twenty-first century.

Robert R. McKay

FOR FURTHER STUDY

Arden, Harvey. "The Land of Northwest Australia: Journey into Dreamtime." *National Geographic* (January, 1991): 8-41.

Australia. Amsterdam, Netherlands: Time-Life Books, 1989.

Ellis, William S. "Queensland, Broad Shoulder of Australia." *National Geographic* (January, 1986): 2-37.

Learmonth, Agnes Moffat. *The Australians, How They Live and Work.* New York: Praeger, 1973.

McKnight, Tom L. *Oceania: The Geography of Australia, New Zealand and the Pacific Islands.* Englewood Cliffs, N.J.: Prentice-Hall, 1995.

Sheil, Christopher, ed. *Turning Point: State of Australia.* St. Leonards, New South Wales, Australia: Allen & Unwin, 1997.

Smith, Roff Martin. "Australia by Bike: A Bloody Long Way Home." *National Geographic* (December, 1997): 48-67.

_____. "Australia by Bike: Closing the Circle." *National Geographic* (April, 1998): 42-60.

PACIFIC ISLANDS

The industries of the Pacific Islands are less developed than those of many other world regions. Reasons for this lack of development are varied and complex. One of the most important reasons is the small population and market of the Pacific region. This has prevented Pacific Island countries from taking advantage of economies of scale that exist in regions with large populations. Another disadvantage is the long distances between the islands and their markets. This often has caused transportation costs for both raw materials and finished products to be high, putting producers at a competitive disadvantage. Another disadvantage is that many of the

countries in the region have limited natural resources.

Mineral, forestry, and agricultural resources are poor throughout the region. In some cases, the political-economic structure has not been conducive to the development of manufacturing. Nevertheless, some industries are found on virtually all of the inhabited islands of the Pacific. The thousands of islands scattered over millions of square miles of the Pacific Ocean can be examined in four major subregions—New Zealand, Melanesia, Micronesia, and Polynesia.

NEW ZEALAND. Compared to the industrialized nations of the world, New Zealand has experienced only modest industrial growth since 1950. Many sectors were dominated by small-scale enterprises. In the 1990's, 80 percent of the manufacturing firms employed ten or fewer workers. Nevertheless, New Zealand remained the dominant Pacific Island industrial power as the twentieth century ended. From an industrial perspective, no other country of the region had the strength or diversity of New Zealand.

Food processing was New Zealand's largest industry in terms of employment and output. The processing of meat and dairy products was the most significant component of this sector. Most of these products were produced for international markets, and the sector accounted for a substantial amount of New Zealand's foreign exchange earnings.

The production of pulp, paper, and other wood products was New Zealand's most rapidly growing manufacturing sector as the 1990's ended. Much of this rapid growth was based on the processing of timber from pine forests on North Island, which had been planted since 1970. At least eight plants were engaged in processing the extensive wood resources in the late 1990's.

One of the basic manufacturing industries that was important to New Zealand's economy was aluminum production. New Zealand has a large surplus of electrical power, derived from its hydroelectric generating facilities, which provided energy for the production of aluminum. Few manufacturing processes require as much electricity as does aluminum production. Alumina, the raw material for the manufacture of aluminum, was imported from Australia; the finished product was sold to Japan and other Asian countries.

New Zealand's steel industry was small but highly competitive. New Zealand's iron ore and scrap metal were used as raw materials. Among the products manufactured in the 1990's were ingots, slabs, rods, and bars. Much of the output was consumed by the domestic market, although some was exported.

In addition to these relatively large-scale industries, New Zealand manufactured a wide range of consumer goods, including appliances, motor vehicles, transportation equipment, printing and publishing, textiles, clothing, and footwear. Many other goods were produced on a small scale. Several niche industries have emerged in recent years. Among the more important were mountain bikes, camping and climbing gear, yachts, and food-processing equipment. These products have found a ready market overseas.

MELANESIA. The islands that make up Melanesia, like most developing countries, had poorly developed industry at the end of the twentieth century. Typically, only a small percentage of the labor force was devoted to industry. The most developed industrial sector was mining and the processing of minerals.

On a number of the islands, mining has expanded substantially since 1970. Papua New Guinea and New Caledonia were Melanesia's leading producers of minerals, which were the mainstays of those economies. Copper, gold, silver, natural gas, and petroleum were being extracted on Papua New Guinea. New Caledonia was the world's third-leading producer of nickel, and also produced significant amounts of chromium, cobalt, manganese, and iron ore. The potential to expand New Caledonia's mining was great, for there were large deposits of copper, lead, silver, gold, mercury, and antimony.

On several of the island countries, tropical hardwood and softwood forests have provided the basis for an incipient wood products industry. Although roundwood (logs) were frequently exported, many sawmills and wood processing plants produced lumber and wood products. Typical of these plants were those on Papua New Guinea, where plywood and wood chips were manufactured. Fiji was noted for its plywood, veneers, pulp, and wood chips. In some areas, small furniture manufacturing plants have opened; elsewhere, wood is used to produce charcoal, which is used for cooking by many rural residents.

Although it is of minor importance, locally grown agricultural products have been processed for decades on many of the islands. The most widespread such industry is the processing of coconuts. Both copra (dried coconut meat) and coconut oil were produced on many Melanesian islands. Other crops included coffee and

palm oil, which were produced on Papua New Guinea and the Solomon Islands, respectively, and require some processing before they are sold. Sugar refining has been the most important industry on Fiji since the 1840's and also was important on several other islands in the 1990's. These industries employed a number of unskilled workers and were important to the local economies.

MICRONESIA. At the end of the twentieth century, the economies of many Micronesian countries were largely dependent on subsistence agriculture; industry was poorly developed. Service industries were frequently the largest employer, and government spending was crucial to the economies of several islands. On the Federated States of Micronesia, the Mariana

Palm oil storage facility in the Solomon Islands. (Tom McKnight/Joan Clemons)

Islands, and the Marshall Islands, the largest employer was the public sector.

In contrast to Melanesia, mining in Micronesia has been of marginal importance. A few widely dispersed deposits of petroleum and other minerals were being exploited, and on Guam, petroleum refining was important. The only Micronesian country where mining has been of significance is Nauru, where the production of phosphate was a mainstay of the economy for decades. This mineral was exported to Australia and several Asian countries, where it was used as fertilizer. By the end of the twentieth century, Nauru's phosphate reserves were virtually exhausted.

Of the other industries that were of some importance to the economies of Micronesia, most are classified as services. An important industry that expanded rapidly in several countries in the 1980's and 1990's was tourism. Other expanding service industries were retail, professional, and personal services.

Manufacturing on most islands was poorly developed and, on many islands, very small scale as the twentieth century drew to a close. Most manufacturing enterprises provided consumer goods for domestic markets. The most widely manufactured consumer goods included food and drink, tobacco, detergents and soap, plastic products, paint, paper and packaging, boats, furniture, and building materials. Food processing remained important on several islands, especially Kiribati, where three-fourths of the income of rural residents was derived from the production of copra. On several islands, handicrafts are made to provide products in demand by tourists. Textile and apparel manufacturing plants have been established to take advantage of inexpensive labor on several islands. Most of the output from these plants was exported, which in turn generated needed foreign exchange.

POLYNESIA. A single industry—tourism—dominated the economies of several Polynesian countries at the end of the twentieth century. On several islands, tourism was the major employer, and it continued to expand as increasing numbers of visitors arrived each year. Tourism was especially important in American Samoa, Easter Island, French Polynesia, the Cook Islands, and Western Samoa. In some cases, local development agencies have only recently recognized the potential for the expansion of tourism. The natural beauty, mild climate, diverse cultures, and even the isolation of the Polynesian Islands are major tourist assets. Efforts were underway to promote tourism on several islands, including Tonga, Tuvalu, and Niue, where tourism was poorly developed. Constraints on the tourism industry, however, included a shortage of facilities to accommodate tourists, especially adequate ports and airports.

The economies of several Polynesian islands were largely dependent on subsistence agriculture and fishing; these islands possessed few natural resources, especially forestry and mineral resources. Partially for these reasons, the development of industry has been retarded. Some effort has been made to exploit the fish resources of the Polynesian Islands. Fish-processing canneries have been built on American Samoa. In order to take advantage of low wages on Tonga and the Cook Islands, small apparel manufacturing plants have been opened.

Robert R. McKay

Nauru Pages 1910, 1976

FOR FURTHER STUDY

Farrow, Cherry. *Pacific Odyssey: The Islands of the South Seas.* London: O'Mara, 1990.

Howard, Michael. *Mining, Politics, and Development in the South Pacific.* Boulder, Colo.: Westview Press, 1991.

McKnight, Tom L. *Oceania: The Geography*

of Australia, New Zealand and the Pacific Islands. Englewood Cliffs, N.J.: Prentice-Hall, 1995.

New Zealand Official Yearbook 1998. Wellington, New Zealand: Statistics New Zealand, 1998.

Nile, Richard. *Cultural Atlas of Australia, New Zealand, and the South Pacific.* New York: Facts on File, 1996.

Oliver, Douglas L. *Native Cultures of the Pacific Islands.* Honolulu: University of Hawaii Press, 1994.

Pacific Island Economies. Washington, D.C.: World Bank, 1996.

Patterson, Carolyn Bennett. "In the Far Pacific: At the Birth of Nations." *National Geographic* (October, 1986): 460-499.

Sahlins, Marshall David. *Islands of History.* Chicago: University of Chicago Press, 1985.

Theroux, Paul. *The Happy Islands of Oceania.* New York: G. P. Putnam's Sons, 1992.

TRANSPORTATION

AUSTRALIA

Australia is located a great distance from Europe and the United States and is almost as large as the United States. Distance means isolation, from other countries and from one place to another within the country. This isolation has shaped the human geography of Australia through its effects on immigration, trade, and even on the national character of Australians today.

EARLY SHIPPING. Early in the nineteenth century, Yankee shipbuilders developed what came to be regarded as the world's most beautiful sailing ships—the clippers. These graceful, slender wooden vessels with their tall masts and great areas of canvas were also the fastest sailing ships ever. Initially, they brought tea from China to America and Europe; later, they carried miners to California. Clipper design reached a peak of perfection in the 1850's, just as they were being replaced by steamships, especially for the Atlantic trade. On the long route from Europe to Australia, however, the clipper ships excelled.

Racing in the Roaring Forties—the fierce westerly winds of the south Atlantic—speeds of 400 miles (640 km.) a day were recorded. The sleek *Champion of the Seas*, designed by Donald McKay of Boston, claimed the record of 465 miles (744 km.) in twenty-four hours, on December 12, 1854, while sailing to Australia at 50 degrees south latitude. James Baines of Liverpool bought many McKay clippers for the Australia passage. His Black Ball Line held the record—from Liverpool, England, to Melbourne, Australia, in seventy-four days—but voyages through great stormy seas with huge areas of sail aloft were a frightening experience for many passengers. The rocky south coast of Australia was particularly dangerous, and many ships were wrecked there as they neared the end of the perilous voyage.

STEAMSHIPS. The invention of the steam engine in England led to the building of steamships, which eventually meant the end of sailing ships to Australia. The opening of the Suez Canal in 1869 shortened the route considerably, so that by 1914 the voyage between Europe and Australia took only five weeks. Coastal shipping around Australia also rapidly made the change from sail to steam, but today road and rail transport have largely overtaken coastal shipping in importance. Most Australian ships are now used for recreation or for commercial fishing. Sea transport remains significant for the transport of minerals, which are carried long distances around the coast by Australian registered vessels.

In 1999 the Australian merchant fleet comprised thirty-one bulk carriers, seventeen tankers, four container ships, nine general cargo, fourteen roll-on-roll-off cargo-landing barges, and one roll-on-roll-

Named after explorer Abel Tasman, the Tassie Ferry transports passengers and goods between Melbourne and the island of Tasmania. (Tom McKnight/Joan Clemons)

off passenger ship. Port Kembla and Gladstone handle the largest total weight of cargo, both loaded and discharged. The most important freight in terms of tonne-kilometers is iron ore and bauxite. Australian coastal freight in 1997-1998 comprised 52,522 kilotonnes, with Western Australia and Queensland accounting for half of the total.

Modern Australian ports use bulk handling for agricultural exports of sugar and wheat, as well as for mineral exports such as iron ore, coal, bauxite, and oil. Container ships are commonly used for transport of manufactured goods, both imports and exports. Australia has few long rivers, so shipping was of only minor importance for internal transportation in the nine-

teenth century, when some steamboats operated on the Murray River.

RAILROADS. The first railways—as they are called in Australia—were built by the government of each separate colony, which caused problems in the twentieth century. Victoria used the wide gauge of Ireland—5 feet, 3 inches—wanting large, safe trains for its passengers. The earliest lines from Melbourne to Bendigo and from Geelong to Ballarat, built in the 1860's, have massive stone bridges and other structures. New South Wales had difficulties crossing the Blue Mountains, but it chose the standard English gauge—4 feet, 8.5 inches—for its tracks. Many lines simply ran inland from a port to the hinterland. The colony of Queensland, which had chosen the economical narrow gauge of 3 feet, 6 inches, was the best example of this—lines ran inland from Brisbane, Maryborough, Bundaberg, Rockhampton, Townsville, and Cooktown, but these towns were connected only by steamship until the 1920's.

In the United States, construction of the railroad linked the continent, spread economic prosperity, and helped to create a powerful nation, but the colonial lines of Australia simply brought agricultural products or minerals to the ports for export overseas. By 1880 Australia had nearly 4,000 miles (6,400 km.) of railways, but there was no connectivity. Rail travelers going from Brisbane to Perth had to change trains five times because of the break of gauge, what one engineer called "the most lamentable engineering disaster in Australia." Railway construction boomed through the 1880's, with lines being laid "from nowhere to nowhere." The trains ran on coal, which Australia has in abundance. Modernization in the 1950's meant conversion to diesel trains and air-conditioned carriages.

The Commonwealth Government was responsible for construction of the rail line from Port Pirie to Kalgoorlie, since this rail link was part of the bargain made to secure the entry of Western Australia into the Commonwealth of Australia in 1901. The extended Perth-to-Adelaide line is now known as the Indian-Pacific and run as a private enterprise. Although the Australian National was sold to private consortia in late 1997, the Australian rail systems are still largely operated by the state governments. There are 20,500 miles (33,000 km.) of government railways in Australia. Queensland, with close to 6,200 miles (10,000 km.) of line, has the longest system; South Australia has only 75 miles (120 km.) of railway operated by the government.

Freight is the most important part of railway operations, earning over three billion Australian dollars per year for carrying over 200,000,000 metric tons per year. Passenger travel by rail accounts for almost 600 million journeys a year, with 97 percent being suburban trips. Suburban commuter trains are an important part of the infrastructure of Australian cities such as Melbourne, Sydney, and Brisbane.

Private freight railway lines have been built in remote parts of Australia to carry minerals such as iron ore and coal. In northern Queensland, a network of narrow-gauge tramways take cut cane to the nearby sugar mills. The Kuranda Scenic Railway in north Queensland is a small, picturesque tourist enterprise that takes

South Australia railway Page 1977

"Transportation" in Australian History

Transportation means the carrying of goods or people from one place to another, but there is also an older meaning for the word. Transportation, in the earliest days of European settlement in Australia, meant the exile of British convicts to the penal colony of New South Wales, a harsh punishment in the eyes of British lawmakers. Prisoners who received this sentence were transported to one of the colonies and not permitted to return to Great Britain. During the nineteenth century some 165,000 convicts were transported to the Australian colonies, especially in the peak years 1820 to 1840. The last British convicts were received in the colony of Western Australia in 1868.

Camels
Page 1978

CAMELS IN AUSTRALIA

Throughout the nineteenth century, places in the interior of Australia far from railroads were served by mules, pack-horses, and donkeys, but the largest area of the interior was served by teams of camels that could cope well with the arid, hot conditions and the tough vegetation. Camels were imported from Pakistan and used in exploration parties. They also were used for the construction of the Overland Telegraph line through the arid heart of Australia from Darwin to Adelaide in 1872. Although many camel drivers came from Pakistan, they were called Afghans. When camel teams were replaced in the 1930's by motorized transport, many of the camels were turned loose and became wild, roaming the center of Australia. The modern train from Adelaide to Alice Springs is named The Ghan in honor of the early camel teams and their masters.

passengers from the humid coastal plains of Cairns up a steep track to the Atherton Tableland town of Kuranda, passing waterfalls and affording spectacular views of coast, gorges, and rain forests.

Rail lines are still being built in Australia, which is unusual by world standards. A super-high-speed train has been proposed to link Sydney and Canberra, designed for speeds of up to 215 miles (350 km.) per hour. Rail links between Adelaide and Darwin have been proposed frequently.

Western Australia highway Page 1977

MOTOR ROADS. While other forms of transport declined in the twentieth century, roads increased in importance, and Australians rapidly adopted automobiles as the preferred mode of travel. In 1998 Australia had 479,000 miles (772,821 km.) of roads; the United States, which covers approximately the same area as Australia, has 4 million miles (6.42 million km.) of roads. Australia has an extensive road system for its small population, however. There are twenty-three people per kilometer of road in Australia, compared with forty-one people per kilometer in the United States.

Australia is flat and has a mild climate, so road construction should have been easier and less expensive than elsewhere, but the small population and the great distances to be covered added to the comparative cost per person and per kilometer. About 40 percent of Australia's roads are paved, compared to 60 percent in the United States. Outside the southeast part of Australia, roads are quite narrow, and maintenance is a persistent problem.

Australia has more than nine million passenger vehicles, one for every two people, making this country one of the world's most mobile. Counting buses and commercial vehicles, there were 630 vehicles per 1000 persons in 1997. Australian cities experience traffic congestion, especially Sydney, where there is only one bridge into the inner city; the outback roads are often empty.

There are one million commercial vehicles in Australia, and most domestic freight is carried by road transport. Huge road-trains carry live cattle throughout the Outback in Queensland and the Northern Territory

COBB AND COMPANY. The discovery of gold in 1851 in several places inland in New South Wales and Victoria led to a gold rush of miners from all over the world. Transportation was needed from the ports to the diggings, and the bullock teams laden with provisions were too slow. Horse-drawn coaches were the solution. In 1853 Freeman Cobb imported four thorough-brace coaches—light coaches with the body suspended on two long leather straps instead of metal springs. This made the passengers' ride more comfortable over the rutted tracks and reduced break-downs. Cobb employed experienced drivers from the United States, changed horses every 10 miles, and achieved speeds of 9 miles per hour between Melbourne and Castlemaine. Within a decade, the company expanded its operations to New South Wales and Queensland, carrying passengers, gold, and mail. Soon robbers, known as "bushrangers," began to hold up the coaches and steal gold shipments or rob passengers.

In the 1870's, Cobb and Company was one of the world's largest coaching firms, with six thousand horses working every day. When railways were built, Cobb continued to operate further inland. The last route, in inland Queensland, closed in 1924. Many of the coaches are preserved in Australian museums today.

AIR TRANSPORTATION. Aviation is a federal responsibility in Australia. The continent is well suited to air transport because of the great distances between cities and the fine weather. The absence of major mountains has contributed to Australian aviation's remarkable safety record. There are 108 airports in Australia, and more than ten thousand registered aircraft, about half of which are privately owned small airplanes. The first domestic air service in Australia began in the remote north of Western Australia in 1921. Early pioneers of aviation include Lawrence Hargrave, who invented the box-kite, the areofoil, and the rotary aircraft engine.

Sir Charles Kingsford-Smith is Australia's best-known aviator and an Australian national hero. With Charles Ulm, Kingsford-Smith was the first to cross the Pacific, flying in 1828 from Oakland to Brisbane in the Southern Cross, with landings at Hawaii and Fiji. They covered seventy-four hundred miles in eighty-three hours flying time. In 1934 Kingsford-Smith made the first west-to-east Pacific crossing. Six weeks later, Ulm was lost near Hawaii; in 1935, Kingsford-Smith vanished on a flight from England to Australia. The Sydney airport is named Kingsford-Smith Airport, and the Southern Cross is preserved at the Brisbane Airport. "Smithy's" portrait was on the old Australian $20 bill.

At the close of World War I, the flight from Britain to Australia took four weeks, and a flight from the United States to Australia took ten days. In 1999 one could fly nonstop from Los Angeles to Sydney in fifteen hours.

QANTAS. In 1920 Qantas (the Queensland and Northern Territory Air Service) was begun in outback Queensland. In 1933 the company became Qantas Empire Airways, an international service to the United Kingdom. Now Qantas is Australia's international airline, with an admirable safety record. Smaller airlines operate within Australia at the regional level. There are many private airplanes, since outback pastoralists are able to have airstrips on their properties. Private airstrips also enable visits by the Flying Doctor Service.

THE FLYING DOCTOR. A Presbyterian minister, the Reverend John Flynn, established the Australian Inland Mission in 1912 in the remote center of Australia, to provide medical assistance to isolated settlers in the lonely outback. He saw the possibilities of using aircraft to cover trackless expanses when there was a medical emergency, and of having the new "pedal radio" in all houses to keep in contact. In 1928 Flynn established the Aerial Medical Ser-

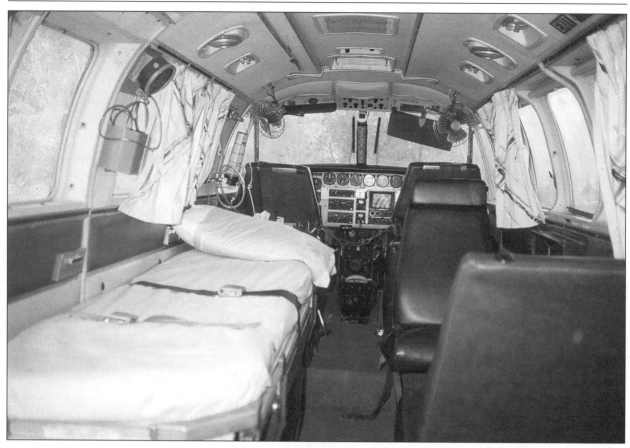

Interior of a Flying Doctor airplane. (Ray Sumner)

vice at Cloncurry in western Queensland, with one small plane leased from Qantas. In 1942 this became the Flying Doctor Service, and the prefix "Royal" was granted in 1955. This was the first comprehensive aerial medical organization in the world, and it continues to provide emergency medical care and routine health services to more than 100,000 people in remote and isolated parts of Australia. The Royal Flying Doctor Service maintains sixteen bases throughout Australia and one Medical Center, served by a fleet of forty-one aircraft.

Ray Sumner

FOR FURTHER STUDY

Austin, K. A. *Cobb and Co.: The Coaching Age in Australia, 1854-1924.* Adelaide, Australia: Rigby, 1977.

_____. *The Lights of Cobb and Co.* Adelaide, Australia: Rigby, 1967.

Barker, H. M. *Camels and the Outback.* Melbourne, Australia: Pitman, 1964.

Blainey, Geoffrey. *The Tyranny of Distance: How Distance Shaped Australia's History.* 4th ed. Melbourne, Australia: Sun, 1974.

"Crossing Australia in a Camel Caravan." *National Geographic* (July, 1989).

Fisher, Ron. *Wild Shores of Australia.* 2d ed. Washington, D.C.: National Geographic Society, 1998.

Gunn, John. *Along Parallel Lines: A History of the Railways of New South Wales, 1850-1986.* Carlton, Australia: Melbourne University Press, 1989.

_____. *The Defeat of Distance: Qantas, 1919-1939.* St Lucia: University of Queensland Press, 1985.

Kelly, Robert C., Debra Ewing, Stanton Doyle, and Denise Youngblood. *Australia Country Review 1999/2000*. Houston, Tex.: CountryWatch, 1999.

Parnell, N. M., and Trevor Boughton. *Flypast: A Record of Aviation in Australia*. Canberra, Australia: Australian Government Publishing Service, 1988.

PACIFIC ISLANDS

The Pacific Islands, also known as Oceania, can be divided into three groups: Melanesia, Micronesia, and Polynesia. Approximately thirty thousand islands make up the Pacific Island region of the Pacific Ocean. Fifty thousand years ago, the first inhabitants of the Pacific Islands are believed to have traveled by canoe from somewhere in Southeast Asia. It was not until the sixteenth century that the first Europeans arrived in the South Pacific. As modes of transportation have evolved, it has become somewhat easier for the Pacific Islands to be more fully integrated into the rest of the world.

While the Pacific region has remained far removed from many advanced centers of the world, the advent of air travel has made getting there take far less time. However, the cost of maintaining links with the Pacific Islands is high for the airlines. Ironically, because of the cost of air travel, the Pacific Islands may have been more isolated from the rest of the world in the 1990's than they were in the 1950's, when less expensive sea travel was more common.

Within the Pacific's many island groups, there are various modes of transportation from which to choose, including air travel, car, canoe, bicycle, motorboat, and freighter. An islander who wishes to travel to places such as Canada or Japan must use an international airline. Before air travel, steamships were the primary mode of transport for people traveling to or from the islands. Because the Pacific Island chains are quite spread out, air and sea travel are the only ways to travel from island to island. Automobiles are used primarily in urban centers. Except for New Zealand and Hawaii, there are no well-developed road systems in the Pacific Islands. The native population traditionally relied on the canoe for traveling short distances. For longer journeys, motorboats were used.

TERRAIN AND TRANSPORT. Most of the islands of the Pacific region are relatively small. The average size of a South Pacific island is approximately 23 square miles (60 sq. km.). In the Pacific, there are three types of islands: continental, volcanic, and coral. New Caledonia, New Guinea, and New Zealand are examples of continental islands. All continental islands were connected to an adjacent continent at one time in their history. The terrain of the continental islands varies, with some combination of mountains, plateaus, and alluvial plains appearing.

Volcanic islands can be found throughout the Pacific region. Most of the islands of Micronesia and Polynesia are of volca-

Automobiles lining up to board the ferry at Wellington, on New Zealand's North Island, to cross the Cook Strait to South Island. Ferryboat transportation provides a vital link between New Zealand's islands. (Corbis)

*Kilauea
Pages
1903, 2034*

nic origin. These islands are extremely rugged. One of the world's most active volcanoes, Kilauea, is located on the island of Hawaii. Coral formations make up a large number of Pacific Islands. While volcanic islands may rise high out of the Pacific Ocean, coral islands do not rise much above sea level. The island of Nauru, with

an elevation of approximately 210 feet (65 meters), is considered a raised coral island. Each type of island has its own challenges for inhabitants. Because of the limitation of useable land in the Pacific Islands, air and sea transport have become the most common.

MARINE TRANSPORTATION. The Pacific Islands are by their nature linked to the sea. The first people to settle in the Pacific Islands traveled by sea from Southeast Asia. These settlers had to be navigators at heart. The canoe is the oldest mode of transport in the region. The ancient sailing canoes could travel great distances. Paddling canoes were used to travel shorter distances. During the sixteenth century, the first Europeans arrived in the South Pacific by ship.

By the late nineteenth century, the United States, Great Britain, France, Spain, and Germany all had interests in the South Pacific. Shipping lanes to the Pacific Islands were created and used by traders, settlers, and missionaries. During the 1960's, several Pacific island groups became independent. In 1971 the Cook Islands, Fiji, Nauru, Tonga, and Western Samoa formed the South Pacific Forum in order to cooperate on such important issues as trade and international relations.

Before World War II, steamships were the primary mode of transport from Europe or the United States to the South Pacific. During the war, many steamships were sunk and that mode of transportation became obsolete. Outside of private yachts and expensive cruise ship tours, few passengers traveled by boat or ship to the Pacific Islands after the 1960's. Cargo was still transported, however, on container ships or freighters to places such as Japan, Australia, and New Zealand.

Except for Tokelau, all the Pacific Island countries and territories have ports. French Polynesia had four in the year 2000, including its capital, Papeete. It also had 4 cargo ships in its merchant marine fleet. Vanuatu had three ports in 2000, as well as 78 merchant marine ships, including cargo ships, tankers, and vehicle carriers. The Marshall Islands had only one port, Majuro, in 2000, but it had 143 merchant marine ships. In 2000 New Zealand had five ports and 10 merchant marine

ships. While the majority of Pacific Island nations had ports in 2000, only a few had navigable waterways, including Fiji, Kiribati, Papua New Guinea, and New Zealand. During the 1990's, Pacific Islanders called for more modern facilities for both travel and commercial expansion. While air traffic had grown, there still was a demand for ships, both to move cargo and for islanders and vacationers alike to seek adventure on the sea.

AIR TRAVEL. In the second half of the twentieth century, air travel became the most efficient mode of transportation to and from the Pacific Islands. In the year 2000 most air traffic flying to the Pacific Islands came from North America, Australia, and New Zealand. Air New Zealand

Containerized cargo piled up at Kiribati's chief port, Tarawa. (Tom McKnight/Joan Clemons)

and Qantas are but two of the major airlines with daily flights to the Pacific Islands.

While air travel makes it possible to travel long distances in relatively short periods of time, profitability was a major problem in 2000 for international airlines thinking about adding routes to the South Pacific, and also for Pacific Island countries and territories that were funding regional airlines. Pacific Island nations came to believe that regional cooperation initiatives were a viable solution to the profitability problem. In the mid-1990's, the Marshall Islands, Nauru, Tuvalu, and Kiribati agreed to share aircraft in order to cut the massive losses that they had been incurring. Other Pacific Island nations were considering the same solution during the late 1990's.

While such well-known destinations as Hawaii, Tahiti, Fiji, and New Zealand were connected to the outside world in 2000 by international airlines, many less well-known South Pacific destinations made use of small commuter planes. Most Pacific Island countries and territories have more than one airport. The only territory that did not have an airport in 2000 was Tokelau: It was served by an amphibious aircraft from Samoa that had to land in a lagoon. In 1999 Papua New Guinea had 492 airports, of which 473 had unpaved runways. New Zealand had more than one hundred airports in 1999, forty-four of which had paved runways.

The Cook Islands are spread out over a vast distance in the South Pacific. In 1999 they had seven airports. Only one domestic airline, Air Rarotonga, served the Cook Islands in the year 2000, making three daily flights from Rarotonga to Atiutaki. In Fiji, several airlines operated among the principal islands. There were twenty-five airports in Fiji in 1999. Two of the local airlines that served Fiji were Air Fiji and Sun-

flower Airlines. The principal islands of French Polynesia were served primarily by Air Tahiti. In 1999 French Polynesia had forty-five airports. Air Moorea and a number of smaller charter airlines also provided occasional air transport in French Polynesia.

ROADS AND MOTOR VEHICLES. The size of a particular island, and how advanced economically was the country or territory of which it is a part, have greatly influenced what kind of highway system could be built on that island. Since New Zealand is one of the most developed countries in the world, let alone in the Pacific region, it has a far more elaborate highway system than any of its Pacific Island neighbors. Although the terrain is primarily mountainous, which makes road construction both hazardous and expensive, New Zealand has invested a large sum of money in order to have first-rate roads. It has spent more on the construction of roads than on any other mode of transport. By the late 1990's, New Zealand had more than 57,000 miles (92,000 km.) of roads, almost 60 percent of which were paved. During the same time period, New Zealand had a total of 1.6 million cars and 315,000 trucks or buses.

By comparison, Papua New Guinea—which is also mountainous—had only about 12,000 miles (20,000 km.) of roads, only 400 miles (686 km.) of which were paved. The terrain and a poor economy have worked against Papua New Guinea having a truly adequate highway system. Still, several towns are linked by roads. The longest road in Papua New Guinea is the Highlands Highway, which runs 350 miles (563 km.) from Lae to Mount Hagen in the central highlands.

Motor vehicles are a common mode of transportation in the urban areas of the Pacific Islands. Papeete, located on the island of Tahiti and the capital of French

Polynesia, had a four-lane freeway connecting it to the suburbs in 2000. The area around Papeete had become so urbanized that it took commuters as much as two hours to go to and from work during the week. While other Polynesian islands remained less developed, Tahiti became the hub of the area and one of its most popular tourist locations. Because land is at such a premium, the introduction of roads and motor vehicles created major problems on islands, such as Tahiti, where economic growth necessitated their use. In Honolulu, Hawaii, with a metropolitan population of more than 850,000, traffic congestion was extremely heavy.

The Polynesian country of Tonga is a small, relatively poor island country, comprising an archipelago of 170 islands, of which only 36 are inhabited. With a population of little more than 102,000 in the year 2000 Tonga had 420 miles (680 km.) of highways, only 115 miles (184 km.) of which were paved.

RAILROADS. The small size of the islands and the hazardous terrain have made rail travel impractical on the majority of the Pacific Islands. The most sophisticated rail system of the South Pacific exists in New Zealand. In 1993 New Zealand Rail was privatized and became known as Tranz Rail. Tranz Rail carried 11.57 million passengers and 11.5 million metric tons of freight in 1997. A twenty-four-hour freight link between Auckland and Christchurch was started in 1994. In Fiji, a 370-mile (597 km.) rail line was run by a government-controlled corporation in 2000.

New Zealand train station Page 1978

"Le Truck," a popular form of urban transportation in Tahiti's crowded capital, Papeete. (Tom McKnight/Joan Clemons)

New Zealand's TranzAlpine Express. (New Zealand Tourism Board)

The only other rail line of note in the South Pacific was in Nauru. In the year 2000 it had a 2.4-mile-long (3.9 km.) rail line that transported phosphates. Without financial backing from government or overseas investors, it is unlikely that rail transport will make inroads into the Pacific Islands in the twenty-first century, where size or terrain make it already a difficult proposition.

Jeffry Jensen

FOR FURTHER STUDY

Gascoigne, Ingrid. *Papua New Guinea.* New York: Marshall Cavendish, 1998.

Henderson, Andrea Kovacs, project ed. *Asia and Oceania.* Vol. 4 in *Worldmark Encyclopedia of the Nations.* 9th ed. Detroit: Gale Research, 1998.

NgCheong-Lum, Roseline. *Tahiti.* New York: Marshall Cavendish, 1997.

Smelt, Roselynn. *New Zealand.* New York: Marshall Cavendish, 1998.

Stanley, David. *South Pacific Handbook.* Emeryville, Calif.: Avalon Travel, 2000.

Stevenson, Robert E. and Frank H. Talbot, eds. *Islands.* Emmaus, Pa.: Rodale Press, 1994.

Ward, R. Gerard. "Remote Runways: Air Transport and Distance in Tonga." *Australian Geographical Studies* 36, no. 2 (July, 1998): 177-186.

The World Factbook 2000. Washington, D.C.: Central Intelligence Agency, 2000.

TRADE

AUSTRALIA

From the earliest days of European settlement in the late eighteenth century, Australia was regarded as a place for the extraction and exploitation of natural resources. Throughout the nineteenth century, the British colonies on the Australian continent maintained this typical trade relationship with the home country, exporting raw materials and natural products and importing manufactured goods.

Wool was the first commercially successful product exported from Australia, soon followed by wheat and animal hides. The invention of the steamship and refrigeration expanded the exports to include frozen meat and fruits. Even after gaining independence, Australia remained a member of the British commonwealth of nations and participated in trade agreements, predominantly with the United Kingdom. Wool and wheat continued to dominate Australian exports until the 1960's, when discoveries of rich mineral deposits occurred. Iron ore and coal quickly became valuable exports, and new markets in Asia overtook traditional European markets, especially as the Japanese economy rebounded in the 1960's. At the close of the twentieth century, Australian trade still maintained this pattern of exports, with minerals and agricultural products dominating exports.

As a high-income economy, Australia has a high demand for manufactured goods. This presents the country with the economic problem of an imbalance of trade: The value of imports is greater than the value of exports. Although Australia's exports of goods and services grew steadily in the late 1990's, the country continued to record a negative balance of trade. In 1999 Australia had a trade deficit of $A16.8 billion. Australia imports large volumes of consumer goods, such as textiles, toys, books, entertainment and leisure products, and shoes. It also imports such capital goods as telecommunications equipment, aircraft, and oil. In 1999 the largest Australian imports by value were automobiles, computers, and petroleum.

The role of Great Britain as a trading partner has been greatly reduced. In 1999 the major countries to which Australia exported goods and services were Japan, the United States, New Zealand, South Korea, and Taiwan. The major countries supplying imports to Australia were the United States, Japan, China, Germany, and the United Kingdom. The United States accounted for 20 percent of Australian imports in 1999, with a value of $A21 billion. In return, Australia exported only $A8.4 billion worth of goods to the United States. Germany, China, and the United Kingdom also export a higher value of goods to Australia than they import. Countries with which Australia had a positive trade balance include Japan, New Zealand, South Korea, and Taiwan.

This imbalance of imported goods and services over exported goods and services is the result of several uniquely Australian factors. The manufacturing industries of Australia have the disadvantages of a small domestic market and a long distance to overseas markets, together with an Australian system of high wages and strong trade unionism. On the other hand, Australia has the advantages of being a stable and democratic country with a highly educated, urbanized workforce and a rich resource base. Australian agriculture and mining are highly productive, using the most modern technology and employing only 3 percent of the workforce.

Australia has encouraged the growth of high technology and information technology, as well as tourism, which is regarded as an export industry. The Sydney Olympic Games in 2000 provided invaluable opportunities for advertising Australia's attractions to the world. Australia has become increasingly popular as a film location, which also enhances the music, software, and associated industries. Foreign companies have invested strongly in Australian industry, especially the United States and Japan. Overseas students are another growing sector of the Australian service economy.

INTERNATIONAL TRADE AGREEMENTS. The Australian government actively seeks new markets for Australian goods and services through trade agreements at different levels. The necessity for these kinds of trade agreements became obvious in Australia in the 1960's when access to the traditional market, the United Kingdom, was restricted by that country's joining the European Economic Community (later called the European Union). This forced Australia to look for new markets, especially in Asia, where several countries had rapidly developing economies. In bilateral initiatives, Australia seeks to make trade deals with individual countries. At a regional level, Australia is a member of the Asia-Pacific Economic Cooperation (APEC), which was established in 1989. It has twenty-one member countries. Its aims include free and open trade and investment among member countries by the year 2020.

Other important trade agreements are the Asian Free Trade Area (AFTEC) and the Australia and New Zealand Closer Economic Relations Trade Agreement (CER). Trade negotiations are also in progress with South American regional trade groups. In 1986 Australia formed the Cairns Group, eighteen agricultural exporting countries, mostly on the Pacific Rim, whose aim is fair trade in agricultural exports. At the global level, Australia is a member of the World Trade Organization.

ASIAN MARKETS. Australia has pursued Asian markets vigorously, and in 1999 seven of the top ten markets for Australian exports were Asian countries. Japan is still the largest market for Australian goods, but these are raw materials, whose price can be manipulated by the buyer or undercut by other supplier countries. Trade with Europe has declined comparatively, as a result of increased trade with Asia. As a reflection of closer ties with Asia, immigration to Australia has changed from predominantly European until the 1970's to predominantly from Asian countries in 2000. The reliance on Asian markets is precarious, however, as was shown when the Asian financial and economic downturn in the late 1990's caused the value of Australian exports to Asia to decrease sharply.

Ray Sumner

FOR FURTHER STUDY

Blainey, Geoffrey. *The Tyranny of Distance: How Distance Shaped Australia's History.* 4th ed. Melbourne, Australia: Sun, 1974.

Bryan, Dick, and Michael Rafferty. *The Global Economy in Australia: Global Integration and National Economic Policy.* St. Leonards, Australia: Allen & Unwin, 1999.

Dyster, Barrie, and David Meredith. *Australia in the International Economy in the Twentieth Century.* New York: Cambridge University Press, 1990.

Islam, Iyanatul, and Chowdhury, Anis. *Asia Pacific Economies: An Analytical Survey.* London: Routledge, 1997.

Langmore, John, and David Peetz, eds. *Wealth, Poverty, and Survival: Australia in the World.* Boston: Allen & Unwin, 1983.

Meredith, David, and Barrie Dyster. *Australia in the Global Economy: Continuity and Change.* New York: Cambridge University Press, 1999.

Wiseman, John Richard. *Global Nation? Australia and the Politics of Globalisation.* New York: Cambridge University Press, 1998.

PACIFIC ISLANDS

The Pacific Islands consist of more than twenty thousand separate islands, ranging from lone specks of barely visible rock to landmasses covering thousands of square miles. They are traditionally divided into three categories. Melanesia, meaning the "black islands," is located in the southwestern Pacific Ocean off the northern and eastern coast of Australia and includes New Guinea, Fiji, and the Solomon chain. Micronesia, meaning the "small islands," is situated just south of Japan and contains key strategic military installations on Guam and Wake Island. Polynesia, meaning "many islands," stretches all the way from the northern Pacific Islands of Midway and Hawaii to the southern tip of New Zealand. These latter islands historically have relied on agricultural exports such as coffee, bananas, pineapples, and coconut oil and dominate the region's economic infrastructure, but with the advent of jet air travel, a global tourist industry has transformed many of the islands, including Fiji, Tahiti, Samoa, New Zealand, and the Hawaiian chain, into international vacation getaways.

EARLY TRADE CONTACTS. Approximately two million years ago during the Pleistocene period, sea levels were low and landmasses were connected. About fifty thousand years ago, people began to emigrate from Southeast Asia to the Pacific Islands, facilitating the evolution of civilizations in the region. Beginning with the early settlements in Australia and New Guinea, various tribes systematically moved outward from Melanesia into New Caledonia, Fiji, Tonga, Samoa, and Hawaii; others sailed north and relocated in parts of Micronesia as well. The development of outrigger canoes and the sail helped spread agricultural commodities such as sweet potatoes, coconuts, and pigs

Papua New Guinea market Page 1979

throughout the region, and profitable trade relations developed throughout the chains. Trade networks stretched from Fiji to Tahiti and connected New Caledonia and New Hebrides. In Hawaii before European colonization, the islanders formed an interdependent trade system that furnished various communities with goods and services from each inhabited island.

The introduction of European traders drastically altered the nature of trade relations in the Pacific Islands. While earlier Spanish, Portuguese, and Dutch missions established the first western contact in the Pacific Islands as far south as New Zealand, the explorations of English captain James Cook from 1768 to 1779 revolutionized trade in the region and expedited the integration of the region into the international political economy. Cook and others discovered that the islands contained vast quantities of sandalwood, which could be exchanged in China for a handsome profit. Indigenous resources were quickly exploited and devoured as islanders swapped sandalwood for European cloth, guns, tobacco, and liquor.

This trade also produced profitable networks among the islands, since Europeans often paid for sandalwood with indigenous products. In Melanesia, traders obtained tortoise shells in the Solomons and exchanged them for pigs in Fiji. These pigs, along with stores of tortoise shells and whale teeth, were used to purchase sandalwood in the Vanuatu islands, advancing the growth of interisland exchanges. However, these contacts also intensified military conflict and political unification in the islands. Many island chiefs desired firearms to further their own ambitions, and the sandalwood trade enhanced the distribution of guns in the region.

Hawaii's King Kamehameha I was able to consolidate his hold over the Hawaiian Islands after securing control of hundreds of muskets, some small cannons, and sailing vessels from European merchants. In Tahiti, Tu sold pigs to Australia for weapons, conquered his opponents, and established a kingship. This same process occurred in Fiji and the Marquesas, as pigs were swapped for firearms. Although the sandalwood trade had been depleted by the 1860's, it helped integrate the Pacific economies and led to a vast movement of people and products from New Zealand to Hawaii.

As a result of European and U.S. imperialism during the nineteenth century, the Pacific Islands were systematically incorporated into the global economy. However, for the most part, this process retarded development and led to the emergence of one-crop export economies, tourism, and military bases in the region. As a result, much of the wealth was drained from the local economy and many islands became structurally dependent upon foreign trade for their survival.

MICRONESIA. These islands are often referred to as the small islands, are sparsely populated, and for the most part, play an inconsequential role in the global economy. Wake Island is an emergency military base for ships and aircraft. The Marshall Islands contain a plentiful supply of fish among their coral reefs, but with the exception of coconuts, few plants can survive in the sandy soil. The Mariana Islands possess considerable precious mineral resources, including phosphate and manganese ore, but are mainly used to provide the United States with naval bases.

Guam is the most vibrant island in Micronesia. It is a principal vacation spot for Japanese tourists, and since it has been established as a duty-free port, it has emerged as an important trading and clearing house in the South Pacific. In addition to providing the United States with one of its most integral military bases in the region, Guam benefits from a fruitful fishing and ship-building industry and exports various textiles and clothing goods. Overall, Micronesia's small population base has failed to attract or generate large-scale world trade.

MELANESIA. Located off the northern coast of Australia, the Melanesian islands are situated in some of the most strategic shipping lanes in the Pacific Ocean. As a result, these islands experienced fierce amphibious battles during World War II. However, most of the islanders continue to rely on subsistence farming for their livelihood, and this region remains highly underdeveloped. The Solomon Islands export fish, timber, and coconut meat to Japan, but they are dependent upon imports from Australia, Great Britain, Malaysia, Singapore, and Japan for most of their food supply, manufactured goods, and fuel. The Bismarck Archipelago suffers from the same problems. Its export economy consists of coconut oil, cocoa, coffee, palm oil, and timber, but most of its inhabitants are committed to traditional tribal ways and small-scale farming.

New Guinea and Fiji have enjoyed a limited economic takeoff and have sustained higher levels of economic development, especially from the rise of tourism in the area. New Guinea benefits from profitable cacao, coffee, and coconut exports, and with the discovery of copper and gold in the 1970's, it also has a lucrative mining industry. Oil and natural gas reserves have been uncovered as well, but overall, this island's economy is still dominated by small-level subsistence farming.

Fiji's major industry is tourism, and its airport at Nadi is an important hub for South Pacific travel. Other islanders devote their time and energy to agriculture. Fijians export sugarcane and coconuts, along with manufactured products such as

beer, cigarettes, and cement. While these islands contain some of the world's best natural harbors and are stationed alongside some of the Pacific's busiest shipping lanes, Fiji's main economic resources continue to be its exotic beaches, remote island locations, and comfortable tropical climate.

POLYNESIA. The Polynesian islands are the heart of the Pacific Island economy. Based on a long-standing, interactive, historical relationship with Asia, the United States, and Europe, this region possesses the most modernized infrastructure and has prospered from a more diversified economic background than the other islands. It is the cornerstone for the Pacific tourist industry, and its import-export trade has created many profitable links throughout the global economy.

Some islands, however, are still quite similar to other underdeveloped sites in the territory. Midway Island has few residents, and its only function is to serve as a military and communications base for the United States. Despite exporting stores of bananas and coconuts to New Zealand and Australia, most of Tonga's inhabitants still practice subsistence farming. The Marquesas share a comparable situation. Following the construction of luxury hotels and a jet airport in the 1960's, American Samoa has experienced a limited economic takeoff due to the rise of tourism. Tuna canning and fish exports have also sparked growth on the island. Tahiti has reaped some of the same benefits as Samoa. Long considered a tropical paradise, jet air travel has allowed Tahiti to become one of the most exotic vacation spots in the world.

Hawaii and New Zealand are the two most developed and sophisticated economies among the Pacific Islands. Hawaii's economy has been directly tied to the United States since the mid-nineteenth century, leading to formal annexation of the island in 1898 and statehood in 1959. Initially explored and settled by U.S. shippers and sugarcane plantation owners, Hawaii has evolved into the most important military base in the Pacific, and a large percentage of its people are employed in a rapidly expanding tourist industry. While some islanders remain extremely critical of the U.S. presence in the islands and claim that the United States has destroyed indigenous rights in exchange for a system of dependency that leaves countless Hawaiians in a perpetual state of poverty, these islands are the official U.S. outpost in the Pacific Ocean.

Sugar and pineapples are Hawaii's two principal agricultural exports. By the 1980's, more than one million tons of sugarcane were produced annually on the islands of Oahu, Kauai, Maui, and Hawaii, and the Polynesians are largely responsible for introducing sugar into the Western economy. Pineapple production emerged as a profitable crop following the creation of the Hawaiian Pineapple Company by James Dole in 1901. As a result, Honolulu has one of the largest fruit-canning businesses in the world. Other products, such as Kona coffee and macadamia nuts, are becoming increasingly important to Hawaii's export economy.

An insufficient supply of cheap power and the lack of raw materials has hindered Hawaii's manufacturing base, and most of the islands' finished products are related to its primary economic activity—tourism. Many clothing manufacturers produce Hawaiian shirts for the millions of tourists who frequent the islands every year. Other goods include jewelry, local handicrafts, souvenirs, and indigenous artifacts that compete in the billion-dollar tourist industry. The spread of tourism has sparked considerable controversy in the islands because many activists argue that the industry has decimated local culture and destroyed natural landmarks, but it continues to provide the people with their most consistent economic activity.

Largely a pastoral and agricultural nation, New Zealand has achieved the most significant economic success of any of the Pacific Islands. New Zealand farmers benefit from a mild climate and have efficiently utilized modern scientific farming techniques to create a profitable business in meat, dairy, and wool exports. Sheep provide a variety of products, including wool, mutton, sausage casings, and animal fat. Beef and dairy cattle also help fuel the nation's economy. Other crops include barley, wheat, and potatoes, and the country is one of the world's most important suppliers of kiwi fruit.

Fishing, forestry, and manufacturing are also significant in New Zealand's economy. Barracuda, lobster, red cod, and snapper represent key exports, and oyster farming is becoming more prominent. Timber grows quickly in North Island's volcanic region, and the nation exports considerable amounts of pine and evergreen wood. Despite its limited supply of mineral resources, New Zealand has developed a manufacturing base that includes steel, aluminum, iron, and textile production. Its exports are sent primarily to Australia, Japan, Great Britain, and the United States, and it conducts only a small amount of trade with other Pacific Islands.

Robert D. Ubriaco, Jr.

FOR FURTHER STUDY

Belich, James. *Making Peoples: A History of the New Zealanders from Polynesian Settlement to the End of the Nineteenth Century.* Honolulu: University of Hawaii Press, 1996.

Diamond, Jared. *Guns, Germs, and Steel: The Fates of Human Societies.* Reprint. New York: W. W. Norton, 1999.

Howe, K. R. *Where the Waves Fall.* Reprint. Honolulu: University of Hawaii Press, 1991.

McKnight, Tom L. *Oceania: The Geography of Australia, New Zealand, and the Pacific Islands.* Englewood Cliffs, N.J.: Prentice-Hall, 1995.

Price, A. Grenfell. *The Explorations of Captain James Cook in the Pacific: As Told by Selections of His Own Journals, 1768-1779.* New York: Dover Publications, 1971.

Salmond, Anne. *Two Worlds: First Meetings Between Maori and Europeans, 1642-1772.* Honolulu: University of Hawaii Press, 1991.

Shineberg, Dorothy. *The People Trade: Pacific Island Laborers and New Caledonia, 1865-1930.* Honolulu: University of Hawaii Press, 1999.

Stephen, Ann, ed. *Pirating the Pacific: Images of Trade, Travel, and Tourism.* Haymarket, Australia: Powerhouse Books, 2000.

Thomas, Nicholas. *Entangled Objects: Exchange, Material Culture, and Colonialism in the Pacific.* Cambridge, Mass.: Harvard University Press, 1991.

Trask, Haunani Kay. *From a Native Daughter: Colonialism and Sovereignty in Hawaii.* Monroe, Maine: Common Courage Press, 1993.

COMMUNICATIONS

AUSTRALIA

Satellite tracking station Page 1979

Australia, the only country in the world that occupies a whole continent, is approximately the same size as the continental United States in landmass. It is the sixth-largest nation in area, but is sparsely populated. Australia is a nation of extreme differences: 80 percent of the population live within 125 miles of the eastern shoreline and the southwestern coast of Western Australia; the rest of the people live in the remote rural area referred to as the Outback, which is approximately 90 percent of Australia's landmass.

Communications have always been a major concern for the people of Australia because of the remoteness of the rural population. The federal government played a prominent role in the development of the wire communications system in rural Australia. Since the completion of the Overland Telegraph system in 1872, the government has maintained and strengthened the telegraph and telephone infrastructure. It is a technical challenge for residents in the remote areas.

New technologies are embraced with enthusiasm by Australians. Color television, videocassette recorders, and mobil telephones are common. Computer technology is growing in acceptance, especially in the urban community. The agricultural area has not been as receptive to new technologies, but has taken a keen interest in the world trade in wool, which is one of Aus-

tralia's main export commodities. The Internet is well accepted in Australian society and continues to gain interest groups.

During the 1990's the Australian government worked to ensure that the rural community was not left off the Information Superhighway and established projects for public access to online services. In 1997 the federal government's Information Policy Advisory Council (IPAC) released a report that dealt with the rapid change of the new technologies and the telecommunications industry. The IPAC report was to stimulate interest among rural society in the benefits of the advanced communications systems. As a result, the Australian government established telecenters across the country.

Telecenters, copied after the systems that were developed in Scandinavia in the 1980's, are publicly accessible spaces furnished with computers, fax machines, printers, satellite dishes, photocopiers, Internet connections, and software. The telecenters were established in abandoned or unused buildings that were structurally sound. Each telecenter is funded by public and private bodies and has a coordinator who makes sure things run smoothly.

MEDIA. Australians enjoy the same types of media that are available in the rest of the world. Persons who live in the cities have access to more media than those who

Broken Hill headquarters of Australia's School of the Air, which uses radio communications to reach school-age children in the Outback. (Tom McKnight/Joan Clemons)

live in rural regions. In the year 2000, approximately 99 percent of Australian homes had television sets, and there were nearly 29 million radios. Of the four hundred radio stations in the country, a little more than half are commercial operations. Public funding pays for the noncommercial stations.

By the year 2000 Australia had twelve metropolitan daily newspapers, with a combined daily circulation of nearly 2.5 million. The *Melbourne Herald Sun* had the largest daily circulation, and the *Sydney Sunday Telegraph* had the largest Sunday circulation. Australia also had 38 smaller regional daily newspapers, and 155 suburban newspapers that were distributed from once to three times a week.

Magazines play a major role in the media process for Australians. Thirty dominant magazines have circulations ranging from 100,000 to more than a million copies per issue. There also are many minor magazines that serve a limited clientele. In the year 2000 the largest-circulation magazine in Australia was *The Women's Weekly*, and the biggest magazine publisher was Australian Consolidated Press.

The Rupert Murdoch News Limited chain was Australia's largest, with eleven metropolitan newspapers, followed by the Fairfax family chain, which owns the oldest capital city publication—the *Sydney Morning Herald*—which began publication in 1842.

BROADCASTING. The electronic media, radio, television, and online communications are regulated by the Australian Broadcasting Authority. This group oversees the rules and regulations of both public and private operations. The Australian Broadcasting Authority functions in the same manner as does the Federal Communications Commission in the United States. Ownership and limiting foreign investment is of major concern for this authority.

There are two nationwide public broadcasting systems in Australia. One broadcasts in English and the other has programs in other languages. Both systems are financially supported by the government, but are free from government control of programs. The Special Broadcasting Service of Australia broadcasts both radio and television programs in approximately seventy languages. The service supplies limited news information to overseas news outlets.

The Australian Broadcasting Corporation, the larger of the two public broadcasting systems, has four radio networks, a television service, and the short-wave radio international service, Radio Australia. The corporation has a vast news-gathering capability and provides a major service for international communications. The federal government finances the operation and guarantees editorial and programming freedom.

Australia has three national commercial television networks that operate in a similar manner as those in the United States. They have affiliates throughout the country that also broadcast regional and local programming. Both the public and private television networks buy programs from local and international suppliers.

Australia's media controls itself by self-regulation. The Australian Press Council, which is financed by the magazine and newspaper industry, responds to complaints made by the general public. The council's main concern is that of freedom of the press, and they aim to address any issue that threatens press freedom. The Australian Journalists' Association section of the Media, Entertainment and Arts Alliance reviews material that is viewed, listened to, and read. They are bound by a code of ethics to evaluate materials in a prudent, honest manner. It is a voluntary independent review.

TELEPHONE SYSTEMS. Australia's telephone system underwent a major change in direction, from a monopoly to competition. There are two national telecommunication carriers and three national mobile telephone carriers. In 1997 the federal government allowed unlimited competition for telephone usage similar to the methods instituted in the United States in the early 1980's. The federal government's telephone regulatory agency, Austel, strictly regulates everything that deals with the telephone industry. Australians enjoy the same benefits from their telephones that people around the world enjoy. They have call-waiting, third-party-conference calls, free calls (008 numbers like the U.S. 800 numbers), and the other normal additions that are supplied by the telephone provider. The mobile telephone service is exceptionally important for the rural people of Australia because of the vastness and general openness of the land.

The Australian telephone industry continues to grow strongly. In the three years after the federal government deregulated the telecommunications industry, revenue increased by more than 40 percent, and usage was up substantially. The five major telephone carriers have several subcarriers that provide regional support for the citizens of Australia. The subcarriers are investing in the infrastructure. It is estimated that about six hundred Internet service providers support the telecommunications industry.

Continued on page 2047

Brisbane, the state capital, major port of Queensland, and Australia's third-largest city, was built along the banks of the Brisbane River, twelve miles (19 km.) inland from Moreton Bay. (Corbis)

River near Honiara, the capital of Guadalcanal in the Solomon Islands. (Tom McKnight/Joan Clemons)

Hawaii's Seven Sacred Pools on the island of Maui. (PhotoDisc)

Honolulu, the largest city in the Hawaiian Islands and one of the largest and most prosperous cities in the Pacific Islands. (PhotoDisc)

The Bay of Islands, the site of New Zealand's first permanent European settlement, is located on the east coast in the Northland region of North Island. (New Zealand Tourism Board)

Rugged coast of Kauai in the Hawaiian Islands. (Digital Stock)

Kilauea's great, perpetually simmering, caldera. (Clyde L. Rasmussen)

McMurdo Station, a U.S. station built during the International Geophysical Year (1957-1958), is situated on the east side of the Ross Sea off Victoria Land in McMurdo Sound. (AP/Wide World Photos)

The Marquesas Islands' Ua Pu is one of ten volcanic islands in the Marquesas group, which is part of French Polynesia in the South Pacific. (American Stock Photography)

Milford Sound's Mitre Peak, part of New Zealand's spectacular Fiordland National Park, rises 5,560 feet (1,695 meters) out of the sea. (New Zealand Tourism Board)

Mount Tautuapae on the island of Mooréa. (American Stock Photography)

*North Island,
New Zealand.*
(PhotoDisc)

The Northern Territory's unusual rock formations include the Olgas, a group of isolated sandstone monoliths in the territory's southwestern corner. (Tom McKnight/Joan Clemons)

Kakadu Waterfall in Australia's Kakadu National Park is part of a World Heritage Site. (Corbis)

An ash plume from the Pagan volcano in the Marianas is visible in this September, 1984, photograph of the Pacific Ocean taken from the space shuttle Discovery. (Corbis)

Perth, the capital of Western Australia and Australia's westernmost major city. (Digital Stock)

Papua New Guinea's Rouna Falls, near Port Moresby. (Tom McKnight/Joan Clemons)

Upper reaches of the Snowy River in New South Wales, Australia. (Tom McKnight/Joan Clemons)

The Snowy River below its main dam. (Tom McKnight/Joan Clemons)

South Island's Lake Tekapo, one of the Southern Alps's many glacier-fed lakes in New Zealand. (Corbis)

Sydney's harbor is famed for its futuristic opera house, designed by Danish architect Joern Utzon. (PhotoDisc)

Stewart Island's Paterson Inlet. (Clyde L. Rasmussen)

Tahiti tourist resort. (Clyde L. Rasmussen)

Tahiti is a lush mountainous country, in which scenes such as this are not uncommon. (Tom McKnight/Joan Clemons)

New Zealand's largest glacier, Tasman, flows down the eastern slopes of Mount Cook on South Island. (Digital Stock)

Hot springs in New Zealand's Tongariro National Park. (New Zealand Tourism Board)

Located on the shores of a natural harbor on the southern tip of New Zealand's North Island, Wellington is built on hilly terrain similar to that of San Francisco. (New Zealand Tourism Board)

One of most unusual physiological sites in the world is the Pinnacles Desert in Western Australia's Nambung National Park. The "pinnacles" are large limestone pillars rising from a field of yellow sand. (Corbis)

KEY DATES IN AUSTRALIAN COMMUNICATIONS

1803:   First newspaper, *Sydney Gazette and New South Wales Advertiser,* appears.

1842:   First capital city newspaper, *Sydney Morning Herald Daily,* is established.

1843:   First rural newspaper, *Maitland Mercury,* is established.

1872:   Overland Telegraph is completed.

1923:   Shortwave radio is introduced.

1927:   Radio is introduced.

1932:   Australian Broadcasting Commission Act establishes national broadcasting presence.

1950:   Black and white television is introduced nationally.

1953:   Television Act of 1953 establishes broadcast regulations.

1974:   Color television is introduced.

1992:   Federal government initiates Telecenter program.

1997:   National telephone service is deregulated.

2000:   One hundred Australian newspapers have Web sites on the Internet.

The impact on Australian society of new technologies, including the various levels of telecommunications, computers, and the Internet, is hard to forecast, but at the expansion rate of the late 1990's, it appears to be great. The World Wide Web has made the world a smaller place, because almost everything is just a fingertip away.

Earl P. Andresen

FOR FURTHER STUDY

Cunningham, Stuart, and Elizabeth Jacka. *Australian Television and International Mediascapes.* New York: Cambridge University Press, 1996.

Cunningham, Stuart, and Graeme Turner, eds. *The Media in Australia: Industries, Texts, Audiences.* St. Leonards, Australia: Allen & Unwin, 1993.

Docherty, James C. *Historical Dictionary of Australia.* Landham, Md.: Scarecrow Press, 1999.

Lewis, Glen, and Graeme Osborne. *Commu-nication Traditions in Twentieth-Century Australia.* New York: Oxford University Press, 1996.

Moyal, Ann Mozley. *Clear Across Australia: A History of Telecommunications.* Melbourne, Australia: Nelson, 1984.

Shawcross, William. *Murdoch: The Making of a Media Empire.* New York: Touchstone Books, 1997.

INFORMATION ON THE WORLD WIDE WEB

A good starting place for Internet research on Australian communications is the National Library of Australia Web page, which provides information from the national government as well as from each of the separate states and territories. (www.nia.gov.au/niac/mfm/nplan.html)

PACIFIC ISLANDS

The communications systems found among the scattered islands of the Pacific Ocean are shaped by the unique geographic situation in which they exist. These far-flung islands, many of them tiny coral atolls with only a few hundred people, are separated by thousands of miles of open ocean. Communications between them have generally been difficult, and the low population densities prevented the development of economies of scale that reduced communications costs in larger societies.

OBSTACLES TO COMMUNICATION. Communications among the islands have been further complicated by the enormous variety of languages within the region. Linguists estimate that as many as twelve hundred languages have been spoken in the Pacific Islands. However, many of these languages have an extremely restricted range, often confined to a few hundred people on one or two coral islands. Almost none of them had a written form before the arrival of Western missionaries. Many of these languages are considered to be moribund, with no children learning them and their use restricted to an ever-shrinking elderly population. It is likely that as many as half of these languages will be dead by the year 2050.

English, in both British and American forms, has become a trade language in many areas of the Pacific Islands, enabling people from various tribes to do business. Japanese serves a similar function in many areas of the western Pacific, particularly in those islands given to Japan as trust territories after World War I. French is used in a few islands controlled by France. Although many people continue to use their native languages at home, it is not uncommon for those who want to enter the wider world to speak English exclusively.

Two striking exceptions to the general patterns of communications systems in the Pacific Islands are New Zealand and Hawaii. These archipelagos of volcanic islands were both originally settled in prehistoric times by Polynesian seafarers— the Maori in New Zealand and the native Hawaiians in Hawaii. However, both of them have been so thoroughly integrated into Western culture (New Zealand is a member of the British Commonwealth, and Hawaii is the fiftieth state of the United States) that they have modern, Western-style economies. They are both unusually large in comparison to the tiny coral atolls, and thus have the resources to sustain such an economy.

POSTAL SYSTEMS. Postal service to the various Pacific Islands has often been spotty and unreliable. Until the second half of the twentieth century, the only way to get letters and parcels between the various islands was by ship, which was often slow and always subject to the vagaries of wind and weather (particularly in the days of sailing ships). By the 1950's, air mail became available, but was often expensive, particularly for the people of smaller islands. Because their small populations made it uneconomical to set up regular postal service, mail deliveries to those islands were generally irregular and dependent upon tramp merchant ships.

Many of the small island nations' postal systems are best known for their colorful stamps, which are prized by collectors. Many of the smaller independent islands have obtained a significant portion of their revenue through the sales of mint-quality stamps to collectors abroad.

New Zealand and Hawaii were notable exceptions to this pattern. Their large populations and links to major Western powers gave them access to excellent postal systems. New Zealand has its own privately owned and operated postal system based upon a British model. Hawaii, as a state of the United States, is served by the United States Postal Service, which regularly airlifts mail to the mainland without additional charge.

TELEGRAPHS AND TELEPHONES. New Zealand and Hawaii both have enjoyed First-World telegraph and telephone services almost from the beginning of telephony. New Zealand's telegraph and telephone systems are privately owned and operated, and generally enjoy a high stan-

dard of quality. Hawaii, as a territory and then a state of the United States, has benefited from U.S. telecommunications technology. The presence of a major U.S. Navy installation at Pearl Harbor has also been an impetus to establish reliable coaxial cable and later satellite links to the mainland.

By contrast, telegraph and telephone service in the smaller islands has often lagged in its development and remained unreliable. Prior to the development of inexpensive telecommunications satellites and cellular telephones, it was often prohibitively costly to provide telephone service, particularly to smaller islands. Thus radiotelephones were often the only form of two-way telecommunications between islands.

NEWSPAPERS. The large daily newspapers of the Pacific Islands are printed in

THE RONGORONGO SCRIPT OF EASTER ISLAND

Easter Island is one of the most remote Polynesian Islands. Its aboriginal culture, long shrouded in mystery, has become the subject of much speculation. Along with the monumental statues erected along its coasts, the people of Easter Island produced a large number of puzzling wooden boards inscribed with rows of mysterious characters. By the time Western scholars took serious interest in Easter Island's culture, no one survived who could read this script, known as Rongorongo.

Because of the characters' notable similarities to those on seals found in the ruins of the Indus Valley civilization in India, a connection between the two cultures has been posited. Some writers have even suggested that these similarities are evidence of undiscovered ancient civilizations that were destroyed in some catastrophe before the accepted beginning of written his-

tory. However, these theories are often discounted by serious scholars. Some linguists discount the idea that the Rongorongo is a native writing system for Rapa Nui, the language of Easter Island. Instead, they suggest that it is of relatively recent origin, probably imitative of European scripts, and was likely decorative, or at most a memory aid.

In the late 1990's a Russian linguist, Sergei V. Rjabchikov, claimed to have deciphered the Rongorongo. In his analysis, it is a hieroglyphic script containing a combination of ideographic characters—those that represent ideas, rather like Chinese characters—and phonetic characters—those that represent sounds, such as Western alphabets. Rjabchikov suggests that the Rongorongo script was used to record sacred legends and astronomical observations.

English in New Zealand and Hawaii. In the year 2000 New Zealand had about thirty daily papers, the largest of which was Aukland's *New Zealand Herald*. Many of New Zealand's newspapers are independents that provide thoughtful in-depth coverage of local events, but have few foreign correspondents and must rely heavily on wire services for international news.

Hawaii had twenty newspapers, six of which were dailies. The largest were the *Honolulu Advertiser* and the *Honolulu Star-Bulletin*. Although most of Hawaii's newspapers are in English, a few are printed in Asian languages such as Chinese and Japanese. Hawaiian publishers also produced thirty-five different periodicals.

Some of the other islands have their own newspapers, but few are large-circulation dailies and almost none are known beyond their own shores. Most of them rely entirely upon wire services for off-island news.

RADIO. Radio has been an important medium of mass communication for the peoples of the Pacific Islands. Because a radio requires little power and radio signals in certain frequencies can carry over long distances via reflection from the ionosphere, radio has generally been the most cost-efficient means to broadcast to those scattered islands. Many of the islands have their own short-wave stations, although their news programs generally consist of some local material combined with relays of news from Australia and New Zealand. Although most broadcast in English, some broadcast in Pidgin or various native languages. Most of them are low power and cannot be received more than a few thousand miles away. However, Papua New Guinea has a particularly strong short-wave station that can be received by properly equipped receivers around the world.

New Zealand has a large number of radio stations, both public and commercial.

Papua New Guinea radio Page 1980

Some radio stations broadcast in the languages of the various smaller islands for rebroadcast by local short-wave stations. Hawaii, as a territory and later a state of the United States, has a long history of radio broadcasting. Its first radio stations, KDYX and KGU of Honolulu, began operation in 1922. In 2000 it had more than sixty radio stations, most of which were located in Honolulu.

TELEVISION. New Zealand has a small but sophisticated television viewer population that expects high-quality programming. Two television networks are operated by the Broadcasting Corporation, an independent board appointed by the government. New Zealand also does some television broadcasting in the languages of the other Pacific Islands for rebroadcast by local stations, although many of the smaller islands do not have sufficient resources or population to support a television transmitter. As a former British colony, New Zealand uses the Phase Alternating Line (PAL) standard for its television broadcasts.

Hawaii's first television station, KGMB-TV, started broadcasting in 1952. In the year 2000 Hawaii had twenty television stations and three cable television providers. As part of the United States, Hawaii uses the National Television Standards Commission (NTSC) standard for its television broadcasts and the operations of its stations are subject to the regulation of the Federal Communications Commission (FCC).

COMMUNICATIONS SATELLITES. Communications satellites have been a great boon, particularly to the smaller islands of the Pacific. While it was often expensive to run a coaxial cable to an island and keep it maintained, any island with an economy large enough to produce electrical power can operate a ground station and take advantage of communications satellites. It thus becomes easy to receive radio and television broadcasts from a satellite relay and rebroadcast them for local consumption. Islands can also improve their telephone connections with the outside world by renting transponder space on satellites, bringing their telecommunications in line with the rest of the world.

INTERNET. Except for New Zealand and Hawaii, most of the Pacific Islands have generally lagged in growth of the Internet. The populations of many of the small coral atolls are generally too poor to afford computers, and electrical power supplies are often unreliable. However, in the 1990's, Tonga, Fiji, and some other island nations have made concerted efforts to bring their populations Internet access and to bring information about their lands to the outside world. Using coaxial cable and satellite links, they have put their islands on the Internet. Many of them have developed colorful and informative Web sites, although some smaller islands such as Pitcairn, which still lack their own Internet links and servers, have had to rent server space on computers on larger islands.

Leigh Husband Kimmel

FOR FURTHER STUDY

Fischer, Steven R. *Rongorongo: The Easter Island Script: History, Traditions, Texts.* New York: Clarendon Press, 1997.

McLuhan, Marshall, and Bruce R. Powers. *The Global Village: Transformations in World Life and Media in the Twenty-first Century.* Oxford, England: Oxford University Press, 1992.

Stevenson, Bruce. *Pacific Island Communities.* Auckland, N.Z.: Longman Paul, 1992.

Yoder, Andrew. *Complete Shortwave Listener's Handbook.* 5th ed. New York: McGraw-Hill, 1997.

ENGINEERING PROJECTS

AUSTRALIA

*Snowy
mountain
project
Page 1981*

*Snowy
River
Page 2041*

Australian engineers have long been handicapped by the country's small, dispersed population, its great size, and the largely inhospitable physical environment. Prior to World War I, Australia largely lacked trained engineers. It was primarily an exporter of agricultural products and minerals, and its capital resources were limited. As a result, engineering activity was concentrated in mining, transportation, and water supply. Any large-scale projects, in great part conceived and executed by foreigners, were dependent upon imported capital, and in many cases, imported construction materials.

After World War I, this situation changed with construction of the Sydney Harbor Bridge (1923-1932). The Snowy Mountain Project was the next major engineering feat in Australia, followed by the Sydney Opera House. Although the engineering aspects of the Sydney Opera House have been overshadowed by its architectural and cultural fame, engineers agree that because of its design and unique construction techniques, the building stands as a model for engineering, and it remains, along with the Sydney Harbor Bridge and the Snowy Mountain Project, one the most significant engineering monuments in Australia. Although the Murray River Barrage and the Adelaide Aqueduct deserve mention, they have been subsumed in importance. The Dingo Fence, although perhaps the longest fence in the world, is merely a wire-link fence of no particular engineering significance.

THE SNOWY MOUNTAIN PROJECT. Australia's foremost engineering project supplies 2,280,000 megaliters of water to 1.31 million acres (530,000 hectares) of farmland in the Murrumbidgee project on the Murrumbidgee River in New South Wales and in the Murray-Goulbrun Project on the Murray River in New South Wales and Victoria. Additional primary agricultural production is estimated at about 60 million Australian dollars. While falling 2,640 feet (800 meters), the water generates 3,740,000 kilowatts of electricity.

One system of tunnels and reservoirs diverts water from the Eucumbene River, a tributary of the east-flowing Snowy River, into the Tumut River, a tributary of the west-flowing Murrumbidgee River. The Upper Murrumbidgee is diverted into the Eucumbene and the Tooma River, a tributary of the Tumut. Another system diverts Snowy River water directly into the Murray River. The two systems connect through reversible flow tunnels, so that excess water can be diverted to storage.

Sixteen major dams, many smaller dams, seven power stations, 100 miles (160 km.) of tunnels, and 80 miles (130 km.) of aqueducts make up the project. When built, the Eucumbene main storage dam, with a capacity of 3,860,000 acre feet, was the world's largest earthen-rock fill dam.

More than 100 miles (160 km.) of highway and 625 miles (1,000 km.) of secondary roads built for the project opened 2.4 million acres (975,000 hectares) of previously inaccessible wilderness for tourism and recreation. The Kosciusko National Park, which includes 800,000 acres (325,000 hectares) of primitive area surrounding Australia's highest mountain—Mount Kosciusko (7,313 feet/2,229 meters)—is a heritage of the project.

The Snowy Mountains Hydroelectric Authority began constructing the project in 1959. Upon completion in 1974, the Snowy Mountains Council—a joint venture of the Commonwealth, New South Wales, Victoria, and South Australia—took operating control. A major refurbishment of underground power stations Tumut 1 and 2 began in the early 1990's. The federal government financed most of the approximately $800 million (Australian) construction cost. Debt, interest, and operational costs are defrayed by selling electricity.

The project's economics and impacts have been criticized. Providing water for intensive agriculture has been said to yield less return than an equivalent investment in grain-growing. The cost of the massive storage requirements needed to offset Australia's highly variable rainfall has been criticized. Some analysts assert that Snowy River hydropower could be re-

Section of the Dingo Fence. (Tom McKnight/Joan Clemons)

THE SNOWY MOUNTAINS HYDRO-ELECTRIC SCHEME

An innovative hydrological engineering project that began in 1949 was the Snowy Mountains Hydro-Electric Scheme. The Snowy River, which was fed by snowmelt from the Australian Alps, was diverted westward into the Murray River. The project involved construction of twelve long tunnels through the mountains, as well as sixteen dams and seven power-generating plants. Immigrants from more than thirty other countries, many of whom had lost everything during World War II, came to Australia to construct these facilities. The project was therefore not only a tremendous engineering challenge for Australia, but also a great social experiment for a country whose existing population consisted mainly of people of British origin. The workers' living conditions were spartan, and the environment was harsh, but the immigrants saw the project as a wonderful financial opportunity. The work, especially the tunneling, was sometimes dangerous, and some 120 people lost their lives during the construction. The Snowy Mountains Hydro-Electric Scheme has been honored twice by the American Society of Civil Engineers as one of the great engineering achievements of the twentieth century.

---

placed at lower cost by thermal plants. Environmentalists charge that the project has destroyed the Snowy River and violated the wilderness. It is alleged that the projects have not paid for themselves.

SYDNEY OPERA HOUSE. Comprising a series of spherical, shell-like components, the Sydney Harbor Opera House, whose engineering design and unique construction techniques were devised by engineer Ove Arup, is assembled from modular precast concrete elements. It stands as a model for engineering design and construction of large buildings enclosed by curved and rounded exterior shells.

The Sydney Opera House is an entertainment center housing a concert hall seating 2,700, an opera theater seating 1,550, a drama theater seating 500, a cinema-music room, rehearsal and recording hall, exhibition areas, and restaurants. As early as 1947, Eugene Goosens, then conductor of the Sydney Symphony Orchestra, called for construction of a musical center for symphony, opera, and chamber music. In 1954 J. J. Cahill, premier in the Labor government of New South Wales, instigated an international design competition for the center. In 1957 Danish architect Joern Utzon won the opera house competition, although his entry included only rough drawings of the proposed building. Utzon was appointed architect, and the Opera House Executive Committee selected Ove Arup and partners to supervise construction for an estimated 7 million dollars Australian. Cahill, fearing a politically inspired cancellation of the project, insisted that construction begin before the 1959 elections.

Work began in March, 1959, on the massive podium, the foundations and platform upon which the building was to rest. Because the final form of the building and how it was to be built was unknown, work was repeatedly interrupted and much completed design work had to be discarded. In some cases, portions of the building were demolished and rebuilt. When the podium was completed in 1963, estimated costs had increased to more than $24,000,000 Australian.

Sydney Opera House Page 2042

Utzon's original, free-hand sketch of elliptical parabaloid shells were not working plans for the walls and roof of the building. His first plan to cast the shells in place proved impractical. Arup designed shells composed of double skins supported by an internal steel frame, but Utzon rejected this design. Utzon and Arup then designed self-supporting shells composed of radiating ribs, each built of precast concrete sections—an utterly new concept. The original ellipsoidal form was discarded for spherical surfaces of a uniform radius, allowing mass-production of the sections.

Utzon's failure to complete plans for the building's interior, even as shell-construction proceeded, intensified conflicts among Arup, the Executive Committee, and the New South Wales government. In 1965, after a Liberal Party election victory, a new Public Works Director, Davis Hughs, assumed personal control over the project and vetoed Utzon's plans for the interior. Utzon resigned in 1966, and succeeding architects and a new engineering firm redesigned the interior.

The building opened with a performance of *War and Peace* by the Australian Opera Company in September, 1973, after which the Queen formally opened it in October, 1973. Largely financed by state lotteries, it was completed at a cost of $A102,000,000. Unresolved problems, including poor acoustics, led to a 1988 an-

Sydney Opera House. (Corbis)

nouncement of a ten-year renovation plan costing $A66,000,000.

The building is a world-famous engineering and architectural monument, but also has been criticized. Some architects argue that the shells were designed wholly for esthetics and thus cause overwhelming problems in seating, acoustics, and staging. Persistent structural shortcomings arose from the innovative techniques and materials. For example, the tiles on the outside of the building require continuous regrouting.

SYDNEY HARBOR BRIDGE. The Sydney Harbor Bridge spans 1,650 feet (503 meters) of open water from Dawes Point to Milson's Point. Five steel approach spans increase the bridge's total length to 3,770 feet (1,149 meters). The top of the main span is 440 feet (134 meters) above mean sea level, and the crest of the deck stands 160 feet (49 meters) above the water. The 160-foot-wide deck originally accommodated a central six-lane roadway, two tram lines, two rail lines, a footway on the eastern side, and a bikeway on the west. In 1959 the tram lines were removed, widening the roadway to eight lanes.

An English firm began construction in 1923. The two wings of the arch, based on two steel pins in each abutment, were cantilevered outward and built from large creeper cranes advancing on top of the growing arch. After the arch was closed in 1930, the cranes retreated, lifting deck panels from pontoons and hanging them from the arch. A total of 58,000 tons of steel, almost all imported from Middlebourough, England, were used in construction. The completed bridge was opened on March 19, 1932. The bridge

cost $A20,230,000, raised by loans and contributions from local governments. Although the loans were paid off in 1988, tolls remained in effect for maintenance costs.

When built, the bridge was the longest single-span bridge in the world and remained the second-longest steel arch span at the end of the twentieth century. The monumental stone pylons at the ends of the bridge have been criticized as entirely decorative and nonfunctional, and the bridge was called too costly and overdesigned. Nevertheless, the bridge came to symbolize Australia and was commemorated on postage stamps. Although some people thought the bridge was not justified by the expected traffic, by 1999, peak traffic reached 15,000 automobiles per hour in contrast to the designed capacity of 6,000 vehicles. A tunnel paralleling the bridge was authorized in 1992; as of 1999, ferries continued to make the crossing.

M. Casey Diana

FOR FURTHER STUDY

Collis, B. *Snowy: The Making of Modern Australia.* Sydney: Hodder and Stoughton, 1990.

Drew, Phillip. *Sydney Opera House, Joern Utzen.* London: Phaidon Press, 1995.

Holgate, Alan. "Case Study of the Sydney Opera House Design." In *The Art in Structural Design: An Introduction and Sourcebook.* New York: Oxford University Press, 1986.

Unger, M. *Voices from the Snowy.* Kensington, Australia: New South Wales University Press, 1989.

Yeomans, J. *The Other Taj Mahal.* 2d ed. London: Longmans, 1973.

Pacific Islands

Until the mid-1900's, most of the Pacific Islands were under colonial rule. The agricultural economies of the region were largely shielded from industrial development. During the second half of the twentieth century, however, most of the island nations achieved political independence and greater economic diversification. Natural resources and agricultural products still formed the backbone of the island economies, but advanced technologies promoted the growth of new industries and created new employment opportunities for technical and professional personnel.

MINING. The Pacific Rim area ranges from New Zealand through the island chains of the Pacific Ocean to Hawaii and the west coasts of North and South America. It is known as the Ring of Fire because of the earth's continuing geological activity in the area, where more than 75 percent of the world's 850 active volcanoes are located. Substantial deposits of valuable minerals are associated with this volcanic activity; New Caledonia, Papua New Guinea, and Fiji have extensive mineral deposits, including gold, silver, chrome, iron, cobalt, copper, aluminum, lead, and manganese.

Mining and processing gold ore is particularly important in Fiji. The country's largest private employer is the Emperor Mine at Vatukoula. Since opening in 1932, this mine has produced 6 million ounces of gold, and during the 1990's it accounted for more than 6 percent of Fiji's national income. The easily accessible mineral veins have been exhausted, but engineers using diamond-tipped drills have located new reserves of 1.2 million additional ounces of gold. In the year 2000 further testing at

greater depths will be conducted, using hydraulic drilling technology.

Papua New Guinea's mining industry relies heavily on foreign technology. During the 1990's, Australian and North American mining companies used core sample drilling, satellite-based mapping, and other sophisticated prospecting technologies to identify new deposits of gold, aluminum, and other metals. At the end of the decade, deposits of gold and copper were discovered near the Frieda River in remote Sanduan Province. The government of Papua New Guinea is financing the construction of a $1.5 billion mining, ore processing, and shipping complex at the Frieda River site. Roads, quarries, and mechanized ore-processing facilities will be built, and the project is expected to stimulate the growth of other sectors of the economy, including the chemicals, communications, and transportation industries.

Nickel is a plentiful resource in the Pacific Islands. Papua New Guinea has almost 5 percent of the world's known reserves and is developing a huge mining and refinery project known as the Ramu Nickel Project at Basamuk Bay. In the year 2000 new roads, bridges, and quarries were being built to access nickel deposits in the southeastern part of the country. An 83-mile-long (133 km.) ore slurry pipeline will carry unprocessed ore to a new nickel refinery, and processed ore will be exported through a new deep-water port.

Other elements of the Ramu Project are construction of new electricity-generation and sulfur-leaching plants. Australian mining companies will provide most of the engineering expertise and heavy equipment and will train local technicians. The

WASTE DISPOSAL IN THE PACIFIC ISLANDS

Long-term waste disposal options for the Pacific Islands are limited. To protect their fragile environments, island governments attempt to turn wastes into reusable resources, such as fertilizers for agriculture. Island governments are also considering limiting imports of nonbiodegradable and hazardous substances.

Ramu Project eventually will process 3.2 million tons of ore annually, exporting an estimated 32,800 tons of cathode nickel and 3,200 tons of cobalt salts per year, and smaller quantities of magnesium and aluminum. Environmentalists question the planned deposit of chemical and other refinery wastes into deep canyons in the ocean floor off the island. Engineers are designing improved, leak-resistant canisters that should prevent the wastes from entering the marine environment.

A similar nickel-mining complex is under construction in New Caledonia, which has 20 percent of the world's reserves. In 1998 Canadian mining corporations launched a joint venture with French and local firms to build an $800 million nickel ore-processing facility, which will include new quarries, pipelines, and smelters. When the project is completed, New Caledonia will have one of the world's most productive nickel ore processing industries.

PETROLEUM AND POWER ENGINEERING IN NEW ZEALAND. Dwindling world oil reserves and threats of monopoly pricing by the established oil-producing nations have spurred an active oil and natural gas exploration and development industry in New Zealand. Initial exploration efforts in the 1970's identified potentially enormous oil and gas reserves in the 40,000-square-mile (104,000 sq. km.) Taranaki Basin, most of which lies west of New Zealand's North Island. The basin features a stacked configuration of underground domes, or reservoirs, located at depths of up to about 15,000 feet (45,000 meters) below the ocean floor.

In the late 1990's, geologists using satellite-based ocean floor mapping and core sample analysis techniques identified one such natural gas reservoir, with estimated reserves of 1.2 trillion cubic feet of gas. New Zealand's drilling efforts moved offshore, and pipelines were laid on the sea floor to carry gas from drilling sites to storage terminals on North Island. Economic growth in New Zealand has bolstered the domestic market for natural gas. In 1999 the 400-megawatt Otahuhu gas-fired electricity-generating plant near Auckland came on line. The plant uses special turbines and instrumentation imported from Germany, but local engineering firms performed most of the design and construction work. The Otahuhu plant is one of the largest gas-fired plants in the world.

TELECOMMUNICATIONS ENGINEERING. The Pacific Islands face special difficulties in the operation of effective communications systems. Huge distances separate the inhabited islands, and extreme weather conditions interfere with conventional telephone lines. In the late 1990's, North American and Australian companies offered new solutions based on advanced technologies. In Vanuatu, networks of fiber-optic cables have been buried underground, and VHF radio communications have been strengthened by relay stations that boost radio signals, enabling them to travel despite the complex topography of the islands, dense vegetation, and interference from storms and volcanoes. In Tonga, an undersea cable system provides voice, data, and fax transmissions to the five main islands, and international links are provided by microwave communications with satellites. With these new facilities in place, islanders have for the first time been able to connect to the World Wide Web.

Laura M. Calkins

FOR FURTHER STUDY

Cole, Rodney V., ed. *Pacific 2010: Challenging the Future.* Suva, Fiji: University of the South Pacific, 1993.

Howard, Michael C. *Mining, Politics and Development in the South Pacific.* Boulder, Colo.: Westview Press, 1991.

Jayaraman, T. K. *Private Investment and Macroeconomic Environment in the South Pacific Island Countries.* Manila: Asian Development Bank, 1996.

Lockwood, Victoria, et al., eds. *Contemporary Pacific Societies: Studies in Development and Change.* Englewood Cliffs, N.J.: Prentice-Hall, 1993.

McKee, David L. *Developmental Issues in Small Island Economies.* New York: Praeger, 1990.

GAZETTEER

Places whose names are printed in SMALL CAPS *are subjects of their own entries in this gazetteer.*

Adelaide. Capital and largest city of the state of SOUTH AUSTRALIA. Located on a plain 9 miles (14 km.) inland from the Gulf of St. Vincent and at the base of the Mount Lofty Ranges that rise to the east. Has a Mediterranean climate and a 1991 population of 1 million. The Torrens River flows through the city. Known for its beautiful parklands, Adelaide has grown from an early agricultural center (fruit, wheat, wool, and Barossa Valley wines) into an industrial power producing automobile parts, machinery, textiles, and chemicals. A hub of rail, sea, air, and road transportation, it is also connected by pipeline with the Gidgealpa natural gas fields in Cooper Basin, northeastern South Australia. Port Adelaide, its main harbor, is located 7 miles (11 km.) northwest. Established in 1836 and named for Queen Adelaide, wife of British king William IV.

Adélie Coast. See TERRE ADÉLIE.

Admiralty Islands. Island group in the western PACIFIC OCEAN, part of PAPUA NEW GUINEA. The eighteen islands are part of the BISMARCK ARCHIPELAGO. The two largest are Rambutyo Island and Manus Island. The League of Nations mandated the islands to AUSTRALIA in 1920. Japan occupied the islands in 1942, then the Allies in 1944. They were administered by Australia, then became a United Nations Trust Territory before becoming part of Papua New Guinea in 1975.

Akaka Falls. Waterfall along the Hamakua coast of HAWAII ISLAND. Tallest waterfall in the Hawaiian Islands, at 442 feet (135 meters). The stream that forms the waterfall cuts through a layer of ash to the lava below.

Alice Springs. OUTBACK town located in the Red Centre of AUSTRALIA's NORTHERN TERRITORY. The Red Centre is an area approximately 100,000 square miles (260,000 sq. km.) in size of desert and rocky outcrops, flanked by the MacDonnell Ranges. Had a 1989 population of 23,600 and is 954 miles (1,535 km.) south of DARWIN and 1,028 miles (1,654 km.) north of ADELAIDE. Now reached by rail and road, it is a major shipping point for cattle and minerals and an important part of Australia's tourism. It is the gateway to Australia's Outback, to Ayers Rock/ULURU and the Olgas/Kata Tjuta, and to aboriginal lands, and is the regional headquarters for the Royal Flying Doctor Service and the School of the Air. Originally established along the ephemeral Henley River in 1871 as a station for the Overland Telegraph Line.

Alice Springs Page 1980

Alps, Australian. Section of the GREAT DIVIDING RANGE, located in the southeasternmost corner of AUSTRALIA in southeastern NEW SOUTH WALES and eastern VICTORIA. Forms as the divide between the MURRAY RIVER system flowing west and the SNOWY RIVER and other streams that flow east to the PACIFIC OCEAN. Massive and covered with snow nearly half the year, the Alps are the tallest mountains on the continent and include Australia's tallest peak, Mount KOSCIUSKO, at 7,313 feet (2,229 meters).

Ambrim. Active volcano on Ambrim Island on northern VANUATU in the southwestern PACIFIC OCEAN. Reaches a height of 4,376 feet (1,350 meters). One of its most recent eruptions occurred in 1999.

American Samoa. Unincorporated territory of the United States, comprising seven islands in the southern PACIFIC OCEAN: Tutuila, the Manua group

Akaka Falls Page 1982

(Tau, Olosega, Ofu), Aunuu, Rose Island, and Swains Island. Total area of 77 square miles (199 sq. km.); population was 55,223 in 1994. Tutuila, the Manua group, and Aunuu are of volcanic origin; Rose and Swains Islands are coral atolls. Pago, a harbor town on Tutuila, is the seat of government.

Amery Ice Shelf. Ice shelf on the INDIAN OCEAN in southeast ANTARCTICA. About 125 miles (200 km.) wide; fed by the LAMBERT GLACIER, one of Antarctica's largest, it receives more than 8.4 miles (13.5 km.) of new glacial ice annually.

Antarctica map Page 1846

Amundsen-Scott South Pole Station. U.S. research station located at 90 degrees south latitude, directly on the SOUTH POLE. Buildings are covered by a huge geodesic dome to protect them from the punishing winds that howl constantly across the pole. Named for Antarctic explorers Roald Amundsen and Robert Falcon Scott.

Andesite Line. Geological line forming a boundary between the high (continental) and the low (oceanic) islands of the PACIFIC OCEAN. The line follows the island arcs from the Aleutians southward to the Yap and Patou arcs, eastward through the BISMARCKS and SOLOMONS, and southward through SAMOA, TONGA, CHATHAM, and Macquaries to ANTARCTICA.

Antarctic Circle. Imaginary line at 66°32′ south latitude, south of which lies all the Antarctic landmass but a small portion of the ANTARCTIC PENINSULA.

Antarctic Convergence. Point just north of the ANTARCTIC CIRCLE where cold polar waters meet the warmer waters of the ATLANTIC, PACIFIC, and INDIAN Oceans. The cold water sinks, forcing the warmer currents to rise toward the surface. Also called the Antarctic Polar Front.

Antarctic Peninsula. Peninsula that juts north into the South ATLANTIC OCEAN. With water on three sides, it has the most moderate climate on ANTARCTICA, with summer temperatures sometimes reaching 50 degrees Fahrenheit (10 degrees Celsius). Warm enough to have occasional light rainfall and to support the two flowering plants that grow south of 60 degrees south latitude, the pearlwort and grass, as well as several mosses and lichens

Antarctic Polar Front. See ANTARCTIC CONVERGENCE.

Antarctica. World's fifth-largest continent. Has 10 percent of the earth's landmass, covering 5.1 million square miles (13,209,000 sq. km.). Twice the size of Europe or AUSTRALIA, 1.5 times the size of the United States. Earth's highest continent, with an average altitude of about 6,000 feet (1,830 meters), excluding its covering of snow and ice. Its ice and snow cover, with an average thickness of about 8,000 feet (2,440 meters), increases its average altitude to 14,000 feet (4,270 meters), just a little less than Mount Rainier in Washington. The most isolated continent, located 600 miles (960 km.) from the southern tip of South America, 1,550 miles (2,500 km.) from Australia, and 2,500 miles (4,023 km.) from the southernmost point in Africa. Round in shape except for the ANTARCTIC PENINSULA, which juts northward into the South ATLANTIC OCEAN, and the indentations of the ROSS and WEDDELL Seas. Has 18,648 miles (30,010 km.) of coastline.

Arafura Sea. Shallow sea in the western PACIFIC OCEAN. Covers 250,000 square miles (650,000 sq. km.) at depths of 165 to 260 feet (50-80 meters). Located between the north coast of AUSTRALIA and the Gulf of CARPENTARIA and the south coast of New Guinea. Bordered by the TIMOR SEA to the west and connected to the CORAL SEA to the east by the TORRES STRAIT. Known as a navigational hazard because of its many uncharted shoals.

Arnhem Land. Historical region located at AUSTRALIA's Top End in the eastern half of a large peninsula forming the northernmost portion of the NORTHERN TERRITORY. Covers 37,000 square miles (95,900 sq. km.), including islands off the coast. Set aside in 1931 as aboriginal reserves, it has a tropical climate. Named for his ship the *Arheim* (*Aernem*) by Dutch explorer Willem van Colster in 1623.

Arthur's Pass. NEW ZEALAND's highest alpine pass, at 3,032 feet (924 meters). The road-railway pass crosses over the SOUTHERN ALPS of SOUTH ISLAND, linking the CANTERBURY PLAINS on the east with Westland on the west. Named after the surveyor Arthur Dobson, who rediscovered the old Maori alpine route in 1864.

Atherton Tableland. Highly fertile plain, part of the GREAT DIVIDING RANGE (Eastern Highlands) in northeastern Queensland, AUSTRALIA. Covers 12,000 square miles (31,000 sq. km.), bordered by the Palmer River on the north and BURDEKIN RIVER on the south. Originally settled in the 1870's as a mining region.

Atlantic Ocean. The South Atlantic Ocean lies north and east of ANTARCTICA. The ANTARCTIC PENINSULA, the WEDDELL SEA, and QUEEN MAUD LAND in EAST (GREATER) ANTARCTICA all face toward the South Atlantic.

Auckland. Largest city in NEW ZEALAND, and largest Polynesian city in the world. Population was more than one million in 1999. Located on a narrow neck of land in the north of NORTH ISLAND,

surrounded by two harbors, Waitemata to the east and Manukau to the west. Built on forty-eight extinct volcanoes, including Rangitoto, the last and largest of which became extinct eight hundred years ago. Site of the year 2000 America's Yacht Cup Race.

Austral Islands. Groups of islands in FRENCH POLYNESIA, South PACIFIC OCEAN. Small islands form a chain 850 miles (1,370 km.) long. Total area is 54 square miles (140 sq. km.); population was 6,509 in 1998. The islands with residents are Rimatara, Rurutu, Tubuai, Raevavae, and Rapa. Also known as Îles Australes or Tubuai Islands.

Australasia. Loosely defined term for the region, which, at the least, includes AUSTRALIA and NEW ZEALAND; at the most, it also includes other South Pacific islands in the region and takes on a meaning similar to that of OCEANIA.

Australia. Continent occupied by a single nation of the same name, covering 2.97 million square miles (7.68 million sq. km.), including its island state of TASMANIA. Located between the INDIAN and PACIFIC Oceans, Australia is the sixth-largest country and the smallest continent in the world. Population in the late 1990's was 18 million people. Other states are NEW SOUTH WALES, QUEENSLAND, VICTORIA, SOUTH AUSTRALIA, and WESTERN AUSTRALIA. It also has the NORTHERN TERRITORY and Australian Capital Territory, which contains the national capital, CANBERRA. Australia is the flattest and driest continent; two-thirds is either desert or semiarid. Geologically, it is the oldest and most isolated continent.

Australian Capital Territory. Site of CANBERRA and surrounding lands of AUSTRALIA's national capital. Covers 910 square miles (2,350 sq. km.) within the Southern Tablelands of NEW SOUTH

WALES. Established as a result of the British Parliament's passing the Commonwealth of Australia Constitution Act in 1901. The site was chosen in 1908; parliament moved from the temporary capital, MELBOURNE, into the official Parliament House in 1927.

Ayers Rock. See ULURU.

Bagana. Active volcano on south central Bougainville Island, PAPUA NEW GUINEA. Reaches 6,558 feet (1,999 meters). One of its most recent eruptions occurred in 1998.

Balleny Islands. Island group resting precisely on the ANTARCTIC CIRCLE. Unlike such coastal islands as Ross, Alexander, and Roosevelt, is in the sea off VICTORIA LAND. Connected to the mainland by pack ice during the winter.

Bass Strait. Channel separating VICTORIA, AUSTRALIA, from the state of TASMANIA. It is 150 miles (240 km.) wide and 180-240 feet (50-70 meters) deep and known for rough crossing. Bordered by King Island and the INDIAN OCEAN to the west and by the FURNEAUX GROUP to the west. Named in 1798 by the English navigator Matthew Flinders for the surgeon-explorer George Bass.

Bay of Islands. See ISLANDS, BAY OF.

Bay of Whales. See WHALES, BAY OF.

Beardmore Glacier. Largest glacier thus far discovered in the Antarctic. Originates at the SOUTH POLE and continues its flow to the ROSS ICE SHELF, which is roughly the size of France.

Belau. See PALAU, REPUBLIC OF.

Bellinghausen Sea. Sea in West ANTARCTICA. Extends from the eightieth south parallel to the ANTARCTIC PENINSULA. Named after Russian explorer Admiral Fabian Bellinghausen.

Bentley Subglacial Trench. Lowest spot in ANTARCTICA and the lowest altitude on any continent. At 8,325 feet (2,538 meters) below sea level, it is 7,000 feet

Bora-Bora Pages 1843-1844

(2,134 meters) lower than Israel's Dead Sea. There is little snow, and the earth is often exposed.

Bikini Atoll. Small atoll in the MARSHALL ISLANDS group in the western PACIFIC OCEAN. In the 1940's and 1950's the United States tested nuclear bombs on Bikini and neighboring atolls, forcing their residents to leave the islands.

Bismarck Archipelago. Group of mostly volcanic islands in the west PACIFIC OCEAN, north of the east end of New Guinea; part of PAPUA NEW GUINEA. Total area is 19,173 square miles (49,658 sq. km.); population was 371,400, primarily Melanesian, in 1989. Contains New Britain, New Ireland, New Hanover, ADMIRALTY ISLANDS, and two hundred other islands and islets. There are active volcanoes on New Britain.

Blue Mountains. Section of the GREAT DIVIDING RANGE, NEW SOUTH WALES, AUSTRALIA. Rises to 3,781 feet (1,180 meters). Steep and riddled with waterfalls and ravines, its bluish hue is caused by light rays diffusing through oils dispersed into the air by varieties of indigenous eucalyptus trees. The location of many ancient rock formations, including the Three Sisters and the Jenolan Caves, as well as the Blue Mountains National Park, a 768-square-mile (1,989 sq. km.) nature reserve. SYDNEY is 40 miles (60 km.) to the east.

Bora-Bora. Volcanic island in FRENCH POLYNESIA in the South Pacific. One of the Leeward Islands, SOCIETY ISLANDS group. Area is 15 square miles (39 sq. km.); population was 4,225 in 1988. Leading industries are tourism and copra production; was a U.S. air base during World War II.

Botany Bay. Inlet of the South PACIFIC OCEAN on the southeastern coast of AUSTRALIA. Located 9 miles (15 km.)

south of PORT JACKSON, in the city of SYDNEY, NEW SOUTH WALES. The site of Captain James Cook's first landing on Australian soil, in 1770.

Brisbane. State capital and major port of QUEENSLAND, and AUSTRALIA's third-largest city. Built along the banks of the Brisbane River, 12 miles (19 km.) from where it empties into Moreton Bay. Balmy and tropical, it had a 1990's population of 1.3 million. A shipping and manufacturing hub, its proximity to the agricultural lands of the Eastern Highlands and DARLING DOWNS, and its port, which can accommodate ships of 34,000 tons, have made Brisbane a major exporter of wool, meat, dairy products, sugar, and grains. Industrialization is responsible for more than 50 percent of the state's manufacturing capacity; included are food-processing plants, oil refineries, shipyards, sawmills, and factories that produce automobiles, rubber goods, cement, and fertilizer. Also the gateway to Australia's famous Gold Coast resorts and casinos. Originally established as a convict settlement in 1824; became the capital in 1859.

Brooks Islands. See MIDWAY ISLANDS.

Burdekin River. Largest river in AUSTRALIA's QUEENSLAND state. Enters the sea in a big delta near Ayr, where groundwater makes the cultivation of sugarcane, a principal crop, possible. After flooding in the summer months, it dries up into waterholes for much of the year. Queensland's largest dam was constructed at the Burdekin Falls. Named by explorer Ludwig Leichhardt in 1844 in honor of the Burdekin family, which financed his expedition.

Byrd Glacier. Largest glacier feeding the ROSS SEA and the ROSS ICE SHELF in ANTARCTICA. Wider than the English Channel and produces more ice annually than all the other six glaciers that feed the Ross Ice Shelf. Discharges about 4.3 miles (7 km.) of ice into the Ross Ice Shelf annually.

Byron, Cape. Easternmost point of AUSTRALIA's mainland; located in northeastern NEW SOUTH WALES. Shelters Byron Bay. Originally the main port between the town of Newcastle and BRISBANE, 90 miles (145 km.) to the north. Discovered by Captain James Cook in 1770 and named in honor of Commodore John Byron, the grandfather of British poet Lord Byron.

Cairns. City and port in North QUEENSLAND, AUSTRALIA; gateway to the GREAT BARRIER REEF. Located 860 miles (1,380 km.) north of BRISBANE, with a 1990's population of fifty thousand. Served by international air, rail, and the Bruce Highway. An important tourist center for access to the Great Barrier Reef, coastal resort islands, and big-game fishing. Founded in the 1870's on Trinity Inlet of Trinity Bay; grew as a result of nearby gold and tin mining and sugarcane cultivation.

Canberra. Federal capital of AUSTRALIA, located in the AUSTRALIAN CAPITAL TERRITORY. The country's first planned city; carved from the bush in southeastern Australia, about 150 miles (240 km.) southwest of SYDNEY. Site was chosen in 1909; an international contest was launched in 1911 to find a design for the new capital. Construction began in 1913; in 1927 ceremonies marked the official transfer of the federal parliament from its temporary home in MELBOURNE to the new Parliament House in Canberra. Low buildings, large expanses of park lands, and the artificial lake Burleigh Griffin form the city's core. Name is derived from an Aboriginal word for "meeting place."

*Brisbane
Page 2031*

Canterbury Plains. Largest lowland area in NEW ZEALAND. About 200 miles (320 km.) long and 40 miles (64 km.) wide; located in the east-central region of SOUTH ISLAND. The breadbasket of the country. Once home of the moa, a large flightless bird that was hunted into extinction by the Maori. Home of the nor'wester, a dry, warm wind that blows from the northwest across the plains, similar to the chinook of northwest America.

Cape York Page 1839

Cape York Peninsula. Large triangular portion comprising the northernmost extension of AUSTRALIA's QUEENSLAND state, with the Gulf of CARPENTARIA on the west and the CORAL SEA to the east. A remote area with mostly dirt roads; travel in wet lowlands is made difficult by flooding streams. The four large national parks on the peninsula represent the wide variety of Queensland vegetation and habitats, ranging from tropical rain forest to woodland and tropical grasslands and swamps. Cattle raising and gold mining on the Palmer River were important during the nineteenth century; bauxite mining and tourism now provide for the local economy.

Caroline Islands. Archipelago in the western PACIFIC OCEAN, with more than six hundred islands, atolls, and islets. Area of 350 square miles (1,165 sq. km.) is divided into the Republic of PALAU (1994) and the Federated States of MICRONESIA (1979), consisting of Chuuk, Kosrae, Pohnpei, and Yap. Native inhabitants are Micronesians. The larger islands are volcanic in origin; the smaller are coral atolls. From 1947 to 1979, the islands, previously in Japanese hands, were the Trust Territory of the Pacific Islands, administered by the United States.

Carpentaria, Gulf of. Shallow inlet of the ARAFURA SEA along the northern coast of AUSTRALIA. Covers 120,000 square miles (310,000 sq. km.) with a maximum depth of 230 feet (70 meters). Bordered on the east by the CAPE YORK PENINSULA and on the west by ARNHEM LAND. More than twenty meandering rivers drain into the gulf. The town of Karumba, located on the gulf, is a major center for the prawn-fishing industry; huge deposits of manganese and bauxite are mined in the area.

Chatham Islands. Remote group of islands belonging to NEW ZEALAND. Situated 528 miles (850 km.) east of CHRISTCHURCH. Population was 739 in 1996. Main population center is located at WAITANGI. Island economy is based on the export of sheep, wool, and fish to the mainland. Original inhabitants of the islands were the Moriori, of Polynesian origin. Tommy Soloman, the last full-blooded Moriori, died in 1933.

Christchurch. Largest city on SOUTH ISLAND, NEW ZEALAND. Situated on the coastal edge of the CANTERBURY PLAINS, at the foothills of Banks Peninsula, an extinct volcano. Population was 341,000 in 1999. Founded in 1850 as an Anglican settlement. Most of the city is built on flat terrain, making it ideal for bicycling and walking. The international airport is the primary gateway to ANTARCTICA.

Christmas Island. See KIRITIMATI ISLAND.

Clutha River. Largest river by volume and second-longest river in NEW ZEALAND. Flows southeast 200 miles (322 km.) across central Otago on SOUTH ISLAND, beginning at Lake Wanaka and reaching the PACIFIC OCEAN south of DUNEDIN. Major source of hydroelectric power for NEW ZEALAND. Center of the Otago gold rush in the eighteenth century.

Coober Pedy. Mining town in central SOUTH AUSTRALIA; most of the world's opals come from this area. Located 590 miles (950 km.) northwest of ADELAIDE in the Stuart Range on the edge of the GREAT VICTORIA DESERT. Population was approximately thirty-five hundred in the late 1990's. Its name is derived from the Aboriginal words meaning "white man's hole," referring to miners' practice of building homes underground to escape temperatures as high as 125 degrees Fahrenheit (52 degrees Celsius) during the summer months. The first opals were found here in 1911.

Cook, Mount. NEW ZEALAND's highest mountain peak, at 12,317 feet (3,754 meters). Located in the SOUTHERN ALPS of SOUTH ISLAND. Perpetual snow cap; popular skiing site. Known to the Maori as Aorangi, meaning "the cloud piecer."

Cook Islands. Self-governing islands in association with NEW ZEALAND in the South PACIFIC OCEAN. About 1,600 miles (2,600 km.) northeast of New Zealand. Comprises fifteen islands with a total area of about 90 square miles (240 sq. km.); population was 16,500 in 1998. Northern islands are sparsely populated atolls; southern islands are volcanic in origin and include Rarotonga. Most of the islands' people live on Rarotonga and are of mixed Polynesian and European ancestry.

Cook Strait. Stretch of ocean separating NORTH and SOUTH Islands of NEW ZEALAND. Major interisland shipping link; 16 miles (25 km.) at its narrowest point. Subject to rough seas and site of maritime disasters; acts like a wind tunnel. In 1968 the interisland roll-on, roll-off ferry sank, costing fifty-one lives, during one of the worst storms in the country's history. Named after Captain James Cook, who sailed through the strait in 1770.

Cooktown. Town and port located at the mouth of the Endeavour River on the CORAL SEA in northeastern QUEENSLAND. Population was about one thousand in 1991. Linked by the Mulligan Highway to CAIRNS, 120 miles (190 km.) to the south; faces the GREAT BARRIER REEF. Founded in 1873 during the Palmer River gold rush; today's economy relies on agriculture and some mining. Named after British explorer Captain James Cook, who beached his ship *Endeavour* there for repairs.

Coral Sea. Part of the southwestern PACIFIC OCEAN; extends east from its meeting with the ARAFURA SEA, through the TORRES STRAIT, east of the Australian continent and New Guinea, west of NEW CALEDONIA and the New Hebrides, and south of the SOLOMON ISLANDS. Covers 1,849,800 square miles (4,791,000 sq. km.); named for its many coral formations, particularly the GREAT BARRIER REEF, which extends 1,200 miles (1,900 km.) down AUSTRALIA's northeast coast. Subject to typhoons from January to April; provides a 200-mile (320 km.) shipping channel between eastern Australia and the South Pacific Islands and China. Site of a naval battle in 1942 that prevented the Japanese invasion of Australia.

Darling Downs. Tableland located in southeastern QUEENSLAND, AUSTRALIA. Agricultural and pastoral region covering 5,500 square miles (14,200 sq. km.); a major wheat and dairy belt.

Darwin. Capital city of AUSTRALIA's NORTHERN TERRITORY. Located in the far north, or Top End, it was founded in 1869 on a low peninsula northeast of the entrance to its harbor, Port Darwin, an inlet of the Clarence Strait of the TIMOR SEA. A center for government administration and mining; also a tourist destination, providing access to

Darwin, Australia. (Tom McKnight/Joan Clemons)

Bathurst and Melville Islands. Population was about seventy thousand in 1991. Violence was part of the area's history, as the local Aborigines resisted European settlement. As a result of its proximity to Asia, Darwin was bombed by the Japanese in 1942 during World War II. Port Darwin was named in 1839 by John Lort Stokes aboard H.M.S. *Beagle*, after his former shipmate, Charles Darwin.

Dry valleys. Ice-free valleys in ANTARCTICA that receive almost no precipitation and can sustain some rudimentary plant life. Dry valleys with oases are found in VICTORIA LAND, Wilkes Land, and Princess Elizabeth Land, all in EAST (GREATER) ANTARCTICA. Protected by the Royal Society Mountain Range; consist of the TAYLOR, Wright, and Victoria Valleys, which were once filled by glaciers. Collectively, they cover an area of 9 to 15 miles by 93 miles (15 to 25 km. by 150 km.).

Dunedin. Second-largest city on NEW ZEALAND's SOUTH ISLAND. Located on the southeast coast of Otago; population was 112,000 in 1999. Founded as a Scot-

*Dunedin
Page 1978*

tish settlement in 1848. New Zealand's first university was established there in 1869. The name is Gaelic for "Edinburgh."

East (Greater) Antarctica. Portion of ANT-ARCTICA east of the TRANSANTARCTIC MOUNTAINS. Includes Wilkes Land, Enderby Land, and QUEEN MAUD LAND. The geographic and magnetic South Poles lie in this area. Considerably larger than WEST (LESSER) ANT-ARCTICA.

Easter Island. Chilean island in the South Pacific, about 2,000 miles (3,220 km.) off the coast of Chile. Area of 46 square miles (119 sq. km.); population was 1,928 in 1985. The island, discovered on Easter Sunday in 1722 by Dutch Admiral Jacob Roggeveen, is known for the hundreds of monolithic statues of people, averaging 15 feet (4.6 meters) tall, that dot its landscape. Also known as Isla de Pascua or Rapa Nui.

Ellice Islands. See TUVALU.

Ellsworth Mountains. Range located south of the ANTARCTIC PENINSULA in MARIE BYRD LAND. Some of the world's highest peaks are located there: VINSON MASSIF soars to 16,859 feet (5,140 meters); Mount Tyree reaches 15,500 feet (4,723 meters). Named for the U.S. aviator who discovered their northern portion, SENTINEL RIDGE.

Equator. Great circle of the earth that is everywhere equally distant from the two poles and divides the earth into the northern and southern hemispheres. The direction of the currents and winds around the equator have a profound effect on the Pacific Islands.

Erebus, Mount. Largest active volcano on ROSS ISLAND, ANTARCTICA. Rises to 13,200 feet (4,023 meters) above sea level. Discovered in 1841 by Antarctic explorer Sir James Clark Ross, who named it after one of his ships. When

discovered, it was spewing smoke and flame into the sky to a height that Ross estimated to be 2,000 feet (600 meters).

Eyre, Lake. Great salt lake located in the southeastern corner of the GREAT ARTESIAN BASIN in the state of SOUTH AUSTRALIA. Covers 3,700 square miles (9,300 sq. km.). The surface of the lake bed is covered by a thin crust of salt, the result of deposits made by rapidly evaporating waters.

Federated States of Micronesia. See MICRONESIA, FEDERATED STATES OF.

Fiji. Archipelago in the South PACIFIC OCEAN, comprising about 320 islands in a horseshoe configuration in MELANESIA. Area is 7,056 square miles (18,274 sq. km.). Capital city is SUVA. Population was about 736,000 in 1990, 51 percent native Fijians and 44 percent Asian Indians. This has created continuing ethnic strife. Two main islands are Viti Levu and Vanua Levu. The islands are volcanic in origin, but coral reefs have built up along them. Also known as Fiji Islands.

Filchner Ice Shelf. Enormous ice shelf on the northeastern side of the WEDDELL SEA in EAST (GREATER) ANTARCTICA. Became much smaller in 1986, when all the ice north of its great chasm calved, floating into the Weddell Sea. The area that broke away covered 5,000 square miles (13,000 sq. km.).

Fiordland National Park. Largest national park in NEW ZEALAND. Covers 485,830 acres (1.2 million hectares). Established in 1952 in the remote southwestern corner of SOUTH ISLAND. Its geographical features include fjords, rugged mountain ranges, and vast beech forests. The park is a World Heritage area.

Flinders Island. Largest and northernmost island in the FURNEAUX GROUP, TASMANIA, AUSTRALIA. Located in the

Trans-antarctic Mts. Page 1848

Fiji Pages 1845, 1903, 1917, 1975

eastern BASS STRAIT between Tasmania and the Australian mainland; covers approximately 800 square miles (2,080 sq. km.). Named for English navigator Matthew Flinders, who first surveyed it in 1798.

Fraser Island. World Heritage-listed sand island, located off the southeastern coast of QUEENSLAND state, AUSTRALIA; also called Great Sandy Island. It is 75 miles (120 km.) long and covers 625 square miles (1,620 sq. km.). Named for Captain James Fraser, who was killed there by Aborigines in 1836.

Fremantle. One of AUSTRALIA's largest ports and the principal port of WESTERN AUSTRALIA state. Located on the INDIAN OCEAN at the mouth of the Swan River. Originally a major whaling center; later served the gold fields of Coolgardie-KALGOORLIE; a principal submarine base for the Allies in World War II; now a major industrial center. Known for its role in the America's Cup sailing competition.

French Oceania. See FRENCH POLYNESIA.

Bora-Bora
Page 1843

French Polynesia. Territory of France located in the South PACIFIC OCEAN, comprising 35 volcanic islands and more than 180 coral atolls. Area is 1,261 square miles (3,266 sq. km.); population was 212,000 in 1993. Contains SOCIETY, MARQUESAS, Gambier, and AUSTRAL island groups and TUAMOTU ARCHIPELAGO. Capital is Papeete, located on TAHITI, its largest island. Tahiti is also home to the largest peak on the islands, Mount Orohena, which reaches 7,352 feet (2,241 meters). About 67 percent of the population are Polynesian, 15 percent are mixtures of Polynesian and Chinese or European ancestry, 10 percent are of French origin, and 5 percent are ethnic Chinese. Also known as Polynésie Française. Formerly French Oceania.

Friendly Islands. See TONGA.

Furneaux Group. Cluster of mountainous, rocky islands situated in the BASS STRAIT that separates the Australian mainland from the island state of TASMANIA. Primary used for cattle and sheep raising. Sighted by Tobias Furneaux in 1773.

Gambier, Mount. Mountain located in southeastern SOUTH AUSTRALIA, approximately 280 miles (450 km.) southeast of the capital city of ADELAIDE. An extinct volcano with four crater lakes; rises to a height of 623 feet (190 meters).

Gaua. Active volcano on Gaua (also known as Santa María), one of the Banks Islands, north VANUATU in the southwestern PACIFIC OCEAN. Volcano, which reaches 2,614 feet (701 meters) in height. One of its most recent eruptions occurred in 1982.

Gaussberg, Mount. Only volcano discovered in EAST (GREATER) ANTARCTICA.

Geographic South Pole. See SOUTH POLE.

George VI Ice Shelf. Antarctic ice shelf melting ten times faster than the ROSS ICE SHELF. Located below the George VI Sound west of PALMER LAND on the ANTARCTIC PENINSULA, it receives deep, warm waters that spill over the continental shelf. These waters are 3.6 degrees Fahrenheit (2 degrees Celsius) warmer than those beneath the Ross Ice Shelf, enough drastically to affect the speed at which the ice melts.

Gibson Desert. Vast dry area in the interior of WESTERN AUSTRALIA. Located between the GREAT SANDY DESERT to the north and the GREAT VICTORIA DESERT to the south. First crossed in 1876 by Ernest Giles; named for Alfred Gibson, a member of his party who perished there.

Gilbert Islands. Group of islands with sixteen atolls in KIRIBATI, west PACIFIC

Ocean, across the EQUATOR. Area is 102 square miles (264 sq. km.); population was 63,848 in 1985. Part of the Gilbert and Ellice Islands (*see* TUVALU) Colony until 1976. Major islands are Tarawa, Butaritari, Abalang, Abemama, Tabiteuea, Nonouti, and Beru.

Gippsland. Fertile region of southeastern VICTORIA, AUSTRALIA. Covers 13,600 square miles (35,200 sq. km.). Center of the state's dairy industry. Originally attracted settlers with its gold finds; farmers arrived with the completion of a rail line from MELBOURNE in 1887.

Graham Land. Southern half of the ANTARCTIC PENINSULA; the northern half is called PALMER LAND. Named after a British nobleman.

Grampians. System of mountain ranges extending southwest from the GREAT DIVIDING RANGE in southwest central VICTORIA, AUSTRALIA. Covers approximately 400 square miles (1,035 sq. km.). Mount William, the highest peak, rises to 3,827 feet (1,166 meters). Noted for sandstone rock formations, deep gorges, and colorful vegetation.

Great Antarctic Horst. See TRANSANTARCTIC MOUNTAINS.

Great Artesian Basin. One of the largest areas of artesian water in the world, covering approximately 676,250 square miles (1,750,000 sq. km.). Underlies approximately one-fifth of the Australian continent, including most of QUEENSLAND, with portions extending into NEW SOUTH WALES, the NORTHERN TERRITORY, and SOUTH AUSTRALIA.

Great Australian Bight. Embayment of the INDIAN OCEAN indenting the southern coast of the Australian continent. Its head abuts the arid NULLABOR PLAIN. Has a continuous border of sea cliffs that rise 200-400 feet (60-120 meters) high.

Great Barrier Reef. Limestone formation created by the largest group of coral reefs in the world; extends 1,250 miles (2,010 km.) along the northeast coast of AUSTRALIA. Parts of the reef are more than 100 miles (160 km.) from the coast; the closest point is 10 miles (16 km.) distant. Covers approximately 135,000 square miles (350,000 sq. km.). Thought to have begun growing millions of years ago, the reef is formed from the skeletal waste of tiny marine organisms called coral polyps and hydrocorals. Supports about four hundred species of these organisms, more than fifteen hundred species of fish, and myriad other sea life and birds. Current biggest threat is the crown-of-thorns starfish, which feeds on the living coral. In addition to its scientific interest, the reef is a major tourist attraction. In 1981 it was added to UNESCO's World Heritage list. The Great Barrier Reef was first explored by Europeans in 1770, when British explorer Captain James Cook's ship ran aground on it.

Great Dividing Range. Series of mountain ranges and plateaus that form the main watershed of eastern AUSTRALIA. Also known as the Great Divide or Eastern Highlands, the range begins to the north on the CAPE YORK PENINSULA and parallels the coasts of QUEENSLAND, New South Wales, and VICTORIA, ending in the GRAMPIANS. One section, the Australian ALPS, includes Australia's highest peak, Mount KOSCIUSKO. Several of the country's major rivers form their headwaters in the range, including the Snowy, Darling, and Murrumbidgee Rivers. An important agricultural, lumbering, and mining region.

Great Sandy Desert. Vast, flat expanse of sand hills and salt marshes located in northern WESTERN AUSTRALIA, between the Pilbara and Kimberly ranges.

Great Sandy Desert Page 1851

Sparsely populated, with no significant settlements. Daytime temperatures in the summer are some of the hottest in AUSTRALIA, rising above 100 degrees Fahrenheit (38 degrees Celsius) at times.

Great Sandy Island. See FRASER ISLAND.

Great Victoria Desert. Vast, arid expanse of land in Western and SOUTH AUSTRALIA, situated between the NULLARBOR PLAIN to the south and the GIBSON DESERT to the north, and stretching eastward from KALGOORLIE nearly to the Stuart Range. Composed of salt marshes and hills covered with *Spinifex* grass. First explored by Ernest Giles, who named it.

Hawaiian pools Page 2032

Greater Antarctica. See EAST (GREATER) ANTARCTICA.

Guadalcanal. Largest of the SOLOMON ISLANDS in the South PACIFIC OCEAN. Area is 2,180 square miles (5,646 sq. km.). Population was 60,700 in 1991. Extending the length of the island (92 miles/148 km.) are the Kavo Mountains. During World War II, the site of fighting between U.S. and Japanese forces, beginning in August, 1942, and ending in February, 1943, with a U.S. victory.

Guadalcanal Page 2031

Guahan. See GUAM.

Guam. Largest and southernmost of the MARIANA ISLANDS in the western North PACIFIC OCEAN; unincorporated U.S. territory. Area is 212 square miles (549 sq. km.); population was 143,000 in 1993. Capital is Agana. Its northern part, largely a plateau, was formed by coral; the southern part, hilly with streams, is volcanic in origin. Occupied by the Japanese in 1941 and taken by the United States in 1944. Many U.S. Navy, Army, and Air Force installations are located on Guam, which was an important air base in the Vietnam War. Also known as Guahan.

Hawaii Pages 1853, 1903

Halycon Island. See WAKE ISLAND.

Hamersley Range. Mountains in the Pilbara region of WESTERN AUSTRALIA. Includes the state's highest peak, Mount Meharry (4,111 feet/1,253 meters). Important for mining, particularly iron ore.

Hawaii. State of the United States consisting of a chain of volcanic and coral islands in the North PACIFIC OCEAN. The Hawaiian archipelago contains eight major islands—Hawaii (also known as the Big Island), KAUAI, OAHU, MAUI, Lanai, MOLOKAI, Nihau, and Kahoolawe—and 124 islets, reefs, and shoals. The islands' total area is 6,471 square miles (16,760 sq. km.). Hawaii's population was 1.1 million in 1990. Largest city is HONOLULU, on Oahu Island. The islands are almost all volcanic in origin, with some areas formed from coral reefs. The islands contain mountains rising to more than 13,000 feet (4,000 meters) above sea level, numerous sandy beaches, dense rain forests, arid scrublands, fields, forests, barren lava beds, and canyons. European explorer Captain James Cook arrived in 1778 and named the islands the Sandwich Islands. Originally an independent kingdom created by Kamehameha I in the late eighteenth century, the islands lost their independence in the late nineteenth century, when American planters overthrew the monarchy and declared a republic. Hawaii was annexed to the United States in 1898 and became the nation's fiftieth state in 1959.

Hawaii Island. Largest and southernmost of the Hawaiian Islands, United States, in the North Pacific. Area is 4,021 square miles (10,414 sq. km.); population was 120,317 in 1990. Has four volcanic mountains: MAUNA KEA, Hualalai, MAUNA LOA, and KILAUEA.

Hawke's Bay. Largest production region

of apples, pears, and peaches in NEW ZEALAND. A wide bay located on the east central coast of NORTH ISLAND. Boasts a Mediterranean climate and fertile soils. Contains Cape Kidnappers, the largest known mainland gannet-nesting colony in the world. Named by Captain James Cook after Sir Edward Hawke, then Lord of the British Admiralty, in 1769.

Hobart. Largest city, main port, and capital of AUSTRALIA's island state, TASMANIA. Australia's smallest capital city, with an estimated population of 127,000 in the 1990's. Established as a convict settlement at the mouth of the Derwent River in the southeastern corner of the state in 1804. Existed in conflict with the native Aborigines until the last of them was exterminated in 1876. Situated at the foot of lofty Mount Wellington (4,165 feet/1,270 meters) and blessed with an excellent deep-water harbor, Hobart has prospered, particularly in the whaling trade, shipbuilding, and the export of agricultural products such as corn and merino wool.

Honolulu. Seaport city on OAHU Island, HAWAII, in the PACIFIC OCEAN. Population was 355,272 in 1990. Its convenient location in the North Pacific Ocean and its protected harbor make it a valuable trade port. Located at the mouth of the Nuuanu Valley, with the Punchbowl and Mount Tantalus behind it. A superior beach is located in its southeastern suburb of Waikiki. Main industries are tourism, sugar processing, and pineapple canning.

Howe, Cape. Southeastern point of mainland AUSTRALIA, located at the NEW SOUTH WALES-VICTORIA border, 300 miles (560 km.) southwest of SYDNEY. Named by Captain James Cook in 1770 for Richard, Lord Howe, of the Royal Navy.

Hunter Valley. Fertile agricultural region in east central NEW SOUTH WALES, AUSTRALIA; watered by the Hunter River and its tributaries. Agriculture includes fruit orchards and vineyards; cattle, sheep, and poultry are raised also.

Îles Australes. See AUSTRAL ISLANDS.

Îles Marquises. See MARQUESAS ISLANDS.

Indian Ocean. One of the three oceans on which the coast of ANTARCTICA fronts. The Indian Ocean is off EAST (GREATER) ANTARCTICA, from about the fiftieth to the hundred-twentieth parallel.

Invercargill. Southernmost city in NEW ZEALAND. Located on the Waihopai River at the bottom of SOUTH ISLAND; population was 50,800 in 1999. Has some of the widest streets of any city in New Zealand.

Isla de Pascua. See EASTER ISLAND.

Islands, Bay of. Site of NEW ZEALAND's first permanent European settlement. Located on the east coast in the Northland region of NORTH ISLAND. Contains 150 islands, most uninhabited, within an irregular coastline that stretches 497 miles (800 km.).

Bay of Islands Page 2033

Jervis Bay. Inlet of the TASMAN SEA, in southeastern NEW SOUTH WALES, AUSTRALIA. One of the country's finest natural harbors, 10 miles (16 km.) wide and 6 miles (10 km.) long. Discovered and named in 1770 by Captain James Cook.

Honolulu Pages 1968, 2033

Joseph Bonaparte Gulf. Inlet of the TIMOR SEA indenting the northern coast of AUSTRALIA for nearly 100 miles (160 km.). Site of Wydham, the area's main port; termination point for the Ord, Victoria, and other rivers. Aboriginal reserves are located here.

Kalgoorlie. Historical Gold Capital of the World, located in the OUTBACK northern goldfields of WESTERN AUSTRALIA, 372 miles (600 km.) from PERTH. Population was eleven thousand in the 1990's. Mining began with (Paddy) "Hannans's Find"—the discovery of gold in 1893; production peaked in 1903. Nickel is now the region's chief mineral product. An arid region, its name is a corruption of the Aborigine word "galgurlie," an indigenous plant.

Kangaroo Island. AUSTRALIA's third-largest offshore island. Located at the entrance to the Gulf of St. Vincent in SOUTH AUSTRALIA, 80 miles (130 km.) southwest of the state's capital city, ADELAIDE. Kingscote is the main town; population was twenty-one hundred in the 1990's. A low, cliffed plateau, 90 miles (145 km.) long and 27 miles (44 km.) wide. Separated from the mainland by Investigator Strait. Named by English explorer Matthew Flinders in 1802 for the abundance of kangaroos.

Karkar. Active volcano on a small island in the PACIFIC OCEAN, off the east coast of New Guinea Island, in the BISMARCK ARCHIPELAGO, PAPUA NEW GUINEA. Reaches a height of 4,920 feet (1,500 meters). One of its most recent eruptions occurred in 1979.

Kauai. Island in the northwest part of the HAWAIIAN ISLANDS, North PACIFIC OCEAN. Area is 555 square miles (1,437 sq. km.). Mountainous, with two major

Kauai
Page 2034

Mount Kilauea. (Hawaii Visitors & Convention Bureau/Warren Bolster)

peaks, Kawaikini and WAIALEALE; three major bays are Nawiliwilli, Hanalei, and Hanapepe. Largest city, Lihue, had a population of 5,500 in 1990.

Kavachi. Active submarine volcano in the SOLOMON ISLANDS, south of Vangunu Island, in the PACIFIC OCEAN. Located 18.6 miles (30 km.) from the boundary of the Indian and Australian tectonic plates. Rises from a depth of about 3,250 feet (1,100 meters); base measures about 4.9 miles (8 km.) in diameter. Since the first recorded eruption in 1939, it has created at least eight islands up to about 480 feet (150 meters) in length.

Kerr Point. Northernmost tip of NEW ZEALAND. Situated on North Cape at 34°24' south latitude, longitude 172°59' east. Extends northward into the PACIFIC OCEAN.

Kilauea. Active volcanic crater in Hawaii Volcanoes National Park, on the east slope of volcanic mountain of MAUNA LOA, south central HAWAII ISLAND, Hawaii. Crater is at an elevation of 4,009 feet (1,247 meters), more than 10,000 feet (3,000 meters) below the summit. It began erupting in 1983, spewing 525,000 cubic yards (400,000 cubic meters) of lava per day on average. The lava had added about 5,000 acres (2,000 hectares) of land to Hawaii Island by 1995.

Kimberley Plateau. Sandstone plateau with deep river gorges, located in northern WESTERN AUSTRALIA. Covers 140,000 square miles (360,000 sq. km.). Mining and cattle grazing are primary industries. Several thousand Aborigines live in the region.

Kiribati. Island nation, part of the Commonwealth of Nations, in the central PACIFIC OCEAN. Area is 313 square miles (811 sq. km.); population was 87,000 in 2000. This Micronesian re-

public comprises thirty-three coral atolls in three groups: the GILBERT, PHOENIX, and Line Islands. Seventeen of the twenty-one permanently inhabited islands are in the Gilbert Islands, where its capital, Tarawa, is located. Except for Banaba, the islands are atolls, few rising more than 13 feet (4 meters) above sea level. Kiribati, among other Pacific Island nations, has expressed concern over global warming, which could mean raised ocean levels and the submersion of its islands.

Kiritimati Island. One of the Line Islands of KIRIBATI, in central PACIFIC OCEAN. Largest atoll in the Pacific, at 234 square miles (606 sq. km.); population was 2,537 in 1990. Part of KIRIBATI since 1979. Also known as Christmas Island.

Kosciusko, Mount. AUSTRALIA's highest mountain peak, located in NEW SOUTH WALES. Rises to 7,313 feet (2,229 meters). Snow covers the mountain through the winter. In 1840 explorer Paul Edmund de Strzelecki named the mountain after Thaddeus Kosciusko, a Polish army officer who fought with the Americans in the Revolutionary War.

Lagoon Islands. See TUVALU.

Lambert Glacier. Sizable Antarctic glacier; 25 miles (40 km.) wide and more than 248 miles (400 km.) long. Flowing through the PRINCE CHARLES MOUNTAINS, it drains the interior reaches of the continent of ice and snow, discharging 8.4 miles (13.5 km.) of ice every year into the AMERY ICE SHELF.

Lesser Antarctica. See WEST (LESSER) ANTARCTICA.

Little America. Name of several bases in ANTARCTICA. The first was established by explorer Richard Byrd near the Bay of WHALES in 1928. Four subsequent bases called Little America were built after this one. Little America V was dis-

Kilauea Page 1903, 2034

Richard E. Byrd and members of his Antarctic expedition raise an American flag at Little America in December, 1956. (AP/Wide World Photos)

McMurdo Station Page 2035

McMurdo Sound Page 1910

banded in 1979 after the Geophysical Year.

Lopevi. Active volcano on the island of Lopevi, in south central VANUATU in the southwestern PACIFIC OCEAN. Reaches a height of 4,755 feet (1,449 meters). One of its latest eruptions occurred in 1999.

McMurdo Station. One of six U.S. stations built in ANTARCTICA during the International Geophysical Year (1957-1958). Situated on the east side of the Ross SEA off VICTORIA LAND in the McMurdo Sound. Staffed by twelve hundred researchers and explorers during

the Antarctic summer; about two hundred people remain during the long winter.

Magnetic South Pole. See SOUTH MAGNETIC POLE.

Mariana Islands. PACIFIC OCEAN island group east of the Philippines that comprises the sixteen coral and volcanic islands of the Commonwealth of the NORTHERN MARIANA ISLANDS and GUAM.

Mariana Trench. Deepest seafloor depression in the world, 25,840 feet (10,924 meters) deep. Located just east of the MARIANA ISLANDS in the PACIFIC

OCEAN at 11°22′ north latitude, longitude 142°36′ east. The arc-shaped trench, which averages 44 miles (70 km.) in width, stretches from northeast to southwest for about 1,554 miles (2,400 km.). The Challenger Deep, at the southwestern end of the trench, is the deepest point on Earth at 36,198 feet (11,033 meters).

Marie Byrd Land. Large area in WEST (LESSER) ANTARCTICA. Established near the one hundredth parallel; named for the wife of Antarctic explorer Richard Byrd.

Marquesas Islands. Ten-island group in FRENCH POLYNESIA, in the South PACIFIC OCEAN. Area is 480 square miles (1,243 sq. km.); population was 7,358 in 1988. Major islands fall in three groups: Nuku Hiva, Ua Pu, and Ua Huka (center); Hiva Oa, Tahuata, and Fau Hiva (southeast); and Eiao and Hatutu (northwest). Islands are of volcanic origin. Also known as Îles Marquises.

Marshall Islands. Archipelago and republic in central North PACIFIC OCEAN. Contains more than 24 atolls and more than 867 coral reefs. Area is 70 square miles (181 sq. km.); population was 68,000 in 2000. Manjuro is the capital island of these MICRONESIAN islands. The February, 1944, capture of Manjuro by the United States in World War II was the first seizure by the United States of a Japanese possession. The United

States used BIKINI ATOLL in the Marshall Islands as a nuclear testing ground in 1946. A trusteeship of the United States after 1947; became self-governing in 1979. Officially, the Republic of the Marshall Islands.

Maui. Second-largest of the HAWAIIAN ISLANDS. Area is 728 square miles (1,886

Ua Pu
Page 2035

Haleakala Crater on Maui. (Corbis)

Maui's Haleakala National Park is dominated by the giant crater of Haleakala volcano, which last erupted in 1790. (PhotoDisc)

sq. km.). East end of the island has Haleakala National Park, with a peak, Red Hill, reaching 10,023 feet (3,055 meters); the west end has Puu Kukui, at 5,787 feet (1,764 meters). On its south coast is Maalaea Bay.

Mauna Kea. Extinct volcano in north central HAWAII ISLAND, Hawaii. At 13,796 feet (4,205 meters), the highest island mountain in the world from base to peak.

Mauna Loa. Active volcano in Hawaii National Park on south central HAWAII ISLAND, Hawaii. Reaches 13,680 feet (4,170 meters) in height; is the largest mountain in the world in cubic content. Since the 1830's, it has erupted on average once every three to four years. Large lava flows occurred in 1919, 1950, and 1984.

Melanesia. One of three divisions of the Pacific Islands, the other two being MICRONESIA and POLYNESIA. Located in the western PACIFIC OCEAN. The name Melanesia, or "dark islands," was given to the area because of its inhabitants' dark skins. PAPUA NEW GUINEA forms the westernmost part of Melanesia; the western half, Irian Jaya, is part of Indonesia, and thus considered part of Asia. The other islands include the SOLOMON ISLANDS, VANUATU, NEW CALEDONIA, FIJI, ADMIRALTY ISLANDS, and the BISMARCK ARCHIPELAGO.

Melbourne. State capital of VICTORIA, Australia; country's second-largest city. Situated 3 miles (4.5 km.) inland at the head of Port Phillip Bay on the southeastern coast. Population was three million in the late 1990's. Established in 1835 on the banks of the Yarra River, the cosmopolitan city is the country's financial center. The densely populated city center and outlying suburbs cover approximately 2,359 square miles (6,109 sq. km.). Hosted the Olympic Games in 1956.

Micronesia. One of three divisions of the Pacific Islands, the other two being MELANESIA and POLYNESIA. The name Micronesia means "small islands." The islands are mostly atolls and coral islands; however, many of the islands in the CAROLINES are of volcanic origin. The more than two thousand islands of Micronesia are located in the PACIFIC OCEAN east of the Philippines, mostly above the EQUATOR. Micronesia contains the Federated States of MICRONESIA, NAURU, KIRIBATI, the MARSHALL ISLANDS, the Republic of PALAU, GUAM, and the Commonwealth of the NORTHERN MARIANA ISLANDS.

Micronesia, Federated States of (FSM). Islands of the CAROLINES except PALAU, in free association with the United States. Area is 271 square miles (702 sq. km.); population was 133,100 in 2000. Comprises four states—Kosrae, Pohnpei (formerly Ponape), Chuuk (formerly Truk), and Yap—and is located north of the EQUATOR. Contains more than six thousand islands, many of which are low-lying coral atolls. Pohn-

pei, a volcanic island, is FSM's largest and is home to the capital, Palikir. The islands of Yap state, unlike the others of FSM, are continental (formed by an uplifting of the continental shelf).

Midway Islands. Two islands, Eastern and Sand Islands, parts of a coral atoll in central PACIFIC OCEAN. Area is 2 square miles (5 sq. km.). Unpopulated before occupied by the United States since 1867; administered by the U.S. Navy and has been used extensively by the U.S. Navy and Air Force. In June, 1942, during World War II, U.S. forces defeated a Japanese fleet nearby. Formerly Brooks Islands.

Milford Sound. One of the wettest places in NEW ZEALAND, with an annual average rainfall of 256 inches (650 centimeter). A 10-mile-long (16 km.) fjord located in the remote corner of SOUTH ISLAND. Part of FIORDLAND NATIONAL PARK. Contains a number of rock-sheer cliffs including Mitre Peak, which rises 5,560 feet (1,695 meters) out of the sea. Ending point of the Milford hiking track.

Milford Sound Page 2036

Molokai. One of the HAWAIIAN ISLANDS. Area is 259 square miles (671 sq. km.). Largest city is Kaunakakai; the island has MAUNA LOA at its west end and Kamakou at its east end. A leprosy-treatment center is located on its north coast.

Murray River. AUSTRALIA's major river. Flows 1,609 miles (2,589 km.) across southeastern Australia, from the Snowy Mountains to the GREAT AUSTRALIAN BIGHT on the INDIAN OCEAN. Main tributaries include the Darling and Murrumbidgee Rivers. The fertile Murray Valley, the most irrigated land on the continent, is of great economic importance.

Nauru. Raised coral island and republic in central PACIFIC OCEAN. Area is 8.2 square miles (21.2 sq. km.); population

Nauru Pages 1910, 1976

Nauru from the air in 1986. (Tom McKnight/Joan Clemons)

was 10,700 in the year 2000 most living in a narrow coastal strip around the edges of the island. Naurans are of Polynesian, Micronesian, and Melanesian origin. The island contains large amounts of phosphate rock. Mining of the phosphate, due to be depleted in 2000, has produced royalties that made the republic, per capita, one of the richest in the world, but caused severe damage to the environment. Formerly Pleasant Island.

New Caledonia. French overseas territory in the southwestern PACIFIC OCEAN. Contains New Caledonia Island, Loyalty Islands, Isle of Pines, Chesterfield Islands, and Huon Islands. Total area is 7,358 square miles (19,058 sq. km.); population was 164,173 in 1989, with 43 percent Melanesian, 37 percent European (mainly French), and 20 percent Vietnamese, Polynesian, and Indonesian. Economic activities include mining (nickel, iron, and manganese), agriculture, livestock production, fishing and forestry, and tourism. Officially New Caledonia and Dependencies. Also known as Nouvelle Calédonie.

New Hebrides. See VANUATU.

New Hebrides Basin. Part of the CORAL SEA, located east of AUSTRALIA and west of the New Hebrides island chain. The basin contains volcanic islands, both old and recent.

New Hebrides Trench. Ocean trench in the southwestern PACIFIC OCEAN, about 5,682 miles (9,165 km.) long and 3,936 feet (1,200 meters) deep.

New South Wales. AUSTRALIA's most populous state. Located in the southeastern section of the continent; bounded by the PACIFIC OCEAN to the east, the state of SOUTH AUSTRALIA to the west, QUEENSLAND state to the north, and the state of VICTORIA to the south. Population was more than six million in the 1990's. Climate ranges from tropical rain forests to snow-clad mountains. Geographically, it is a narrow coastal plain bordered in the east by the GREAT DIVIDING RANGE, which runs the length of the state; slopes and plains lie to the west. In 1788 it became the site of the first British settlement on the continent; during the nineteenth century the colonies of VICTORIA, South Australia, TASMANIA, and QUEENSLAND were carved out of its vast original territory. Highly industrialized and economically stable, the state is famous for its beautiful harbor and capital city, SYDNEY.

New Zealand. Large South Pacific island nation, located more than 1,000 miles (1,600 km.) southeast of AUSTRALIA, its nearest neighbor. It was a British colony until 1947. The country comprises two main islands, the NORTH and SOUTH islands, and a number of small islands, which collectively cover an area of about 104,000 square miles (268,000 sq. km.). New Zealand administers the South Pacific island group of TOKELAU and claims a section of ANTARCTICA. NIUE and the COOK ISLANDS are self-governing states in free association with New Zealand. Its economy is based on the export of agricultural products. About 15 percent of its 3,801,000 people (1998) are native Maoris. Capital city is WELLINGTON.

Ninety Mile Beach. Famous beach in NEW ZEALAND, located along the west coast of the top of NORTH ISLAND. Despite its name, it is about 50 miles (90 km.) long. The fringe of the beach is lined by white sand dunes, in places reaching heights of 469 miles (143 meters) and widths of 4 miles (6 km.).

Niue. Raised coral island in the south central PACIFIC OCEAN, east of TONGA, in free association with NEW ZEALAND. Area is 100 square miles (259 sq. km.); population was 1,906 in 1994. Consists of a plateau (200 feet/61 meters) surrounded by a lower level (90 feet/27 meters) and rimmed by uneven, steep cliffs. Most of its residents are Polynesian; about half live in or around the capital, Alofi. Also known as Savage Island.

North Island. Smaller of the two principal islands of NEW ZEALAND, separated from SOUTH ISLAND by COOK STRAIT. North Island has an area of 44,204 square miles (114,489 sq. km.), as well as a majority of the national population. Most of its people are concentrated in the vicinity of the major urban areas, WELLINGTON and AUCKLAND. Its population was 2,553,413 in 1991.

Northern Mariana Islands, Commonwealth of the. Island group in the PACIFIC OCEAN, east of the Philippines, commonwealth of the United States. Area is 184 square miles (477 sq. km.); population was 43,345 in 1990. Consists of sixteen coral and volcanic islands that are the MARIANA ISLANDS minus GUAM. Main islands are SAIPAN (where the seat of government is), Tinia, and Rota. The islands' economy is based on agriculture, light manufacturing, and tourism. Also known as Northern Marianas.

Northern Territory. Self-governing territory of AUSTRALIA. Located in the cen-

North Island Page 2037

New Zealand map Page 1841

*Olgas
Page 2037*

*Kakadu
Waterfall
Page 2038*

tral section of the northern part of the continent; bounded by the TIMOR and ARAFURA Seas to the north, the state of WESTERN AUSTRALIA to the west, QUEENSLAND and the Gulf of CARPENTARIA to the east, and SOUTH AUSTRALIA to the south. Population was 200,000 in 1996. Occupies nearly one-sixth of the Australian landmass. Climate is tropical in the north and semi-arid in the south. Central section is crossed east-to-west by the Macdonnell Ranges; main rivers include the Victoria and the Adelaide. ULURU monolith is located near the southwest corner of the territory. Major towns are DARWIN (the capital) and ALICE SPRINGS.

Nullarbor Plain. Flat, treeless plateau located in the state of SOUTH AUSTRALIA. An ancient limestone seabed rising about 150-500 feet (50-200 meters) above sea level; southern edge is bordered by the GREAT AUSTRALIAN BIGHT and features 124 miles (200 km.) of spectacular eroded sea cliffs. Covers 100,000 square miles (260,000 sq. km.) and is crossed by the world's longest stretch of straight railroad track (330 miles/530 km.); it is also accessed nearer the coast by the Eyre Highway. Has an average rainfall of less than 10 inches (254 millimeters) and is nearly featureless with no surface streams. Name is Latin for "no tree."

Honolulu's Pearl Harbor is home to one of the largest U.S. Navy bases. This floating memorial honors the crew of the battleship Arizona, *which was sunk on this location by Japan's attack on the base on December 7, 1941. (Clyde L. Rasmussen)*

Oahu. Third-largest of the Hawaiian Islands. Area is 600 square miles (1,555 sq. km.). Contains two mountain ranges: the Koolau along the northeast coast and the Waianae along the southwest coast. Honolulu, capital of the state of Hawaii, and Pearl Harbor are located on its south coast.

Oceania. Collective name for the more than ten thousand islands scattered throughout the Pacific Ocean, excluding the Japanese archipelago, Indonesia, Taiwan, the Philippines, and Alaska's Aleutian Islands. The term also generally excludes Australia, while including Papua New Guinea and New Zealand. Oceania has traditionally been divided into four parts: Australasia, Melanesia, Micronesia, and Polynesia. Its total land area, excluding Australia, is approximately 317,000 square miles (821,000 sq. km.); its population (again excluding Australia) was about 9,400,000 people in 1990.

Ord River. River in the Kimberley plateau region of northeastern Western Australia. Flows east then north nearly 300 miles (500 km.) to the Cambridge Gulf. Site of Australia's most expensive and controversial irrigation plan, the Ord River Project, designed to prevent seasonal flooding and store water for irrigating areas subject to drought.

Outback. Name by which Australians refer to any place away from their cities. More specifically, the semiarid region west of the Great Dividing Range (Eastern Highlands), which covers about 80 percent of the continent, including most of Queensland, all of the Northern Territory, and all of Western Australia except the southwest corner. The Macdonnell, Musgrave, and Petermann mountain ranges and the country's four major deserts (Victoria, Great Sandy, Gibson, and Tanamai) are situated in the Outback. Economy is mainly supported by sheep raising, opal mining, and oil production. Home of the Royal Flying Doctor Service, which provides medical assistance to the residents of this area.

Pacific Ocean. Largest body of water on Earth, covering more than one-third of the world's surface. Its area of about 70 million square miles (181 million sq. km.) is greater than the entire land area of the world. It is framed by North and South America in the northeast, Asia in the west, and Australia in the southwest. The equator separates the North Pacific Ocean from the South Pacific Ocean. The ocean's average depth is about 12,900 feet (3,900 meters). Its bottom is more geologically varied than those of the earth's other great oceans—the Indian and Atlantic Oceans. The Pacific has more volcanoes, ridges, trenches, seamounts, and islands. Historically, the vast size of the Pacific was a formidable barrier to travel, communications, and trade well into the nineteenth century.

Pagan. Active volcano on Pagan Island in the Northern Mariana Islands. Reaches 1,870 feet (577 meters) in height. One of its most recent eruptions occurred in 1993.

Pagan from space Page 2039

Palau, Republic of. Republic and group of about two hundred islands and islets in the west Pacific Ocean, in free association with the United States. Area is 188 square miles (488 sq. km.). Its population was about 19,000 in 2000, with about 70 percent of its people living on Koror. Part of Micronesia and considered western part of Carolines. The republic includes islands of Babelthuap (the largest), Urukthapel, Peleliu, Angaur, Eli Malk, and Koror. Palau's is-

*Perth
Page 2039*

*Port
Moresby
Pages
1971, 1979-
1980*

*Rouna
Falls
Page 2040*

lands, the larger of which are volcanic, are encompassed by a fringing reef. Also known as Belau; formerly Pelew.

Palau Trench. Seafloor depression in the western PACIFIC OCEAN; about 250 miles (400 km.) long and 26,425 feet (8,055 meters) deep. Located near PALAU at 7°52′ north latitude, longitude 134°56′ east.

Palmer Land. Northern half of the ANTARCTIC PENINSULA; the southern half is called GRAHAM LAND. Named after Nathaniel Palmer, an American who discovered the SOUTH ORKNEY ISLANDS.

Papua New Guinea. Independent country in the southwestern PACIFIC OCEAN. Area is 178,704 square miles (462,840 sq. km.); population was 3,918,000 in 1993. Capital is PORT MORESBY. Located on the eastern half of New Guinea; contains Bougainville Island, Buka Island, Louisiade Archipelago, Trobriand Islands, D'Entrecasteaux Islands, the BISMARCK ARCHIPELAGO (New Britain, New Ireland, Manus), and hundreds of smaller islands. (The western part of New Guinea is Irian Jaya, part of Indonesia and thus considered part of Asia.) Mountains on the mainland stretch from east to west and rise to 14,793 feet (4,509 meters) at Mount WILHELM in the Bismarck Range. Between this range and the Owen Stanley range in the southeast lie broad, high valleys. North of the valleys is a swampy plain; on its north are coastal mountain ranges, running from west to east. Major rivers include the Fly, Purari, Kikori, Sepik, and Ramu. Located along the RING OF FIRE, a belt of seismic activity circling the Pacific Ocean, it has forty active volcanoes and frequent earthquakes. Formerly known as the Territory of Papua and New Guinea.

Pelew. See PALAU, REPUBLIC OF.

Perth. Capital of WESTERN AUSTRALIA state, AUSTRALIA. Located on the banks of the Swan River, 12 miles (19 km.) from the river's mouth, which forms the harbor of FREMANTLE. A city since 1856, it is now the fourth-largest in the country; more than one million people—nearly two-thirds of the state's population—live there. An important industrial center; has a mild climate nearly eight months of the year. Nicknamed the "city of lights" by astronauts orbiting the earth in the 1960's. Closer in distance to Asia's Singapore than to SYDNEY.

Petermann Range. Low mountain range extending for 200 miles (320 km.) from east central WESTERN AUSTRALIA to the southwest corner of the NORTHERN TERRITORY. Rises to 3,800 feet (1,158 meters). First explored by Ernest Giles in 1874, and named for August Petermann, a German geographer.

Phoenix Islands. Island group consisting of eight small coral atolls, in the central PACIFIC OCEAN; part of KIRIBATI. Area is 11 square miles (29 sq. km.). The Phoenix Islands contain Kanton, Rawaki, Enderbury, Birnie, Manra, Orona, Nikumaroro, and McKean. Formerly a stop on trans-Pacific flights.

Pitcairn Island. Group of islands forming a British dependency in the south PACIFIC OCEAN. Consists of Pitcairn Island and the uninhabited islands of Henderson, Ducie, and Oeno. Area is 18 square miles (47 sq. km.); population was 61 in 1991. Pitcairn, of volcanic origin, contains a single village, Adamstown. It was uninhabited when mutineers of the HMS *Bounty* and a group of Tahitians occupied it in 1790; the remains of their settlement were discovered in 1808. Overpopulation resulted in two hundred islanders moving to

Norfolk Island in 1856; some later returned to Pitcairn.

Pleasant Island. See NAURU.

Pole of Inaccessibility. Point near the sixtieth meridian of east longitude that is farthest from any coast. The ice dome's highest elevation, some 14,000 feet (4,267 meters), is in this vicinity.

Polynesia. One of three divisions of the Pacific Islands, the other two being MELANESIA and MICRONESIA. Group of islands in the central and southern PACIFIC OCEAN. Polynesia means "many islands." Includes AMERICAN SAMOA, the COOK ISLANDS, EASTER ISLAND, FRENCH POLYNESIA, HAWAIIAN ISLANDS, Line Islands, NEW ZEALAND, NIUE, the PITCAIRN ISLANDS, SAMOA, TOKELAU, TONGA, TUVALU, and the WALLIS AND FUTUNA ISLANDS. The islands, mostly small, are predominantly coral atolls, but some are of volcanic origin.

Port Arthur. Inlet of the TASMAN SEA on the south coast of the Tasman Peninsula, TASMANIA, AUSTRALIA. Located 63 miles (101 km.) northwest of the capital city of HOBART. Site of one of the most notorious British penal colonies, established in 1830, the ruins of which have become a popular tourist attraction.

Port Jackson. Inlet of the PACIFIC OCEAN and principal port of NEW SOUTH WALES, AUSTRALIA; also known as Sydney Harbor. Its 1.5-mile-long (2.4 km.) entrance lies between North and South Heads; it is 12 miles (19 km.) long, with a total area of 21 square miles (55 sq. km.), and is spanned by the Sydney Harbor Bridge at its northern end. Comprises three smaller harbors—North Harbor, Middle Harbor, and Sydney Harbor—and the deepwater mouths of two rivers, the Parramatta and the Lane Cove.

Port Moresby. Seaport and capital of PAPUA NEW GUINEA in the PACIFIC OCEAN. Located on the southeast coast of the Gulf of Papua. Population was 193,240 in 1990. Has a large, sheltered harbor; was an Allied base in World War II.

Port Moresby Pages 1971, 1979-1980

Prince Charles Mountains. Area through which the LAMBERT GLACIER in EAST (GREATER) ANTARCTICA flows, annually carrying 8.3 miles (13.4 km.) of ice to the AMERY ICE SHELF.

Queen Maud Land. Section of ANTARCTICA located west of Enderby Land, between 20 degrees west and 45 degrees east latitude.

Queensland. AUSTRALIA's second-largest state. Covers 668,200 square miles (1,730,648 sq. km.) including almost 2,700 square miles (7,000 sq. km.) of islands. The state constitutes 22.5 percent of Australia's total area. In 1999 its population was 3.5 million; the population is heavily concentrated in the southeast. Capital is BRISBANE, with 1.3 million people. The state has a tropical climate and is known for its unusual flora, fauna, and proximity to the GREAT BARRIER REEF. Originally a British penal colony named Moreton Bay.

Queensland Pages 1909, 1912

Rabaul. Active volcano on New Britain Island, in the BISMARCK ARCHIPELAGO, part of PAPUA NEW GUINEA in the PACIFIC OCEAN. Reaches a height of 2,257 feet (696 meters). One of its most recent eruptions occurred in 1999.

Rapa Nui. See EASTER ISLAND.

Red Centre. See ALICE SPRINGS.

Rockhampton. City and commercial center in central QUEENSLAND, AUSTRALIA. Located 38 miles (60 km.) inland at the head of the Fitzroy River, which empties into Keppel Bay. Population was fifty thousand in the 1990's. Regional commercial center served by the deepwater Port Alma; important tourist base for ocean access to the GREAT BARRIER REEF.

Ronne Ice Shelf. Large Antarctic ice shelf in the WEDDELL SEA. Named after Edith Ronne, who spent nearly a year in 1947 on STONINGTON ISLAND with her husband, explorer Finn Ronne. Originally called Edith Ronne Land, the name was later changed to the Ronne Ice Shelf.

Ross Ice Shelf. Largest ice shelf in ANTARCTICA. About 3,000 feet (914 meters) thick, sloping down to 650 feet (198 meters) as it approaches the ROSS SEA. Constantly growing through the activity of the glaciers that feed it, it is four times the size of the state of New York and almost as large as Texas. Presents an impenetrable surface along its entire face, high cliffs of ice totally without openings, making it impossible for early explorers to move from the Ross Sea into the interior.

Ross Island. Large island in the ROSS SEA of ANTARCTICA. Has four volcanoes, Mount EREBUS being the only active one. Covered most of the year by ice that connects it to the mainland. The cold temperatures there prevent rain from falling, but it regularly receives snow. Named after British explorer Sir James Clark Ross,

Ross Sea. Large sea south of the PACIFIC OCEAN on ANTARCTICA's west side; ice-free part of the year. The TRANSANTARCTIC MOUNTAINS run 3,000 miles (4,838 km.) from the Ross Sea across the SOUTH POLE to the WEDDELL SEA. Named after Sir James Clark Ross, who explored the area 1839-1843.

Rotorua. Active thermal region of NEW ZEALAND, situated in central NORTH ISLAND. Site of sulfur fumes, bubbling mud, and hot springs. One of only three areas in the world where geysers

*Samoa
Pages
1845, 1971*

are found, including Iceland and Yellowstone Park in the United States. An important center of Maori culture.

Saipan. One of the NORTHERN MARIANA ISLANDS in the west PACIFIC OCEAN. Area is 70 square miles (181 sq. km.); population was 38,896 in 1990. High cliffs mark the north end of the hilly island. Was included in the Japanese mandate under the League of Nations in 1920; Japan developed it as a naval base. Captured by U.S. troops in 1944 and converted to a U.S. air base for the duration of World War II.

Samoa. Independent island nation in the southern PACIFIC OCEAN. Located on the western part of the Samoan archipelago, west of longitude 171 degrees west. (The part of the archipelago east of this line is AMERICAN SAMOA.) Consists of nine volcanic islands. Area is 1,093 square miles (2,831 sq. km.); 99 percent of this area is Savavi'i and Upolu, the two largest islands, which contain rain forests. The other seven islands are Apolima, Manono, Fanuatapu, Nu'ulopa, Nu'utele, Nu'ulua, and Nu'usafee. Samoa's population was 235,300 in 2000, two-thirds living in Upolu. Samoans make up more than 90 percent of the population. Also known as Samoa Islands; formerly Western Samoa.

Sandwich Islands. See HAWAII.

Savage Island. See NIUE.

Sentinel Ridge. Northern ridge of the ELLSWORTH MOUNTAINS in the Antarctic. VINSON MASSIF, ANTARCTICA's highest mountain, is found there.

Shark Bay. Inlet of the INDIAN OCEAN, WESTERN AUSTRALIA. Bisected by Peron Peninsula and sheltered to the west by Dorre, Benier, and Dirk Hartog Islands. Named in 1699 by the pirate William Dampier after numerous sharks were sighted.

Shirase. ANTARCTICA's fastest-moving glacier. Located in QUEEN MAUD LAND on the Atlantic side of the continent. Moves about 1.2 miles (2 km.) a year.

Simpson Desert. Vast arid region of central AUSTRALIA, situated mainly in the southeastern corner of the NORTHERN TERRITORY. Covers approximately 56,000 square miles (145,000 sq. km.), mostly uninhabited. The last refuge for some of Australia's rarest animal species. Characterized by miles of sand dunes and ridges, some rising 70-120 feet (20-37 meters) in height, and interspersed with growths of *Spinifex* grass. First noted by explorer Charles Sturt in 1845.

Snowy River. River in NEW SOUTH WALES, Australia. Rises from the Snowy Mountains (a section of the Australian ALPS). Fed by melting snow, it flows about 270 miles (435 km.) southeast, then west, and south to the BASS STRAIT. Waters are diverted by the Snowy Mountains Hydroelectric Authority, which includes mountain tunnels, sixteen dams, and several reservoirs; this is one of the world's largest power and irrigation projects.

Society Islands. Group of islands in the west part of FRENCH POLYNESIA in the South PACIFIC OCEAN. Area is 621 square miles (1,608 sq. km.); population was 162,573 in 1988. Volcanic in

Snowy River Page 2041

Snowy Mts. Pages 1906, 1981

Sand ridges in the Simpson Desert. (Tom McKnight/Joan Clemons)

Mooréa
Page 2036

*South
Island
Pages
1854, 2042*

origin. Made up of two island groups, the Windward Islands (TAHITI, Mooréa, and several islets) and the Leeward Islands.

Solomon Islands. Independent nation, member of the Commonwealth of Nations, in the west PACIFIC OCEAN, east of New Guinea. Area is 10,639 square miles (27,556 sq. km.); population was 470,000 in the year 2000, mainly Melanesians. Capital is Honiara, on GUADALCANAL. Comprises thirty islands and many atolls. Includes most of the Solomon Islands group: Guadalcanal, New Georgia, Santa Isabel, Malaita, Choiseul, San Cristóbal, Vella Lavella, Ontong Java Atoll, Rennell, and the Santa Cruz Islands. Mountainous islands, mostly of volcanic origin. Excessive logging may lead to a ban on this industry, which has accounted for as much as more than half of the islands' exports.

South Australia. AUSTRALIA's driest state, occupying about one-eighth of the continent's total landmass. Bounded on the west, north, and east by other mainland states; flanked on the south by the GREAT AUSTRALIAN BIGHT of the INDIAN OCEAN. Covers 379,900 square miles (984,377 sq. km.). Capital is ADELAIDE; population was more than 1,400,000 in the late 1990's. More than 50 percent of the state is pastoral lands; the southeastern section is the economic center and where most of the population resides. The Murray is the only major river; Mount Lofty/Flinders Ranges are the most important mountains.

South Georgia. Island in the South ATLANTIC OCEAN. The Andes Mountains of South America are part of a mountain chain that extends beneath the ocean and continues to the ANTARCTIC PENINSULA. South Georgia was formed

*Southern
Alps
Page 1841*

when the peaks of some of these submarine mountains emerged above the water.

South Island. Larger and more southerly of the two principal islands of NEW ZEALAND in the southwest PACIFIC OCEAN. COOK STRAIT separates South Island from NORTH ISLAND. Its population has grown much less rapidly than that of North Island. Its area is 58,676 square miles (151,971 sq. km.). Its population was 881,537 in 1991.

South Magnetic Pole. Southern pole of the earth's magnetic center, to which compass needles point. Located about 170 miles (272 km.) from the geographic SOUTH POLE, which is the southernmost point on earth.

South Orkney Islands. Islands in the South ATLANTIC OCEAN off the ANTARCTIC PENINSULA. They are the tops of a mountain range that includes the Andes in South America and continues to the mountains on the Antarctic Peninsula. In 1904 Argentina set up a weather station at Laurie Island in the Orkneys.

South Pacific Gyre. Large mass of water, located in the PACIFIC OCEAN in the Southern Hemisphere, that rotates counterclockwise. Warm water moves toward the pole and cold water moves toward the EQUATOR.

South Pole. Point which by definition is the southernmost point on the earth—a point from which the only possible direction is north. The geographical South Pole is at an elevation of 9,200 feet (2,804 meters), which is only slightly lower than Leadville, Colorado, the highest city in the United States. See also SOUTH MAGNETIC POLE.

Southern Alps. Highest mountain range in AUSTRALASIA. The backbone of SOUTH ISLAND of NEW ZEALAND, running almost the entire length of the island in a north-to-south direction. The

New Zealand's Southern Alps. This satellite image of Lake Pukaki (center) reveals the contours of the surrounding mountain range. (PhotoDisc)

highest peak of the Alps is Mount COOK, at 12,317 feet (3,754 meters). The Alps contains 360 glaciers. Permanent snowfields occur throughout most of the mountain range.

Southern Ocean. World's stormiest ocean. Located between 60 and 65 degrees south latitude. The cold continent and the warmer ocean waters meet, creating a low-pressure situation that results in cyclones. The winds blow violently almost constantly from east to west until they spiral toward the coast of ANTARCTICA, where some of their fury dissipates. This is nature's way of distributing tropical heat to the polar regions.

Spencer Gulf. Inlet of the INDIAN OCEAN, indenting the southeastern coast of SOUTH AUSTRALIA. Runs 200 miles (320 km.) with a maximum width of 80 miles (130 km.). Several islands are situated in its 50-mile-wide (80 km.) mouth; major ports include Port Pirie and Port Augusta, which is located near the head of the inlet.

Stewart Island. Smallest of the three main islands of NEW ZEALAND. Located 15 miles (24 km.) south of Bluff, across Foreaux Strait. Population was 387 in 1999. Almost triangular in shape; covers 670 square miles (1,746 sq. km.). Most of the terrain is mountainous and covered by bushland.

Stonington Island. Island near the ANTARCTIC PENINSULA, where Antarctic explorer Finn Ronne and his wife, Edith, spent nearly a year in 1947.

Sutherland Falls. Highest waterfall in NEW ZEALAND, fourth-highest in the world, at 1,903 feet (580 meters). Situated in FIORDLAND NATIONAL PARK, at 44°48′ south latitude, longitude 167°44′ east. Fed by waters from Lake Quill, the falls drop down a rockface in three stages. Named after Donald Sutherland, the Hermit of MILFORD SOUND, who discovered the falls in 1880.

Suva. Seaport town, capital of FIJI, on southeast coast of Viti Levu Island in the PACIFIC OCEAN. Population was 69,665 in 1986. An excellent harbor; major industries are coconut processing and tourism.

Sydney. AUSTRALIA's oldest and largest city and the capital of NEW SOUTH WALES. Established in 1788 as a British penal colony and located on PORT JACKSON, a magnificent deep harbor along the southeastern coast of the continent. Australia's leading industrial city and its major seaport. The city and suburbs cover about 4,700 square

miles (12,000 sq. km.) with a population of nearly 4 million in the late 1990's. A major tourist destination, famous for its mild climate and white sand beaches, the Sydney Harbor Bridge, and the Opera House. In the year 2000 the city hosted the Olympic Games.

Tahiti. Mountainous island in the Windward Islands of the SOCIETY ISLANDS in FRENCH POLYNESIA, in the South PACIFIC OCEAN. Area is 408 square miles (1,057 sq. km.); population was 131,309 in 1988. Largest city is Papeete. Largest of the French islands in the Pacific and the commercial and political center of French Polynesia. Tourism is a major industry. Formerly Otaheite; also known as Taïte.

Tasman Glacier. Largest glacier in NEW ZEALAND. Flows down the eastern slopes of Mount COOK in SOUTH ISLAND. First explored by geologist Julius Von Haast and surveyor Arthur Dobson in 1862.

Tasman Sea. Area of the PACIFIC OCEAN off the southeast coast of AUSTRALIA, between Australia and TASMANIA on the west and NEW ZEALAND on the east. Also called the Tasmanian Sea.

Tasmania. AUSTRALIA's only island state, located about 150 miles (240 km.) south of VICTORIA state across the BASS STRAIT. Comprises the heart-shaped main island (Tasmania) and numerous smaller islands, including Bruny, King, and Flinders in the Bass Strait, and the subarctic Macquarie Island, located 900 miles (1,440 km.) to the southeast. The main island has a maximum width and length of about 200 miles (320 km.) with a cool, Mediterranean-like climate moderated by the SOUTHERN OCEAN. Mount Ossa (part of the GREAT DIVIDING RANGE) is the highest peak at 5,305 feet (1,617 meters). Capital is

Mountain in Tahiti. (Digital Stock)

HOBART; population was approximately 500,000 in the late 1990's. Agriculture and mining form Tasmania's economic base. Originally called Van Diemen's Land by the Dutch navigator, Abel Tasman, who discovered it in 1642.

Taupo, Lake. NEW ZEALAND's largest lake. Located within the Volcanic Plateau in central NORTH ISLAND; covers 235 square miles (606 sq. km.). Considered one of the best trout-fishing spots in the world. Site of one of the largest volcanic eruptions in the world, around 135 C.E.

Taylor Valley. One of the DRY VALLEYS in EAST (GREATER) ANTARCTICA. Dry valleys receive almost no precipitation, so they do not have the ice and snow cover that characterizes 98 percent of the continent. They can support rudimentary plant life.

Terre Adélie. Area that has the thickest covering of ice in ANTARCTICA. Located 248 miles (400 km. from the coast, in EAST (GREATER) ANTARCTICA between Wilkes Land and George V Land. Its enormous subglacial trench has a 15,670-foot (4,766 meters) ice sheet. Also called Adélie Coast.

Terror, Mount. Inactive volcano in ANTARCTICA. Located close to the active volcano Mount EREBUS. Sir James Clark Ross discovered it; nearby, he encountered a perpendicular wall of ice 200 feet (60 meters) high that extended as far as the eye could see and blocked his passage.

Timor Sea. Section of the INDIAN OCEAN, located northwest of AUSTRALIA, and southeast of Indonesia and the island of Timor. Covers approximately 235,000 square miles (615,000 sq. km.) and is about 300 miles (480 km.) wide. Opens east into the ARAFURA SEA and west into the Indian Ocean.

Tinian. Island in the NORTHERN MARIANA ISLANDS in the west PACIFIC OCEAN. Area is 20 square miles (52 sq. km.). Part of the Japanese mandate in 1919; occupied by U.S. troops in 1944 during World War II. Planes sent from its airfield dropped atomic bombs on Hiroshima and Nagasaki.

Tokelau. Group of islands in central PACIFIC OCEAN; part of NEW ZEALAND. Area is 4 square miles (10 sq. km.); population was 1,690 in 1986. Part of the GILBERT and Ellice Islands (*see* TUVALU). Includes islands of Atafu, Fakaofo, and Nukunomu. Formerly Union Islands.

Tongariro Page 2045

Tonga. Independent island nation in the southern PACIFIC OCEAN. Area is 290 square miles (750 sq. km.); population was 108,207 in 1998, two-thirds living on Tongatapu. Capital, chief port, and largest town is Nukualofa. Polynesian monarchy, comprising 150 islands (40 inhabited) divided into three main groups: Tongatapu, Na'apai, and Vava'u. Largest island is Tongatapu. Western islands are of volcanic origin; eastern are coral islands. Active volcanoes dot several islands. Most Tonga residents (98 percent) are Polynesians, and Tonga has retained much of its traditional culture, although the island is Christian. Also known as Tonga Islands or Friendly Islands.

Tonga Trench. Seafloor depression in the PACIFIC OCEAN, 35,433 feet (10,800 meters) deep. Located near TONGA, at 23°16′ south latitude, longitude 174°44′ west.

Tongariro National Park. First national park in NEW ZEALAND. Gifted by chiefs from the Maori Tuwharetoa tribe to the people of Aotearoa (New Zealand) in

Mahuia Rapids in New Zealand's Tongariro National Park. (Digital Stock)

1887. Located in central NORTH ISLAND, covering 32,226 acres (79,598 hectares). Site of three active volcanoes including Mount Ruapehu; highest peak in the North Island at 9,177 feet (2,797 meters).

Torres Strait. Passage through the CORAL SEA to the east and the ARAFURA SEA to the west in the western PACIFIC OCEAN; to the north is New Guinea and to the south lies AUSTRALIA's CAPE YORK PENINSULA. Dangerous to navigate because of reefs and rocky shoals. Nearly 80 miles (130 km.) wide; some of its larger islands are inhabited. Discovered in 1606 by Spanish navigator Luis Vaez de Torres.

Townesville. City, commercial center, and major port of eastern QUEENSLAND, Australia. Located close to the Flinders Passage through the GREAT BARRIER REEF and to the Atherton Plateau inland, making it an important gateway to both areas. Population was about 100,000 in the 1990's.

Transantarctic Mountains. Range of mountains running across Antarctic from the ROSS SEA to the WEDDELL SEA, passing through the SOUTH POLE. Divides ANTARCTICA into EAST (GREATER) ANTARCTICA south of the INDIAN OCEAN and WEST (LESSER) ANTARCTICA south of the PACIFIC OCEAN. Has a trough running alongside it with an accumulation of ice 2 miles (3.2 km.) deep, half of it below sea level. Also called the Great Antarctic Horst.

Tuamotu Archipelago. About eighty islands in FRENCH POLYNESIA in the South PACIFIC OCEAN. Area is 331 square miles (857 sq. km.); population was 11,754 in 1988. Mostly coral atolls; its main islands are Makatéa, Fakarava, Rangiroa, Anaa, Hao, and Reao. France has used it for atomic testing since the mid-1960's. Also known as Low Archipel-

ago, Paumotu, or Dangerous Archipelago.

Tubuai Islands. See AUSTRAL ISLANDS.

Tuvalu. Island country in the western PACIFIC OCEAN; member of the Commonwealth of Nations. Area is 10 square miles (26 sq. km.); population was 10,444 in 1998. Consists of a chain of nine coral islands, none of which rises more than 16 feet (5 meters) above sea level. Funafuti, Nanumea, Nui, Nukufetau, and Hukulaelae are atolls; Namumaga, Niutao, Vaitupu, and Niulakita are single islands with lagoons. About one-third of Tuvalu's people, who are mostly ethnic Polynesians, live in Funafuti. Also known as Lagoon Islands; formerly Ellice Islands.

Ulawun. Active volcano in the Whiteman range, on the island of New Britain, part of PAPUA NEW GUINEA in the PACIFIC OCEAN. Located on the north coast and east end of the island; reaches 7,532 feet (2,295 meters) in height. One of its most recent eruptions occurred in 1993. The volcano is also known as The Father.

Uluru. Giant red sandstone monolith located about 280 miles (450 km.) northeast of ALICE SPRINGS in AUSTRALIA's NORTHERN TERRITORY. The largest in a group of tors (isolated and weathered rock masses) that includes the Olgas/Kata Tjuta; the Uluru-Kata Tjuta National Park is listed as a World Heritage site. Rises more than 1,100 feet (335 meters) from a flat, sandy plateau; it is oval in shape, 2.2 miles (3.6 km.) long, 1.5 miles (2 km.) wide, and 6 miles (9.45 km.) around its base. Its coarse sandstone composition causes it to glow a brilliant red at sunrise and sunset. In 1985 ownership of the rock was returned to the Aborigines, who leased it back to the Australian government for ninety-nine years. The rock takes its

Transantarctic Mts. Page 1848

Uluru Pages 1849, 1906

name from an Aboriginal word for giant pebble; the first European to sight the monolith, Ernest Giles, named it Ayers Rock after South Australian premier Sir Henry Ayers.

Union Islands. See TOKELAU.

Vanuatu. Independent republic in the southwestern PACIFIC OCEAN. Area is 4,707 square miles (12,190 sq. km.); population was 192,800 in 2000. Capital is Port-Vila. Consists of more than eighty islands—70 percent of which are inhabited—in a Y-shaped configuration. The largest island is Espiritu Santo; others are Malakula, Éfaté, Erromango, and AMBRIM. Most of the islands are volcanic in origin; there are several active volcanoes. About 94 percent of the population are ethnic Melanesians (ni-Vanuatu); about 70 percent live on Anatom, Éfaté, Espiritu Santo, Futana, Malakula, and Tanna. Formerly known as New Hebrides.

Victoria Pages 1850-1851

Victoria. AUSTRALIA's smallest mainland state, located in the southeast corner of the continent. Bordered to the north by NEW SOUTH WALES (with the MURRAY RIVER forming a natural boundary), to the east by the Australia ALPS section of the GREAT DIVIDING RANGE, to the west by the deserts of SOUTH AUSTRALIA, and to the south by BASS STRAIT. Covers 87,884 square miles (227,600 sq. km.), with a range of climates. Population was four million in the late 1990's, with most living in the capital city of MELBOURNE and its suburbs. Victoria's major harbor is located in Port Phillip Bay.

Victoria Land. Region of ANTARCTICA that presses against the TRANSANTARCTIC MOUNTAINS east of the ROSS SEA. Named after Great Britain's Queen Victoria.

Vinson Massif. Highest point in ANTARCTICA. Soars to 16,859 feet (5,140 me-

ters), higher than any mountain in the United States except for Mount McKinley.

Vostok. Russian research station near the SOUTH MAGNETIC POLE in ANTARCTICA. Site of the lowest temperature ever recorded: −128 degrees Fahrenheit (−89 degrees Celsius) in 1983.

Waialeale. Mountain in central KAUAI Island, Hawaii, that is the rainiest place in the world, according to the National Geographic Society. Average annual rainfall is 460 inches (1,168 centimeters). Reaches 5,200 feet (1,585 meters).

Waikato River. Longest river in NEW ZEALAND, stretching 264 miles (425 km.). Flows northward across central NORTH ISLAND, from the headwaters at Mount Ruapehu, through Lake TAUPO, reaching the TASMAN SEA 30 miles (50 km.) southwestern of AUCKLAND. A major source of hydroelectric power for North Island.

Waitangi. Modern birthplace of NEW ZEALAND. Located on NORTH ISLAND in the Bay of ISLANDS. Site of the signing of the Treaty of Waitangi on February 6, 1840, between representatives of the British Crown and a number of Maori chiefs. Under the terms of the treaty, the Maori chiefs ceded sovereignty to the Crown and were guaranteed full rights of tribal lands and personal protection as British subjects. Maori word for "weeping waters."

Wake Island. Coral atoll in the central PACIFIC OCEAN, territory of the United States. Area is 3 square miles (7.7 sq. km.); population was 126 in 1997. Consists of three islets (Wake, Peale, and Wilkes) around a shallow lagoon. The United States formally occupied Wake Island in 1898 and built a naval air base and submarine base on the island in 1939. Attacked by the Japanese on December 7, 1941, immediately after

Pearl Harbor. It reverted to the United States after World War II and is administered by the U.S. Army Space and Strategic Defense Command. Formerly known as Halcyon Island.

Wallis and Futuna Islands. Overseas territory of France, in the southwestern PACIFIC OCEAN. Consists of the Wallis Archipelago (Wallis and twenty smaller islands and islets) and the Futuna Archipelago (two mountainous islands, Futuna and Alofi). Total area is 77 square miles (200 sq. km.); population was 13,705 in 1988. Capital is Matâ'utu on Wallis.

Weddell Sea. Body of water formed by an indentation in the continent of ANTARCTICA. Located southeast of South America; bordered by the ANTARCTIC PENINSULA, the Leopold Coast, the Cairn Coast, and Coats Land. Named for James Weddell, a British navigator who laid claim to it in 1823.

Wellington. Capital and second-largest city of NEW ZEALAND. Population was 346,700 in 1999. Located on the shores of a natural harbor, at the southern end of NORTH ISLAND, on a major earthquake fault. Built on steep, hilly terrain, similar to San Francisco.

West (Lesser) Antarctica. Area that lies west of the TRANSANTARCTIC MOUNTAINS. Includes MARIE BYRD LAND, Ellsworth Land, the ANTARCTIC PENINSULA, and the ROSS SEA.

Western Australia. AUSTRALIA's largest state; occupies nearly one-third of the continent. Bounded to the north by the TIMOR SEA, to the south by the Antarctic Ocean, to the west by the INDIAN OCEAN, and to the east by the deserts of SOUTH AUSTRALIA and the NORTHERN TERRITORY. Covers 975,100 square miles (2,525,500 sq. km.), most of which is a semiarid plateau. Has no winter season, only "wet" and "dry." Popu-

lation was more than two million in the late 1990's, more than 70 percent residing in and around PERTH, the capital city.

Western Samoa. See SAMOA.

Whales, Bay of. Bay in the ROSS SEA on ANTARCTICA's west side. Has much less wind than other parts of Antarctica. Over a four-year period, the average wind speed was 11 miles (17.6 km.) per hour, about equivalent to that in Peoria, Illinois, or Kansas City, Missouri.

White Desert. Another name for the polar ice cap. ANTARCTICA is the earth's driest continent. The annual snowfall on the polar ice cap is only 1-2 inches (2.5-5 centimeters); the coastal regions receive 10-20 inches (25-51 centimeters) of snow a year.

White Island. Active volcano in NEW ZEALAND. Located 31 miles (50 km.) off the Bay of Plenty on NORTH ISLAND. Covers 131 acres (324 hectares); characterized by intense thermal activity as steam, noxious gases, and toxic fumes are released into the atmosphere from numerous vents in the crater. In 1914 a violent eruption killed eleven men who were mining sulfur.

Wilhelm, Mount. Mountain in Bismarck Range, New Guinea Island, PAPUA NEW GUINEA, in the PACIFIC OCEAN. Highest peak in New Guinea at 14,793 feet (4,500 meters).

Wilson's Promontory. Granite peninsula projecting into the BASS STRAIT, forming the southernmost point of the Australian mainland. Located in the state of VICTORIA, 110 miles (177 km.) southeast of MELBOURNE. It is 22 miles long and a maximum of 14 miles wide; the 80-mile (130 km.) coastline rises to a mountainous interior, with Mount Latrobe (2,475 feet/754 meters) its highest peak.

Weddell Sea Page 1846

Wellington Page 2046

Wilson's Promontory Page 1911

Western Australia Page 2046

Yasur. Active volcano on Tanna Island, south VANUATU. Reaches 1,184 feet (365 meters) in height. One of its most recent eruptions occurred in 1998.

York, Cape. Northernmost tip of AUSTRALIA, located at 10°41′ south latitude, longitude 142°32′ east. Both it and CAPE YORK PENINSULA were named by Captain James Cook in 1770, in honor of Great Britain's Duke of York. Reaches into TORRES STRAIT, which separates Australia from New Guinea.

Cynthia Beres; Huia Richard Hutton; Dana P. McDermott; R. Baird Shuman; Rowena Wildin

INDEX TO VOLUME 7

See volume 8 for a comprehensive index to all eight volumes in set.

F L A G S O F T H E W O R L D

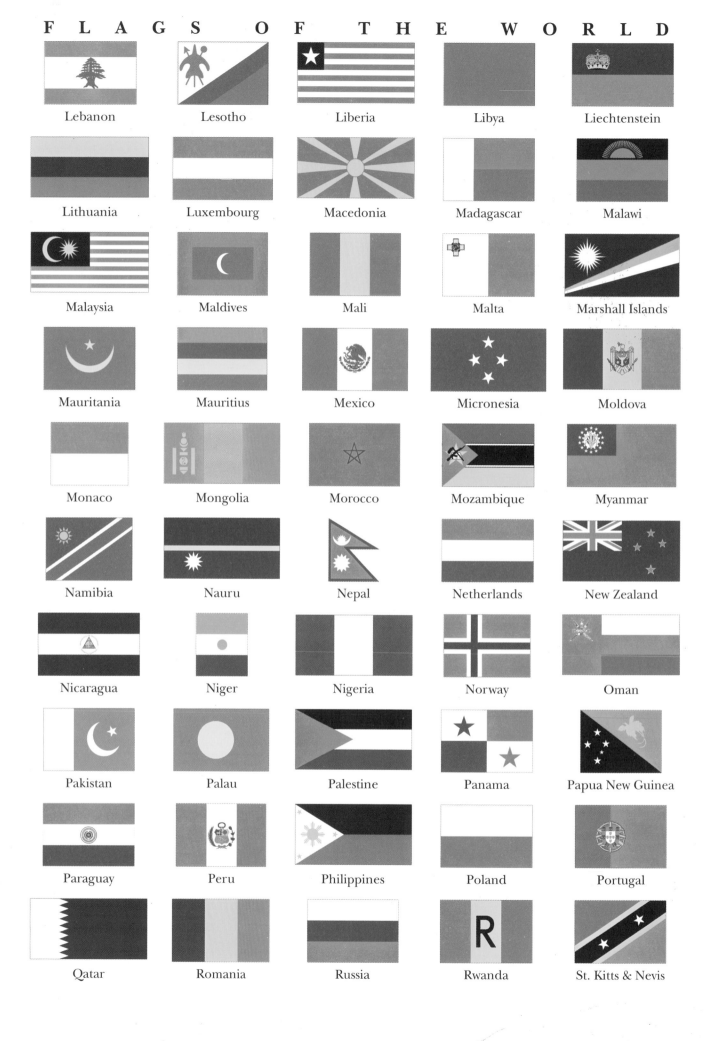

Lebanon	Lesotho	Liberia	Libya	Liechtenstein
Lithuania	Luxembourg	Macedonia	Madagascar	Malawi
Malaysia	Maldives	Mali	Malta	Marshall Islands
Mauritania	Mauritius	Mexico	Micronesia	Moldova
Monaco	Mongolia	Morocco	Mozambique	Myanmar
Namibia	Nauru	Nepal	Netherlands	New Zealand
Nicaragua	Niger	Nigeria	Norway	Oman
Pakistan	Palau	Palestine	Panama	Papua New Guinea
Paraguay	Peru	Philippines	Poland	Portugal
Qatar	Romania	Russia	Rwanda	St. Kitts & Nevis